Perspectives in Psychological Theory

ESSAYS IN HONOR OF HEINZ WERNER

Perspectives in Psychological Theory

ESSAYS IN HONOR OF HEINZ WERNER

Edited by

BERNARD KAPLAN AND SEYMOUR WAPNER

Department of Psychology and Institute of Human Development

Clark University

INTERNATIONAL UNIVERSITIES PRESS, INC.
New York

Contents

Contributors

SILVANO ARIETI, Clinical Associate Professor of Psychiatry at the College of Medicine, State University of New York, is the author of *Interpretation of Schizophrenia*, and Editor of the recent two-volume *American Handbook of Psychiatry*.

SOLOMON ASCH, at the Institute for Advanced Study, Princeton, for the past two years, is Professor of Psychology at Swarthmore College. Among his many contributions to psychology is his book, *Social Psychology*.

JEROME S. BRUNER, Professor of Psychology at Harvard University, has worked extensively in the areas of perception and cognition; he recently co-authored *A Study of Thinking*.

TAMARA DEMBO, Associate Professor of Psychology at Clark University, has worked intensively on the experimental study of emotions and values; most recently she co-authored *Adjustment to Misfortune*.

KURT GOLDSTEIN, currently Visiting Professor at the New School for Social Research, has contributed widely to the fields of neuro- and psychopathology. Among his major works are *The Organism* and *Language and Language Disturbances*. He also co-authored (with Martin Scheerer) the monograph, *Abstract and Concrete Behavior*.

MAURICE D. HULING is staff psychologist at Winter V.A. Hospital, Topeka, Kansas.

ROMAN JAKOBSON is the Samuel F. Kross Professor of Slavic Languages and Literature at Harvard University; and Visiting Institute Professor at the Massachusetts Institute of Technology. Among his publications are the book *Kindersprache, Aphasie und allgemeine Lautgesetze*, and the forthcoming book *Sound and Meaning*.

BERNARD KAPLAN, Associate Professor of Psychology at Clark University, is author of various articles on language and symbolization. He is at present collaborating with Heinz Werner on a book on *The Development of Symbolization*.

GEORGE S. KLEIN, Professor of Psychology and Director of the Research Center for Mental Health, New York University, has worked intensively in the area of perception-personality relationships. He is the editor of the new monograph series, *Psychological Issues*.

NORMAN R. F. MAIER, Professor of Psychology at the University of Michigan, worked in many areas, including higher processes in animals and humans, behavior under frustration and behavior in industrial settings. His publications include *Frustration, Psychology in Industry, Prin-*

ciples of Human Relations, and (with T. C. Schneirla) *Principles of Animal Psychology.*

ABRAHAM H. MASLOW, Professor of Psychology at Brandeis University, has worked chiefly in the areas of motivation and normal and abnormal personality. His publications include *Principles of Abnormal Psychology* and *Motivation and Personality.*

GARDNER MURPHY, Director of Research at the Menninger Foundation, is the author of many books, including *Historical Introduction to Modern Psychology,* and *Personality: a Biosocial Approach.*

HARRIET NERLOVE, formerly at Swarthmore College, is a graduate student in the Department of Social Relations at Harvard University.

DAVID RAPAPORT, Research Associate at the Austen Riggs Center, Stockbridge, is widely known for his theoretical contributions to psychoanalysis and his attempts to integrate the findings of experimental psychology and psychoanalysis. Among his many publications are the books *Emotions and Memory, Diagnostic Psychological Testing,* and *Organization and Pathology of Thought.*

MARTIN SCHEERER, Professor of Psychology at University of Kansas, is co-author (with Kurt Goldstein) of *Abstract and Concrete Behavior* and (with Robert Reiff) of *Memory and Hypnotic Age Regression,* and author of numerous articles on cognitive theory, developmental psychology, etc.

THEODORE C. SCHNEIRLA, Curator at the Museum of Natural History, and Adjunct Professor, Graduate Department of Psychology, New York University, has worked intensively in the field of comparative psychology. Among his publications, he co-authored (with N. R. F. Maier) *Principles of Animal Psychology.*

SEYMOUR WAPNER, Professor of Psychology at Clark University, is author of numerous articles on perception. He is co-author (with Heinz Werner) of *Perceptual Development*, and is one of the collaborators in *Personality Through Perception*.

HERMAN A. WITKIN, Professor and Director of the Laboratory of Psychology at the College of Medicine, State University of New York, has worked for many years in the area of perception-personality relations. Some of his work is described in the book *Personality Through Perception*.

Acknowledgment

We wish to express our deep appreciation to the many people who have helped in the publication of this volume. We owe much to the patient labors of Mrs. Lottie M. Newman of International Universities Press; Mr. Tilton M. Barron, Librarian at Clark University; our colleagues in the Department of Psychology, Clark University; and Miss Helen Dedes, Secretary in the Institute of Human Development.

B. K.
S. W.

Introductory Remarks

BERNARD KAPLAN, Ph.D.

SEYMOUR WAPNER, Ph.D.

Clark University

This volume, "Perspectives in Psychological Theory," is dedicated to Heinz Werner, one of the outstanding figures in contemporary psychology. With the approach of his seventieth birthday (February 11, 1960) a few of us, representing the many who hold him and his work in deep affection and high regard, took this occasion to communicate these feelings in a form most commensurate with his way of life: namely, a *Festschrift* consisting of experimental and theoretical papers in various areas of psychology.

We, who have enjoyed the advantages during the past decade of close collaboration with this outstanding scientist and teacher, and who—because of this intimate contact—have been most in a position to catch him at those moments when present work reminded him of past events, have arrogated to ourselves perhaps the most pleasant task in this volume, namely, that of shaping the fragments we have overheard during the past ten years into some sort of coherent picture of the highlights underlying a long scientific career which is consistently marked by that rare combination: a wide range of interests, a striking originality of thought, and an immense productivity in experimental research.

Among Heinz Werner's major interests during his long career, two principal ones stand out: an involvement in problems of aesthetics (broadly conceived, i.e., as including perception, expression, etc.) and a concern with the developmental aspects of phenomena.

These interests were manifested even during his very early youth: at the age of seven, he began the study of the violin; at the age of ten, he began to read avidly the popular "pocket-books," then available in Vienna, on the evolution of the cosmos, the evolution of animals, the evolution of man, etc. The interaction of these two interests was reflected at the age of sixteen in a paper he wrote while at the technical Gymnasium he attended. In this paper, entitled "The Development of 'Truth' in Ibsen's Plays," he attempted to demonstrate that there was a dialectical process underlying the expression of the idea of "truth" in certain of Ibsen's plays.

After a very brief stay at an engineering school, at which many of the graduates of the technical Gymnasium continued their training, his compelling interests led him to the University of Vienna, with the intention of becoming a composer and a historian of music. While at the University he was exposed to a ferment of philosophic and scientific ideas deriving from Kant, Hegel, the empiricist-positivist tradition and evolutionary theory. He soon found himself directed more toward philosophical and psychological issues.

Heinz Werner's increasing concern with philosophy and psychology did not lead to a neglect of his interests either in the evolutionary aspects of phenomena or in aesthetics; instead there resulted an integration of these various interests, as manifested both in his initial journal article and the topic he chose for his doctoral dissertation. The article, written in 1912, presented, in embryo, his later formulations regarding the sensorimotor bases of conceptual thought; it was entitled, "A Genetic Table of Conceptual Forms." The doctoral dissertation, which appeared subsequently (1916) in monograph form, dealt with *The Psychology of Aesthetic Enjoyment.*

In 1914, Heinz Werner was awarded the Ph.D. degree from the University of Vienna, with highest honors. After he received his degree, he stayed on at the University of Vienna, in the famous Institute for Physiology, directed by S. Exner, as an assistant in psychophysiology. During this period, he published a paper, on "the blind spot," for which he received the Trebitsch Prize. Following his postdoctoral stay at the Institute for Physiology, and a brief period of military service, he joined the Psychological Laboratory at Munich, a place which provided the facilities enabling him to continue his experimental studies.

At the same time as he was pursuing his experimental researches in Munich, he also commuted to Vienna, in order to carry out investigations at a children's day school in that city. These latter inquiries were directed toward an analysis of the melodies spontaneously produced by children between the ages of two and a half to five. They were summarized in his monograph (1917) on *The Invention of Melodies in Early Childhood:* this research once again reflected his combined interests in aesthetics and development.

The extensive and intensive contact with these preschool children gave an added impetus to his already great interest in the developmental analysis of all phenomena. He turned increasingly to the writings of child psychologists and the anthropologists studying primitive forms of behavior in nonliterate peoples. At this time (1917) he left Munich to join the Psychological Laboratories at Hamburg, under the direction of William Stern.

During his early years at Hamburg, he published many articles and three lengthy monographs, *The Origins of the Metaphor* (1919), *Basic Problems in the Psychology of Intensity* (1922), and *The Origins of the Lyric* (1924). At the request of E. Kretschmer—who was then editing a series of monographs in psychology and psychiatry—he also began to work on another monograph, devoted to the problems of developmental psychology. This latter work soon exceeded monograph size, and in 1926 there appeared the first German edition of his well-known work, *Einführung in die Entwicklungspsychologie*, which, elaborated and expanded, is familiar to us as *Comparative Psychology of Mental Development*.

The Hamburg environment during Heinz Werner's fifteen-year stay was a center of vigorous intellectual activity, not only in psychology but also in a number of other disciplines very near to his heart: he had close contact with such outstanding figures as William Stern in child psychology, Ernst Cassirer in epistemology and the philosophy of language, Carl Meinhof in comparative linguistics, Erwin Panofsky in the history of art and comparative aesthetics, and Jakob von Uexküll in comparative psychology. With von Uexküll,—the well-known pioneer in ethology—Heinz Werner taught a number of seminars on animal behavior. Other contributors to this rich environment at Hamburg were younger colleagues and students—among them Fritz Heider, Martha Muchow, Martin Scheerer, Alfred Storch, and Karl Zietz.

During the later part of his stay at Hamburg his dual interests in aesthetics and development were once again unified in his focus on the problem of the aesthetic-expressive aspects of speech. He carried out a number of experiments in this area, and finally published this research in a monograph, *Fundamental Problems in the Physiognomics of Language* (1932).

With the advent of Nazism, Heinz Werner left Germany. On an invitation from Walter Pillsbury, he came as Visiting Professor in Psychology to the University of Michigan. He immediately became deeply involved in experimental research, working on such problems as the establishment of contour phenomena, the dynamics of binocular depth perception, etc. After a short stay at the University of Michigan, he went as Visiting Professor to Harvard; concerned with the over-emphasis on end products in a large bulk of the psychological literature in the United States, he there wrote his provocative article, "Process and Achievement."

In 1938, he returned to Michigan, doing some teaching, but focusing mainly on research with feeble-minded children at the Wayne County Training School. On the basis of this research and later work deriving from it, Heinz Werner published—often in collaboration with other investigators—almost three dozen articles on behavior of different kinds of feeble-minded children.

In 1945, Heinz Werner joined the faculty at Brooklyn College. At Brooklyn, where several of the contributors to the present volume were privileged to know him, he continued his research on brain-damaged children (with Zelda Klapper) and initiated new inquiries on the problem of the acquisition of word meaning (with Edith Kaplan).

In 1947, Heinz Werner was called to Clark University, where he was appointed as G. Stanley Hall Professor of Genetic Psychology and Chairman of the Department of Psychology, positions which he holds today. During the more than ten years he has held these two roles, "psychology" has once again begun to assume a central place in the over-all structure of the University.

Due both to his own example and the influence he has exerted on his colleagues and students, there has been, during this past decade, an enormous expansion in the range and quantity of research activity within the department. Despite the many administrative burdens which attend his position as chairman, Heinz Werner has continued to maintain—and indeed to increase—his remarkable research productivity. In collaboration with the authors of this brief note, he developed long-range programs of experimental research in two areas which have been of major interest to him throughout his academic career, viz., expressive-symbolic processes (including language), on one hand, and perceptual processes, on the other. His manner of formulating and analyzing problems has also spread to some of his other colleagues, who have found developmental conceptualization valuable in their own areas of interest. Naturally enough, with this expansion of research there has been a correlative increase in the size of the department of psychology, so that it is now the largest department in the University.

Heinz Werner has also been instrumental in activating the long-dormant Clark University Press: first for the publication of the fourth volume of the History of Psychology in Autobiography of which he was a co-editor; then for the publication of two monographs in a series he inaugurated entitled Clark University Monographs in Psychology and Related Disciplines. The first of these monographs comprised papers presented at a symposium "On Expressive Language," held at Clark in 1955; among the participants at that symposium were several contributors to the present volume (S. Arieti, S. Asch, B. Kaplan) and, from other disciplines, such outstanding scholars as Roman Jakobson, Susanne Langer, and Hans Sperber. The second monograph summarized a considerable amount of research carried out in collaboration with S. Wapner; this monograph, which appeared in 1957, was entitled *Perceptual Development*.

Finally, in 1958, in conjunction with Leslie Phillips and Seymour Wapner, Heinz Werner realized a desire which had been close to his heart for many years: the founding, at Clark University, of an Institute of Human Development, an Institute which—through training, research, and interdisciplinary collaboration—would once again make Clark an international center directed toward the developmental analysis of phenomena in all the life sciences.

It is fitting that the Chairman of the Board of Directors of this new Institute is a man who has done and is doing so much to promote the developmental point of view throughout the world—the man whose work, past and present, has evoked admiration from the invisible society of scholars and research workers everywhere—Heinz Werner.

The Experiences of Inner Status

SILVANO ARIETI, M.D.

State University of New York

THE EMERGENCE OF AWARENESS

Irritability is one of the fundamental properties of life, necessary to maintain the intactness of the organism in a predominantly inorganic and adverse-to-life universe.

With the evolution of animals the property of irritability is delegated to the nervous system: i.e., what is irritability in some vegetables and in very low animal species evolves to the level of sensation. However, a distinction must be made which is of fundamental importance in biology, but which is nevertheless seldom considered: the distinction between physiological and psychological sensations.

Sensation, in the sense in which the word is generally used, implies a subjective experience or awareness. But this element of awareness, which is so important for the psychologist, is not a necessary ingredient in physiological "sensation." For the physiologist and neurologist sensation is only an impression made on an afferent nerve, an impression which as a rule is transmitted through an ascending tract. This impression may or may not be accompanied or followed by awareness. Actually awareness accompanies only a small proportion of physiological sensations. And I am including among these sensations without awareness not only the many thousands of sensations of the autonomic nervous system (i.e., the afferent parts of the autonomic reflex arcs) but many others which involve the central nervous system. For instance, the important information transmitted through the spinocerebellar tracts never reaches the level of awareness; again only a small proportion of kinesthetic or proprioceptive sensations reaches consciousness.

In this paper, the extremely important problem of why physiological sensation at times becomes also psychological sensation will not be discussed; our present knowledge concerning the neurological substratum permitting the manifestation of this phenomenon does not enable us to explain the emergence of awareness.

As long as physiological sensation is not psychological the organism is not too dissimilar from an electronic computing machine, or a transmitter of information. When sensation becomes accompanied by awareness we have *experience*. With the emergence of experience in the form of psychological sensation psychic life begins.

Before sensation is accompanied by awareness we are still only in the physical (although biological) order of things. One physical event (the stimulus) produces another physical event, the response (although in the body of the organism). Awareness introduces the factor, *psyche*. Physicists who are interested in the study of things as physical phenomena try to remove from their research the disturbances produced by this subjectivation (for instance, they are not interested in the subjective experience of a color but in the wave length which brings about the sensation of that color). What to the physicist is a complicating disturbance is on the other hand for the psychologist one of the foundations of his study matter. We do not imply here that psychic life is confined to awareness. On the contrary, we shall see later that psychic life expands to a certain extent also to the realm of unawareness. We merely want to stress that it starts as awareness.

However, we must point out also that awareness, i.e., consciousness, is only one of the many neurological functions, or rather is one of the many qualities that neurological functions may have. As a matter of fact, the majority of neurological functions is not accompanied by awareness; it is unconscious. Moreover, even what appears to us as conscious phenomena are only the end results, the last steps of a long series of unconscious phenomena: for instance, a conscious thought or a willed complicated movement of our hands are only the end results of a series of thousands of mechanisms, of which only the terminal ones reach consciousness. By demonstrating that some psychic processes are unconscious Freud actually did no more than point out that some of the functions of the nervous system lose this quality of consciousness and become more similar to the rest of the functions mediated by the nervous system. The contribution of Freud was a revolutionary one, because psychic functions were considered as a class *sui generis*, and not as part of neurophysiology.

Awareness of the sensation enables the organism to take action, or to change the environment with the response. But this important aspect of life will not be taken into consideration in this paper. What concerns us here is that the sensation has a purpose (i.e., is retained in evolution because it is a trait necessary to the perpetuation of animal life), namely, the response which follows the sensation tends to maintain homeostasis.

Let us take as an example a thirsty animal. This animal searches for water. The animal is not aware of the danger that dehydration presents for its survival. The animal wants to remove the unpleasant sensation of thirst. The ability to experience thirst has been retained in evolution for its utilitarian purposes.

TWO CATEGORIES OF EXPERIENCES

Thirst, like pain, and, as we shall see later in greater detail, other sensations, when they reach the level of perception, can be seen as having two experiential aspects:[1] (1) the subjective apprehension of a physical state or change of state (for instance, a specific state of discomfort which we call thirst); (2) a mirroring of an aspect of reality. Both aspects lead to some responses. At this point we encounter another basic dychotomy (similar in importance to that between physiological and psychological sensation). On one side is the sensory aspect, or the subjectivization of a bodily change; that is the experience of an inner status, the experience *qua* experience. Even when the experience is recognized and therefore is more properly called a perception, it remains fundamentally a subjectivization of a state of the organism. On the other side we have the function of mirroring reality, a function which generally expands into numerous ramifications which have to do with cognition.

Now if we examine the various perceptions, we recognize that the importance of these two components varies tremendously. The experience of inner status is very important in the perceptions of pain, hunger, thirst, temperature. It becomes less pronounced in other perceptions in which the organism is of necessity in contact with some stimuli (tactual, gustatory

---

[1] After completion of this paper I have read Schachtel's recent book *Metamorphosis* (1959) and noticed considerable similarity between some of the conceptions expressed here and his conceptions of autocentricity and allocentricity. Although I have reached these conclusions independently, there is no doubt in my mind about Schachtel's priority on this important contribution. However, the reader who is acquainted with Schachtel's work will notice that my views and his have only one point of contact. After this point the two conceptions expand in different directions, which are not antagonistic but complementary. Schachtel is fundamentally interested in perception, I in emotion.

and, less obviously, olfactory) coming from the external world. In these perceptions the subjectivization of the alteration of the organism plays the predominant role, but the reality of the external stimulus is generally also acknowledged. In auditory and visual perceptions the experience of a change of inner status plays a minimal role. What is most important in them is the awareness they give us of what happens in the external world, thus enabling the organism to deal more appropriately with this world. They become to a great extent the foundation of cognition; they develop connections with the symbolism of language; they are elaborated to the levels of apperceptions, and become increasingly removed from their sensorial origin. Their importance will no longer lie in their sensorial nature but in their meaning. Both kinds of experiences are purposeful: but whereas the experiences of inner status have an immediate survival value and are fundamentally not symbolic, the experiences of mirroring of reality have more symbolic function and less immediate survival value.

At this point we must indicate that for expository reasons we have oversimplified this complex matter. No experience, especially at a human level, is ever exclusively of one type or another, but only predominantly of one type. Let us take, for instance, a painful experience, a toothache. A toothache is experienced not only as pain but also as an indication that a tooth is in an abnormal state and that a consultation with a dentist is advisable. The cognitive, symbolic elements are, however, secondary to the experience of inner status. The pain is there, as a status, independent of the meaning attached to it. Any meaning attached to pain generally consists of images which are derived from visual or auditory perceptions.

On the other hand when we say that a visual perception has predominantly a cognitive function, inasmuch as it leads to apperception and to higher order phenomena, we do not deny the occurrence of a bodily change. The change can be registered objectively by the electroencephalogram. However, the visual experience, the *qua* experience, is only the initial and subordinate part of a complicated process. The process becomes symbolic almost immediately because of the cortical associations that it brings about.

Moreover, even if we take into consideration man's most cognitive experience, for instance, reflective or inner thought, we recognize in it the two elements. Not only do we think, but we are aware of our thoughts. In a certain way we experience our thoughts as auditory images and less frequently as visual images. Cognitive awareness is a big topic, and we shall not deal with it in this paper.

The present classification of these two types of experience is not arbitrary or based purely on introspection. It has also anatomical foundations: sensations which lead to symbolic activities subsequently become mediated in large neopallic areas; sensations which are predominantly experiences of inner status have much smaller subsequent cortical mediation.

The rest of this paper will deal mainly with the experiences of inner status and only secondarily with the experiences which mirror reality, or cognitive experiences. However, we shall first devote a few sentences to the cognitive experiences to highlight the differences from the experiences of inner status.

The field of cognitive experiences becomes symbolic, that is, it acquires the property of making things stand for others, and therefore it becomes potentially endless. It is a constantly enlarging system, which must be fully evaluated not only as a capacity of the individual but also as a social and a historical phenomenon in the spatial dimension of the community and in the temporal dimension of the history of man. Symbols are in fact created continuously, and they become more and more detached from the original perceptual foundation. What started as a simple perception continues as a prober of wider and wider horizons. The finitude of man seems temporarily overcome by the use of the symbolic process. The impression of overcoming the finitude is of course illusory: no matter how much man knows, his knowledge will be finite and cannot comprehend the infinity of the universe. Yet symbolism may portray the world in infinite ways. Thus man becomes potentially capable of an infinite number of finitudes.

In contrast to this unlimited scope, it would at first seem that the experiences of inner status play only a secondary role, at least in the human organism. They are in fact not symbolic; they cannot expand endlessly, and seem forced to be concerned with the here-and-now reality, a reality restricted to the boundaries of the organism.

Is this really so? Has the organism neglected the first type of experiences? I do not think so. As a matter of fact I will try to explain how the whole phenomenon of motivation depends on these experiences. I will also try to demonstrate how these experiences evolve to different levels. A brief outline of these levels will be given. Needless to say, nature does not jump from level to level, and therefore all these classifications are artificial inasmuch as they abstract levels and ignore intermediary and overlapping stages.

SIMPLE SENSATIONS AND PERCEPTIONS

The first level consists of the simple localized sensations and perceptions, like pain, temperature, etc. We have already briefly discussed these experiences.

PHYSIOSENSATIONS AND PHYSIOPERCEPTIONS

The second level consists of what I call physiosensations[2] (or physioperceptions, if they are elaborated to the degree of perception). They are states of awareness reflecting a particular

---

[2] The names *physiosensations* and *physioperceptions* are proposed to distinguish this group of experiences from simpler sensations. Physiosensation means sensation of a natural state. In certain ways even simple sensations are of this order, but in physiosensations the emphasis is on certain regulatory mechanisms of the body. It is questionable whether physiosensations are phylogenetically older than some simple sensations. Some of them probably are. Some sensations are intermediary between simple sensations and physiosensations: for instance, the subjective experience of one's body temperature.

condition of the organism (for instance, hunger, thirst, fatigue, sleepiness, etc.). What interests us here is not the condition of the organism (for instance, the state of dehydration) but the subjective experience (for instance, the experience of thirst).

Let us take hunger as an example of physiosensations. Nobody would deny that hunger is a sensation which has some similarities to a simple sensation like pain. Nevertheless it has different characteristics:

1. Although it may be localized in the stomach, or represented to a large extent by a feeling of emptiness in the stomach, it is not easily localized, as pain is.

2. It consists of, or has inherent in it, a particular generalized state of the organism, viz., deprivation of food.

Like pain, however, hunger is an uncomfortable status. With little variations similar things could be stated for other physiosensations like thirst, sleepiness, fatigue, etc. The physiological mechanisms of these phenomena are not well known, but we may assume that, for instance, in the states of hunger and thirst, a particular condition of some mucous membranes of the organism, or an inner state of the organism, is able to activate some nerve endings, which transmit the information to nervous centers, where such information acquires consciousness. What is an alteration of the homeostasis for the organism will become a state of discomfort for the psyche. The removal of the discomfort becomes a need. The removal of the need becomes a satisfaction. The discomfort, the need, and the satisfaction are not symbolic. It is true that for the biologist the discomfort is symbolic of altered homeostasis, but not for the subject who experiences the discomfort *qua* discomfort.

Do physiosensations require cognitive processes? They do not: they are experiences of inner status, although generalized. The experience of physiosensation leads of course to some kind of activity, which may require learned behavior, but the awareness per se does not require any cognitive function. Even if we take into consideration physioperceptions as perceptions, we recognize that the cognitive element is minimal.

A large bulk of evidence is now available proving that physiosomatic states are regulated mostly by the hypothalamus (Cobb, 1950). It is, however, more than doubtful that the awareness of physiosensations occurs in the hypothalamus. Primitive receptive centers are located in the ventral thalamus, in the pars optica and in the tuber cinereum. According to Papez (1937), impulses through the ventral thalamus reach the hypothalamus and through the mamillary bodies and the anterior thalamic nuclei go to the gyrus cinguli. It is also possible that what MacLean (1949, 1955) calls the visceral brain has a great deal to do with the experience of physioperceptions.

INSTINCTUAL EXPERIENCES

We must consider now a group of phenomena of inner experiences which are more complicated: the instinctual experiences. In these cases an alteration of the inner status of the organism comes to awareness and leads to action when an external stimulus releases an inner mechanism.

These phenomena are particularly prominent in infrahuman animals. This category of experiences is connected with those previously described. Instinctual experience implies awareness of a status, like that of a physiosensation, but is brought about by the presence or by the propinquity of a specific external stimulus. Sexual instinct belongs to this category. Instinct (of which instinctual experience is only a part) may be divided into several components: (1) the priming, or inner state of preparedness, which is based on hormonic, humoral, or other biochemical excitement, impinging on a congenital nervous apparatus; (2) the external stimulus which is the releasing object, e.g., a member of the opposite sex; (3) a prearranged set of motor and visceral activity which constitutes the instinctive behavior; (4) the subjective experiences which accompany these phenomena.

The study of all these components pertains to ethology.

We are interested chiefly in the experiences of inner status which are part of priming and become the motivation of a certain fixed behavior, a need to follow a prearranged set of motor mechanisms which lead to the extinction of the need. According to Tinbergen (1951), priming is the foundation of motivation. As we know, and as Fletcher (1957) and Ostow (1957, 1959) have recently pointed out, Freudian psychoanalysis also explains human dynamics as based to a large extent on instinctual motivation. Instinct acts not only directly but also indirectly; that is, when it is inhibited it produces a tremendous discomfort in the animal, so that its motivational power increases. The fulfillment of the instinct becomes also a pleasant experience not only because it leads to the extinction of the need and of the discomfort, but also in a positive way, by being pleasant per se, a characteristic which is not always remembered in theoretical discussions of instincts.

An important point for our consideration is the following: how is instinct connected with cognition? Inasmuch as the instinct needs an external object, by which it is released, at least perception and recognition of the stimulus are implied. (Perhaps conscious recognition is not necessary in low animal forms.)

We see thus the difference from physioperceptions. Whereas physioperceptions *qua* experiences need the most minimal cognitive component, instincts need more. They belong to a more complicated level and represent one of the first important interconnections in the psyche (intrapsychic connections) between cognition and affect.

Although in low animal species, the emotional-cognitive apparatus is subcortical, in higher species, starting with the amphibians, the cognitive becomes cortical; that is, the releaser of the instincts becomes more and more a stimulus which is perceived and recognized by the cortex.

Summarizing we may state that physiosensations and instincts are experiences of inner status, which tend not to be

localized but diffuse. Motivationally they may lead to definite
and specific motor responses, but as experiences they tend to
be general in character.

PROTOEMOTIONS

We come now to a higher level which seems almost unrelated
to the previous one, that of the protoemotions.

Protoemotions (1) are experiences of inner status which
cannot be localized but involve the whole organism; (2) include a set of bodily changes, mostly muscular and humoral;
(3) are elicited by specific external stimuli, which are perceived by the animal as important in a positive or negative
way for the safety of the organism. Among protoemotions
are such experiences as fear, rage, short-circuited anxiety, etc.

Let us take, as an example, one of the easiest to understand:
fear. The cognitive element in fear is much more important
than in the previous categories of experiences of inner status.
The stimulus (the feared object) is not only perceived and
recognized, but its capacity to affect the organism is apprehended. Such apprehension elicits an unpleasant experience
which constitutes the fear.

Here we can observe something *in statu nascendi* that is of
extraordinary importance: it is not something having a physical impact on the organism, it is not a physiosensation which
reveals itself or a special somatic internal state brought to
consciousness from a releasing stimulus; it is rather an external stimulus which elicits an inner status, that experience
of inner status which is the status of fear. It is a "wireless
transmission." Fear is registered. Its unpleasantness or discomfort actually stands for the unpleasantness which the animal would undergo if the fear materialized (for instance, if he
would become prey of a bigger animal). It is therefore in a
certain way symbolic and purposeful, because no matter how
unpleasant it is, it is less harmful and less unpleasant than the
realization of the feared act. Nevertheless the experience of
the protoemotion *qua* emotion is not symbolic; it is present,

actual, a subjective reality. The animal develops the need to remove the protoemotion. The cortical network which mediates the perception of danger is immediately connected with an archipallic network, probably in the hippocampus or in the gyrus cinguli, which gives this flavor of experience as a status or the qualitative experience.

As soon as the subjective experience takes place, associative patterns lead to a hypothalamic response. The hypothalamic response coordinates all the visceral, humoral, and muscular reactions which lead to the specific behavior aimed at in the satisfaction of the need.

All the protoemotions are somewhat similar in their basic mechanisms. Fear leads to motor responses predominantly suitable for flight. Rage leads to motor responses predominantly suitable for fight. Like the simple sensations, physiosensations and instincts, protoemotions have a purpose: they are part of the self-regulatory mechanisms necessary for the preservation of the individual and/or of the species. In all these experiences the subjectivity tremendously enhances the chances of re-establishing or maintaining homeostasis. Whereas ethologists exclusively study instincts, physiologists, because of the wealth of physiologic responses, have more characteristically studied protoemotions. A great part of the theoretical framework of orthodox Freudian psychoanalysis is based on the model of the instinct. Many theories of academic psychology are based on the model of protoemotion.

EMOTIONS

However, another category of experiences of inner status exists, the category which has the greatest importance for the psychiatrist: emotion.[3] In this category are included the highest emotions of which the human being is capable: such

---

[3] As will be more clearly illustrated in this section, in this paper the term "emotion" has a more restricted meaning than is customary, being limited only to high-level experiences and not to the types of inner experiences described above.

experiences as (long-circuited) anxiety,[4] depression, shame, guilt, joy, love, happiness, etc.

Let us first compare emotions with protoemotions. Whereas in protoemotions the cognitive element[5] is constituted by the perception of a definite and circumscribed set of present stimuli, often indicating an imminent or threatened change of homeostasis, in emotions the cognitive element is much more extended. No emotion exists as naked emotion, that is, as an experience of inner status which is not accompanied by extended conscious or unconscious cognitive elements. Such feelings as long-circuited anxiety, depression, guilt, shame, love, contempt, loyalty, awe, etc., can exist only if they are engendered by cognitive processes.

To be specific, an unpleasant emotion, for instance, is not elicited by a direct attack on the intactness of the organism or by a threatened change in homeostasis, but by cognitive processes which stand for such an attack. For instance, if I have to take an examination tomorrow and I am not prepared, I experience anxiety. The thought of the examination is the equivalent of a direct physical attack on my organism; it is an attack on my emotional homeostasis. However, such a stimulus exists only inasmuch as my cognitive faculties permit me to conceive the thought of the examination.

The thought of the examination stands for an attack that is not present, it is symbolic of a direct attack. It is not only

---

[4] An emotional status which is intermediate between fear and (long-circuited) anxiety is what I have called short-circuited anxiety (1947). Short-circuited anxiety is an emotional reaction to a danger which is not yet present, but is imminent or expected very soon. It may be elicited only by a *sign*, that is, by something which indicates the forthcoming or imminent presence of the stimulus. Short-circuited anxiety is also determined by lack of satisfaction of a need, when such satisfaction is expected. Another form of short-circuited anxiety is elicited by the inability to react to one of two present conflictful stimuli.

[5] The designation "cognitive element" is incorrect inasmuch as the cognitive process which leads to an emotion is not yet part of the emotion itself. We should rather use the terms "cognitive associations" or "cognitive inner status." For sake of simplification, however, we shall retain the term "cognitive element" to mean those cognitive processes which are necessary to elicit an experience of inner status.

symbolic in space; it is also symbolic in time. The examination
will take place tomorrow, but the emotional attack is already
here. Experience has only one tense: present. My cognitive
process transports into the present what belongs to the future.
But more than that. The cognitive process transcends my
body boundaries: if, for instance, I am afraid not that I will
flunk the examination but that my child will flunk the examination, a disturbance occurs in me on account of what
may happen to another organism. In previous types of experiences only what happened to the subject was subjecti-
vized. Thus, because of the cognitive process, the emotion
enters the interpersonal field. Actually only an interpersonal
environment can offer the individual the symbolic elements
which are necessary for complicated cognition and therefore
for high emotions. We cannot go into this topic here, because
we would have to examine the relation between symbolism
and socialization, which I have done elsewhere (1955).

To be sure, in protoemotions, too, primitive interpersonal
elements enter at times, but they are rudimentary and not
always necessary. They involve the present or the immediate
future of the individual, and the other person or animal is
important only inasmuch as it changes the individual's state.
For instance, a cat may be important to a mouse, but only
inasmuch as it may change the status of the mouse, and not
per se. The mother may be important to a newborn baby,
but only inasmuch as she may convey pleasure or displeasure
to the baby.

Summarizing, the cognitive elements of emotions become
stimuli capable of transcending space, time, and the intra-
personal. As a matter of fact, they usually concern, or are a
reflection of, the interpersonal world. This expansion is of
the greatest psychiatric significance. We know, especially as a
result of the teachings of the neo-Freudian schools, that the
greatest emotions which move people occur at this level.
Love is as important as sex, or more important than sex, in
moving human beings; and fear of losing self-esteem or self-

identity is just as intense as fear of castration. But these high emotional states cannot occur without complicated cognitive and interpersonal processes that are necessary to elicit these emotions. The foregoing does not imply that high emotions cannot occur early in life: on the contrary, they do. Indeed, the fact that they do may engender complications and become sources of psychiatric disturbances. The cognitive elements in young age are relatively few and may become connected with inappropriate or too-intense emotions. The child may be led to wrong assumptions and generalizations, to restrictions of intellectual functions, to inability in finding conflict-free areas, and may become more involved with primitive types of emotion, like excessive sexual preoccupations, phobias, etc.

One of the main differences between the orthodox Freudian and the interpersonal schools of psychiatry is the following: whereas the orthodox Freudians emphasize the importance or the strength of instincts and of protoemotions, the interpersonal school emphasizes the disturbance at the highest level. The primitive emotion which returns pathologically is seen as symptomatic of a disturbance occurring at a high level— disturbance which prevents the manifestation of a more adequate form of emotion.

Now let us compare emotions and protoemotions at the second point: the somatic response. We have seen how rich protoemotions are in somatic, that is, endocrine, muscular, and visceral, responses. Considerable somatic responses occur in emotions too, especially in anxiety, but far less than in protoemotion. In fear and rage, for instance, there is a large discharge of adrenaline, whereas in depression the secretion of adrenaline is almost inhibited; the nervous excitement selects other neuronic patterns, which expand in the central nervous system rather than in the autonomic and have a central response rather than a somatic one. Recent studies, e.g., Whatmore and Ellis (1959), have revealed microactivity in the muscles of very depressed persons, for instance, in patients who are in depressed stupors. Such activity, which may be seen only with special techniques, probably has the purpose of inhibiting more adequate muscular responses.

We come now to the third point: the emotion as felt experience. Whereas in protoemotion the experience leads almost immediately to a motor or visceral outlet and to the extinguishing of the feeling itself, in emotion the feeling lasts longer, leads less rapidly to discharging outlets, and seems to expand as feeling per se. This felt experience is for our purposes the most important element. It is actually what connects these high emotions with the more primitive types of experiences of inner status, such as pain, hunger, sexual urge, fear, etc.

Somebody could object to our putting together all these experiences, in the belief that high emotions belong to an entirely different universe of experience and have nothing in common with the above-mentioned lower experiences. On the other hand emotions have many characteristics in common with the other experiences of inner status. They are feeling-states, felt within the boundaries of the organism; they have a qualitative nature. They cannot be localized as easily as sensations and cannot be verbalized too easily because intrinsically they are subjective experiences and not cognitive or symbolic processes.

Why are such high emotions as anxiety and depression often referred to as mental pain? Because they are similar to pain. No wonder the word *pain* connotes both physical and emotional or mental pain. This is not a peculiarity of the English language. In all the languages with which I am familiar, the word for pain has these two meanings.

Physical pain is the result of a direct attack on the continuity or intactness of the organism. As a rule it can be localized.[6] Mental pain stands for such a physical pain; it is in a certain way the equivalent of such a pain. Like a physical

---

[6] Thalamic pain cannot be localized and is in some ways similar to an emotional experience.

pain it has a purpose; it demands removal. Unless pronounced
to a very pathological degree it leads to responses which are
beneficial for the organism.[7] It is a warning signal as well as
an experience of discomfort.

It is chiefly its qualitative nature which leads us to classify
emotion as an experience of inner status. Let us take into
consideration anxiety or depression. Some anxious or depressed people experience peculiar sensations within their
chest, abdomen, throat, back; others experience numbness,
paresthesias on their skin, etc. Some of these feelings are the
results of those autonomic alterations which accompany emotions (for instance, blushing in a state of shame) and are part
of the somatic response. The majority of these feelings, however, cannot be localized, has no peripheral or somatic bases.
They are central in origin; they are not the peripheral con-
stituent of the emotion as the disproved James-Lange theory
advocated. They are almost attempts at reproducing the
equivalent of a physical pain. They are part of the subjective,
qualitative aspect of emotion.

This flavor, or affect, is mediated in the archipallium, possibly in the gyrus cinguli and in the hippocampus.

Emotion is thus a change in inner status. If the change is
experienced as unpleasant, the organism is directed toward
the removal of the factor which has caused the change; if
the change is experienced as pleasant, the organism is directed
toward behavior which tends to perpetuate or at least to pro-
long the new inner status. Whereas even pleasant physioperceptions, instincts, and protoemotions tend to exhaust
themselves in the act of consummation or in the immediate
outlet, the pleasant emotion aims at the prolongation of itself. Thus it becomes an end in itself.

Emotions thus become motivational forces of tremendous
importance. What Freud calls *cathexis*, investment of energy
or libido, actually is nothing else but the motivational value

---

[7] Elsewhere (1959) I have illustrated the purposefulness of depression.

of the experiences of inner status, as Freud himself used to think before he wrote *The Ego and the Id*. It is the affect or emotion which accompanies any percept. Although these experiences of inner status act *as if* they were powerful physical forces, it is inexact to consider them as manifestation of an energy, resembling kinetic or thermic energy.

For example, as Fromm (1947) has illustrated, if I love a person, this emotional status of mine does not imply that I spend my libido on the object of my love, or that I am impoverished in energy because I love. Experiences in life contradict this fact. Love is a pleasant experience of inner status: an experience that by being pleasant motivates behavior which enhances its perpetuation.

We cannot equate in any quantitative way the intensity of an affect with the cognitive process with which it is associated, or with the intensity of the perceptual stimulus which originated it or with the intensity of the nervous impulse. Neither can we equate the intensity or extension of the nervous impulse with the consequent muscular effort or hormonic behavior determined by such an impulse. We cannot equate the energy change involved in the production of the stimulus with its stimulus value. We cannot equate energetically the work of neurons with the consequent work of muscles. There is no evidence that these processes can be transformed into each other in accordance with the physical law of conservation of energy. Although these processes are based on a physical substratum and must follow each other in certain sequences, each of them evokes an emerging order of different phenomena. If we must resort to a reductionist approach, the best is still the neurophysiological one which teaches us that there is no transferable energy within the nervous system but only a nervous excitement which is transmitted "through the interaction of specific neural elements" (Lashley and Colby, 1957).

By considering now how cognition and affect are connected, we may understand their reciprocal influence. The emotional accompaniment of a cognitive process becomes the propelling drive not only toward action but also toward further cognitive processes. Only emotions could stimulate us to overcome the hardship of high cognitive processes and lead to those complicated symbolic, interpersonal, and abstract processes of which man is rightly proud. Thus a circular process originates. No high emotions exist without cognitive processes, but no cognitive process can exist, expand, or ramify without emotion.

If man studies complicated mathematical problems or looks at the distant stars, or thinks of things which occurred in the remote past or are expected to occur in the distant future, not only does he attempt to mirror events regardless of space and time, not only does he search for a coherent relationship among the apparently unrelated parts of nature, but his inner self, his inner status, his highest level homeostasis are altered, as a result of these endeavors. Thus every cognitive process becomes an inner experience. The spectator of all the times and of all the existences is "touched inside" by all the times and by all the existences. Whatever is perceived touches the core of man. The highest experiences of inner status (predominantly of the inner self) and the cognitive experiences (predominantly of the external world) are necessary to each other. Only those who do not understand this reciprocity can give prominence to one or the other category. The experience of the inner world is necessary to understand the external world, the experience of the external world is necessary to understand the inner world. Such questions as, "Does the heart speak before the intellect or does the intellect speak before the heart?" have no meaning in the circular process of the human psyche. Every emotion has a secret logic behind it, every logical thought rests on a secret emotion.

However, such experiences are not endless. We have already mentioned that cognitive experiences are limited by the finitudes of the symbolic ways; we must add that the possible emotional responses are much smaller in number than those of the symbolic order. This disparity is in fact very important in psychopathology. People tend to respond emotionally in similar ways to different cognitive processes, perpetuating a tendency established in the early years.

The foregoing can also be interpreted anatomically and physiologically. The archipallium which originated in evolution as the center of olfaction was later converted into an emotional center, when the importance of olfaction declined in the highest animal species. Although it is often emphasized that the neopallium is the part of the central nervous system which has undergone the most conspicuous growth in the human species, let us remember that in an absolute sense the archipallium too is larger in the human species than in any other. The neopallium would not have expanded to the human size if it had not been accompanied by an expansion and reorganization of the archipallium. There is a functional equilibrium between archipallium and neopallium. In schizophrenia, this equilibrium is altered (Arieti, 1955, 1956; Gerard, 1956). The archipallium has the function of giving an inner qualitative or affective tone not only to some of the lower experiences of inner status that we have described but also to the cognitive processes, as if such cognitive processes would alter the homeostasis or the inner status. Thus the emotional experience is not the result of a changed status in the soma, should not be confused with the somatic resonance (James-Lange theory), but is mediated by a central excitement of the archipallium. If the emotional experience seems to involve the soma, it is not only because all central experiences must be projected either to the soma or to the external world, [8] but also because phylogenetically in emotion there is an attempt at mimicking the lower forms of experiences of inner status which are substituted by the emotion. [9]

---

[8] For instance, if I see a book in front of me, the visual experience of the book occurs around my calcarine fissure, but I project the existence of the book to the external world. I project other experiences to my soma.

[9] Seeing the totality of the emotional experience as "central" means considering the phenomenon as another example of what neurophysiologists call encephalization. With this name neurophysiologists designate the process by

EMOTION AND THE STATE OF UNCONSCIOUSNESS

What we have so far outlined leads to many areas of fruitful psychiatric investigation: for instance, to the study of how certain emotions may disturb cognition and lead to regressive forms, how emotion may be displaced, or generalized or substituted by lower forms of experiences of inner status. It is beyond the purpose of this paper to illustrate these points. I shall briefly discuss one point, however, which is of great interest to the psychologist and the psychoanalyst: whether experiences of inner status and especially emotions can be unconscious. Perhaps the greatest merit of psychoanalysis is to have demonstrated how certain cognitive processes may become totally or partially unconscious. If, for instance, a patient experiences free-floating anxiety, it is because the cognitive processes connected with this emotion have been repressed. This mechanism is relatively clear, and almost universally accepted today. What we do not know is the physiological process by which conscious ideation becomes unconscious. No physiological interpretation of repression is possible with the data available at present. But what is also unclear is the relation of affect to consciousness and unconsciousness. Freud (1915) has dealt with this problem in his paper, "The Unconscious." Freud writes that although in psychoanalytic practice we are accustomed to speak of unconscious emotions like love, hate, etc., and for practical purposes we may continue to do so, actually there are no unconscious affects. Affects may be displaced, or suppressed altogether; but if they exist, they exist in a state of consciousness. In *The Ego and Id* (1923) Freud writes, "Certainly the qualities of feeling come into being only by being felt." Fenichel (1945) and most orthodox analysts follow Freud. All this makes very good sense and is logically tenable if we ac-

---

which functions that in lower species are mediated by lower or more caudal centers shift toward higher centers. In encephalization higher levels not only "go beyond" lower levels, but in a certain way they also "mimic" the lower levels.

cept the fundamental premise of traditional psychology that emotion is a felt experience. There are some difficulties, however. For instance, what do we mean by unconscious motivation, a concept we cannot dispense with in dynamic psychiatry and psychoanalysis? Do we mean that only the cognitive part of motivation is unconscious or that motivation is only a cognitive process? These points of view cannot be upheld. Although motivation has undoubtedly a very important cognitive element, it is also loaded with affect. Indeed we have seen that it is the experience of inner status that constitutes the motive as motive, as drive toward a goal. As I have just mentioned, this difficulty cannot be overcome if we maintain the premise that emotion is only a felt experience. However, the reader will remember that at the beginning of this paper we have gone to considerable length to demonstrate that neurophysiology teaches that sensation is not necessarily accompanied by consciousness, needs not be felt. Later we have shown how emotions and sensations belong to the same category of mental activities. There is thus no logical reason to assume that unconscious emotions are not possible, i.e., that in some cases not only the cognitive element but also the emotional element of the apperception is made unconscious.

Clinical practice discloses that in pathological conditions both sensations and emotions may become unconscious, i.e., remain as they are, except that they lose the element of awareness.

In hysteria, large areas of anesthesia, functional blindness, deafness, etc., may occur.[10] The fact that the hysterical patient retains reflexes in the anesthetized areas (they might even be exaggerated) discloses that the sensation has not been suppressed but only the awareness of it. I have reported (1945, 1955) loss of awareness of sensation in very regressed schizophrenics, although the reflex reactions were retained.

---

[10] Good descriptions of them are found in some psychiatric books (Abse, 1959) but especially in some textbooks of neurology (Purves-Stewart and Worster-Drought, 1952).

Cases of depersonalization, of self-alienation, of preservation of intellectual sphere with loss of the affective one are too well known in psychiatry to be mentioned here. All these cases deserve further study. The displacement of the emotional components of cognitive processes is certainly one possibility. But there is no sufficient reason to deny that at least in some of these cases the emotional components are retained in a state of unconsciousness. The fact that they may suddenly reacquire consciousness in the usual patterns of thought, either in awakened life or in dreams, seems to indicate that they exist and that only the awareness of them has been lost. Thus it would seem that not only cognitive processes but also emotional ones may regress or return to the big unconscious neurological matrix.

CONCLUDING REMARKS

As simple as the above considerations may seem to some people, they are liable to disturb others. For instance, some academic psychologists may think that a return to an associationist or atomistic point of view is advocated. In the present framework emotion and cognition are first divided and then associated again, whereas the psyche works as a whole. I do not deny at all that the psyche works as a well-organized unity. But to consider only this total or synthetic aspect is in itself a partial approach. It is also important to know how the different parts of the psyche work and influence each other unless we want to ignore completely the anatomical, physiological, neurological (and I would add some psychological) evidence which makes us believe in the existence of such parts.

A different type of criticism may come from a second group of people: the existentialists, Zen-Buddhists, and related groups. Since they put the emphasis on, or try to reduce everything to, immediate experience, they may resent the assertion that cognitive processes are necessary for high-level emotions. I want to stress that in the present work, too, emotions are considered to be felt experiences. They are felt experiences once they are in existence, but their existence is determined by other processes which are not so immediate. Moreover, the certitude of the immediate experience is only the certitude of experience *qua* experience but not of the meaning of the experience.

A third criticism may come from the orthodox Freudian school. What I have tried to express indeed casts doubts on several of their tenets: the libido theory and also the existence of the id. In fact the id is not at all necessary as a reservoir of energy if the motivational force is affect, affect which may be conscious or unconscious, but which may occur at any level of the psyche.

Actually it seems to me that these preliminary remarks of mine could be deepened by a multidisciplinary approach to which all the schools I have mentioned could contribute. The academic psychologist, including the associationist, may throw further light upon the relation between learning and emotion; the existentialist more than anybody else could investigate the richness of the individual emotional experience; the orthodox Freudian may again reaffirm the importance of the development of the psyche and of the phenomenon of repression; the interpersonal school may throw further light on the high-level emotions even in the very early life of man. Such a multidisciplinary approach might well be patterned after the many examples of that pioneer in the various fields of psychology, Heinz Werner.

SUMMARY

1. Neurophysiology discloses that many "sensations" are not accompanied by awareness or subjective feelings. When sensation is accompanied by awareness "experience" occurs, psychic life begins.

2. Experiences may be divided into two broad categories: (a) those whose main function is the subjectivization of an inner status; (b) those whose main function consists of mirroring reality.

3. The second category expands into increasingly complicated mechanisms of cognition, especially symbolic processes. The first category expands into different forms of psychological processes which are predominantly not symbolic.

4. The experiences of the first category (of inner status) may be divided into different groups: (a) single sensations and perceptions like pain, temperature, etc.; (b) physiosensations and physioperceptions, or experiences of a diffuse state of the organism, like hunger, thirst, fatigue, etc.; (c) instinctual experiences, i.e., diffuse bodily urges released by external stimuli; (d) protoemotions, like fear, rage, etc.; (e) emotions.

5. Proceeding from one group to the next, these experiences of inner status become less localizable and more diffuse, less somatic and more central, and more and more connected with cognitive processes and less and less with alteration of the somatic homeostasis. High emotions are elicited only by cognitive processes (conscious or unconscious), which stand for the alteration of the homeostasis and tend to elicit "a central homeostatic alteration." The anatomical foundations of some of these groups of experiences are briefly discussed.

6. High emotions determined by symbolic, interpersonally engendered cognitive processes, are, in the human psyche, the most prominent experiences of inner status and consequently the most important for the field of psychiatry.

7. There is considerable evidence suggesting that not only cognitive but also affective processes may become unconscious. Conscious or unconscious motivation, as an affective process, may be sufficient to explain psychodynamic processes without the need of the concept of psychic energy.

BIBLIOGRAPHY

Abse, D. W. (1959), Hysteria. In *American Handbook of Psychiatry*, ed. S. Arieti, *1*: 272-292. New York: Basic Books.
Arieti, S. (1945), Primitive Habits and Perceptual Alterations in

the Terminal State of Schizophrenia. *Archives of Neurology and Psychiatry*, 53:378-384.

———— (1947), The Processes of Expectation and Anticipation. *Journal of Nervous and Mental Disease*, 106:471-481.

———— (1955), *Interpretation of Schizophrenia*. New York: Robert Brunner.

———— (1956), The Possibility of Psychosomatic Involvement of the Central Nervous System in Schizophrenia. *Journal of Nervous and Mental Disease*, 123:324-333.

———— (1959), Manic-Depressive Psychosis. In *American Handbook of Psychiatry*, ed. S. Arieti, 2:444-446. New York: Basic Books.

Cobb, S. (1950), *Emotions and Clinical Medicine*. New York: Norton.

Fenichel, O. (1945), *The Psychoanalytic Theory of Neurosis*. New York: Norton.

Fletcher, R. (1957), *Instinct in Man*. New York: International Universities Press.

Freud, S. (1915), The Unconscious. *Collected Papers*, 4:98-136. New York: Basic Books, 1959.

———— (1923), *The Ego and the Id*. London: Hogarth Press, 1947.

Fromm, E. (1947), *Man for Himself*. New York: Rinehart.

Gerard, R. W. (1956), Brain Physiology: A Basic Science. In Rado, S. and Daniels, G. E. *Changing Concepts of Psychoanalytic Medicine*, New York: Grune & Stratton.

Lashley, K. S. and Colby, K. M. (1957), An Exchange of View on Psychic Energy and Psychoanalysis. *Behavioral Science*, 2:230-240.

MacLean, P. D. (1949), Psychosomatic Disease and the "Visceral Brain." Recent Developments Bearing on the Papez Theory of Emotion. *Psychosomatic Medicine*, 11:338-353.

———— (1955), The Limbic System ("Visceral Brain") and Emotional Behavior. *American Medical Association Archives of Neurology and Psychiatry*, 73:130-134.

Ostow, M. (1957), The Erotic Instincts. A Contribution to the Study of Instincts. *International Journal of Psycho-Analysis*. 38:305-324.

———— (1959), The Biological Basis of Human Behavior. In *American Handbook of Psychiatry*, ed. S. Arieti; 1:58-87. New York: Basic Books.

Papez, J. W. (1937), A Proposed Mechanism of Emotion. *Archives of Neurology and Psychiatry*, 38:725-743.

Purves-Stewart, J. and Worster-Drought, C. (1952), *The Diagnosis of Nervous Diseases* (Tenth Edition). London: Arnold & Co.

Schachtel, E. G. (1959), *Metamorphosis.* New York: Basic Books.

Tinbergen, N. (1951), *The Study of Instinct.* Oxford: Oxford University Press.

Werner, H. (1940), *Comparative Psychology of Mental Development.* New York: International Universities Press, 1957.

Whatmore, G. B. and Ellis, R. M. (1959), Some Neurophysiologic Aspects of Depressed States. *American Medical Association Archives of General Psychiatry, 1*:70-80.

The Development of Double Function Terms in Children

An Exploratory Investigation

SOLOMON E. ASCH, Ph.D.

HARRIET NERLOVE, M.A.

Harvard University

Most, probably all, of the terms that describe psychological activities or the properties of persons also describe the properties and activities of things. Words such as *hard, deep, bright* are obvious examples; we will call them "double-function" terms since they refer jointly to physical and psychological data. Their presence in speech is far from coincidental or occasional; a previous study (Asch, 1955, 1958) has demonstrated that languages belonging to different families possess such terms, and that the languages agree significantly in the meanings assigned to them.

Such double-function terms are important for several reasons. They promise to clarify the cognition of psychological events, and its relation to the cognition of physical events.

They are also an elementary instance of metaphorical thinking, which is essential to the understanding of language.

The purpose of this investigation was to trace the development of the use and understanding of double-function terms
in children, as they improve in the mastery of their native
tongue. The children were English-speaking. Our aim was
exploratory rather than definitive; we will formulate the
relevant problems, the developmental trends we were able to
observe, and some questions that await further study.

The historical evidence often fails to show how the double
reference accrued to a given term—whether the physical or
psychological reference came first, or whether both were
present jointly from the start. But to judge by the available
evidence, the extension of terms is a frequent occurrence; and
probably many terms, particularly those that designate ubi-
quitous properties in the environment, referred first to the
physical domain. Of this, however, we can be relatively certain: when a term that has exclusively referred to one region,
say, the physical, is first "extended" to the other, this is the
consequence of a directly experienced similarity between the
respective data. Whoever first called a person *brittle* was at
the time sensing a resemblance between a property of certain objects and of a certain way of acting. This is another
way of saying that double-function terms are distinct from
homonyms or homophones.

One can, however, establish more directly the course of this
development in the individual. This was the aim of the present
study: to observe whether children mastered double-function
terms first in their physical or psychological sense, or simultaneously in both. Accordingly, we attempted to observe the
earliest usages of these terms and the changes they undergo
subsequently. We were particularly concerned to establish how
children understood the nexus between the physical and
psychological meanings, and whether the awareness of duality
coincided with dual usage.

(It was not our intention in this genetic study to throw

light on the historical problem mentioned earlier. The questions are indeed different; one has only to consider that the child is engaged in mastering a relatively completed product, of whose past he has no inkling.)

THE EXPERIMENT

To trace this development it is necessary to establish the meanings of the terms in question at different ages. This we undertook to do with five groups of children, ranging in age from three to twelve years. The most direct procedure would have been to observe and record the natural flow of speech; we followed a more controlled design, questioning the children directly about a limited set of terms. There were ten children in each of the age groups studied. It was not our intention in this first study to establish norms or a scale but rather to seek a trend; for this purpose the small number of children was adequate. Since the particulars of observation and recording varied according to age, they will be described separately in connection with the findings for each group.

The Three- to Four-Year Group

The youngest group, consisting of six boys and four girls, ranged between 3:1 and 4:11. The children, who were from predominantly upper middle-class homes, attended a nursery school in Swarthmore. Specific information concerning mental level was not available, but they were at least of normal intelligence.

The observations were made in a nursery school room set aside for the purpose. The experimenter (who was somewhat known, having previously visited the playground) met each child individually and invited him to play a game of words. In the course of the game the experimenter displayed a number of familiar objects, each of which illustrated a particular physical property. (Among these objects were a cube of sugar, iced water, hot water, a wooden block, a gold-colored metal disk, a branch, a powder puff and a cylinder.) The properties on which we centered were: *sweet, hard, cold, soft, bright, deep, warm,* and *crooked.* The child was shown each object in turn; after some discussion the experimenter mentioned one of the words, asking the child to pick an object that the word named. He was then asked to name a few other objects that the term described, to ascertain whether he had a firm grasp of the physical meaning. If he had (not every child knew the physical meaning of each term), he was asked whether the term could describe persons. This involved a series of questions phrased as follows: "Are people, too, *sweet?* Do you know any *sweet* people? How do you know they are *sweet?* What do they do or say when they are *sweet?*" Since the discussion could become lengthy and trying, each child was questioned on one half of the list, but each was asked about the term *sweet.*

The results can be summarized as follows:

1. Most of the double-function terms were known only in relation to physical objects. The children readily called blocks and boxes *hard,* milk *cold,* water *deep,* and trees *crooked.*

2. In the few instances in which the terms were used to describe persons, the reference was most often to *physical* properties of persons. In explaining how they knew that a person had a given quality, the children gave such replies as: "Poor people are *cold* because they have no clothes"; "Daddy and Mommy are *deep* because they look big"; "Santa Claus is *warm* because he has a long beard"; "If there were gold people, they would be *bright.*"

3. *Sweet* was the only word applied to persons in a sense other than physical. Seven of the ten children applied it to persons, and all of them did so to mean generally "good," "nice," "likable."

4. Several of the children were surprised and indignant at the suggestion that some of the terms could be used to describe persons: "No people are *cold!*" "I never heard of *deep* people anyway!" This strong denial of applicability disappeared in the older groups.

The Five- to Six-Year Group

The children, six girls and four boys, ranging in age from 5:10 to 6:1, attended the kindergarten of the Swarthmore public school.

Since we could rely at this age on a knowledge of the terms, the objects employed with the younger group were discarded. The experimenter mentioned one of the terms, asking the child to name an object to which it applied; all were able to do this. Thereupon they were asked whether the term could also apply to persons (e.g., "Are people *soft?* Do you know any *soft* people? How can you tell if someone is *soft?* What does a *soft* person do?"). If a child used the term in the psychological sense, we proceeded to question him further about its relation to the physical meaning (e.g., "Why do we call sugar *sweet,* and kind, nice people *sweet?*"). Each child was questioned about all eight terms.

1. As with the three-to four-year-olds, these children understood and used the terms mainly in their object reference.

2. When they applied the terms to persons they did so predominantly in their physical sense, as did the younger children.

3. There were only ten instances (out of a possible eighty) in which a term was used to describe a psychological property. Five of these occurred for *sweet,* which continued to stand for what is generally good ("Debby is a *sweet* girl because she is nice." "*Sweet* people are nice; they play with you and give you candy."). The psychological sense of a few other terms began to appear at this stage: *hard* and *soft* each occurred twice, and *bright* once. The terms tended to have a strongly affective charge; *hard* was described as "bad," *soft* as "kind."

4. In only a small proportion of the few cases in which the terms appeared with a psychological reference, could the children suggest a basis for the double function. When they did so, the explanations were also in global, affective terms ("Nice people and sugar are both *sweet* because we like both of them.").

5. At this age we introduced a further step, questioning
the children about the homonym, *ring*. They were asked to
suggest why the same word named jewelry worn on the finger
and the sound of the telephone. This question, which was
also put to all later groups, was included in order to check
whether the children would distinguish between homonyms
and double-function terms. Eight children disclaimed any
similarity; one invented a similarity, suggesting that both
might be black. One child proposed that the similarity re-
sided in the name.

From this point on, the step referring to the object sense
of the terms was omitted. The children were asked to give
examples of the application of each term to persons; when
they did so, they were to describe the meaning. They were
then questioned about the relation between the object and
person meanings. If they gave evidence of understanding the
double function, we inquired whether they knew or had
thought of this relation earlier.

The Seven- to Eight-Year Group

The children were five boys and five girls, ranging in age
from 7:6 to 8:0, all pupils in the second grade of the Swarthmore public school.

1. This group showed evidence of a great increase in the
use and understanding of the psychological sense of the terms.
They showed an adequate understanding in forty-seven (out of
a possible eighty) cases. ("*Hard* people are tough and soldier-
like"; "*Soft* people are gentle and nice"; "*Soft* people are
weak and don't fight"; "*Bright* people are cheerful and
friendly"; "*Crooked* people do bad things.")

2. Although they frequently understood the application
of the terms to persons, the children had great difficulty in
formulating a connection with the physical meanings. A
very few came up with more or less adequate formulations:
rocks and *hard* people are alike in that "they don't move
easily," or "you can't get into the main thing in them";

or, pillows and *soft* people both "give to the touch," "both are comfortable." Most of the children could think of no reason why the same word had two meanings, and several suggested that there was no similarity: "They are two different kinds of *deep*"; "Ice cubes and people are a lot different" (referring to *cold*). These children have moved from a rejection of the psychological applicability of the terms to not acknowledging a relation between the several meanings.

3. The children rarely reported having thought about the double function. They could not explain the homonym *ring*, although a few tried to force a similarity.

The Nine- to Ten-Year Group

These were four girls and six boys, age 9:3 to 10:0, in the fourth grade of the Swarthmore public school.

They showed a further marked increase in comprehension of the psychological meanings. Five children adequately understood each of the eight terms. There was an equally strong increase in ability to state the dual function. "The sun and *bright* (gay) people are both beaming, both look happy"; "*Soft* things and *soft* people are both easy to reach, are not remote"; "Neither *crooked* people nor *crooked* things are upright, straight"; "*Hard* things and *hard* people are alike in that neither of them break." There was no evidence that they had been aware in the past of the double function.

The Eleven- to Twelve-Year Group

These were sixth-grade children, five boys and five girls, ranging in age from 10:11 to 12:1.

Their understanding of the psychological meanings was not much more advanced than that of the preceding group. But this age group showed a noticeable advance in the comprehension of the dual function. This is evident in the cogency of their comments: "*Hard* things and *hard* people are both unmanageable." "*Bright* things and *bright* people are alike in that they are both outstanding, you notice them first."

"*Crooked* things and *crooked* people are roundabout and may be dangerous." The ability to state the relation does not keep pace with the understanding of the terms, but the progress in this direction is striking. We also noted a change when the children responded inadequately. Rather than employ the terms to denote physical properties of persons, they erred by assigning faulty psychological meanings to them: "A *deep* person is gruff and abrupt"; "A *cold* person is independent."

There were few reports of having earlier thought about the dual meanings, surely no more than in the younger groups. But the distinguishing feature of these children was their interest in the questions and in the general subject of the investigation. Many were completely fascinated by the problem and often turned from the consideration of one term to another with great reluctance.

TABLE 1

Frequencies of Psychological Meanings

Age	Number of Words									Total	Per cent
	0	1	2	3	4	5	6	7	8		
3-4	3	7								7	—
5-6	4	3	2	1						10	13
7-8			2	1	2		3	2		47	59
9				1		2	2	1	5	72	90
11							1	1	8	77	96

The results for the several age groups are summarized in Tables 1 and 2. Table 1 contains the frequencies with which the terms were correctly employed to name psychological qualities of persons; the last column gives the mean frequencies in percentages. Excepting the three-to four-year group, for which the observations were more limited than for the others, there is a marked increase at each age up to nine. (The lack of substantial increase between the ages of nine and eleven need have no general significance; it may only reflect the ease of the particular terms that were studied.) Table 2 gives the frequencies with which each age group adequately explained the relation between the physical and psychological meanings. The percentage values of the last column were obtained by dividing the totals at each age by the corresponding totals of Table 1; they thus give us the proportion between the comprehension of the double meaning and the comprehension of their relation. (a) There was a continuous increase at each age level, which corresponds in general to the increases of Table 1. (b) As was to be expected, understanding of the dual relation lagged behind knowledge of the dual meanings. (c) Most noteworthy, though, is the lack of detailed parallelism between the age changes recorded in Tables 1 and 2 (see last columns). Up to and including the age of nine, the relative frequency with which the double function was understood remained appreciably constant; a marked change is observable only at the age of eleven, in clear contrast to the rate of growth of the psychological meanings.

TABLE 2

Frequencies of Comprehension of the Dual Relation

	Number of Words									Total	Per cent
Age	0	1	2	3	4	5	6	7	8		
3-4										—	—
5-6	7	2	1							4	40
7-8	2	3	2	2	1					17	36
9	2	1	1	2	1	1	1		1	32	44
11				1	2	2	2	3	1	62	81

DISCUSSION

We found the following trends in the course of the preceding observations: (1) Children first master the object reference of double-function terms. (2) They acquire the psychological sense of these terms later, and then apparently as a separate meaning, as if in independence of the object reference the term already possesses. (3) The dual property of the terms is realized last, and then not spontaneously as a rule.

How are we to account for the first finding, namely, the prior mastery of the object reference of such terms? One might propose that this is a direct effect of teaching, since adults are far more likely to call the child's attention to these properties in things; for example, children are more often warned to avoid *sharp* or *cold* things than persons. Although the effect of such teaching should not be ignored, it is not convincing as a complete explanation. One should also consider the possibility that the physical properties in question are less complex than the corresponding psychological properties. A term such as *deep* organizes a more inclusive and intricate set of events in persons than in things. It is not as easily isolable from the flux of accompanying events, and may on this account be more difficult to name. Here we must guard against a misunderstanding. The failure to use or understand a term is not evidence of failure to have the corresponding experience. It would indeed be strange to hold that children are insensitive to a person's properties such as *warm* or *cold* on the ground that they have not yet included them in their speech. This comment suggests that the present finding is part of a larger problem, which concerns the conditions that determine the naming of experiences, and particularly those pertaining to persons.

The striking finding is not that psychological meanings appear later in development, but that they are initially divorced from the corresponding object reference. The acquisition of psychological meanings does not, it appears, make contact with the physical meaning that the terms already possess. Taken at face value, this result signifies that, for the child, double-function terms are initially homonyms, and that only later he reaches a stage when he can discern the relation between them.

Instances of failure to experience the identity of a term occurring in systematically different contexts are by no means rare. A proper name, say *Robert*, is imbued with the character of its bearer to such a degree that it seems not to be the same name when it identifies a different person. Homonyms generally are excellent examples of this effect. They illustrate the role of context as a segregating condition, or the strength of part-whole determination. Stated different-ly, the perceived identity of a term is a function of its phonetic and contextual properties; apparently the constancy of the former does not suffice to preserve identity against variations of the latter. But the double-function terms are, unlike the preceding examples, not only phonetically identical but also similar in meaning when they occur in different contexts. To be sure, adults too are most often not aware of these rela-tions, but once their attention is called to it, they are quite capable, as were the older children in this study, of realizing and explaining them. The younger children, however, most often failed and at times firmly rejected the relation. The segregation of the dual meanings is much stronger at earlier stages of development, as if the name were less a conventional symbol and more an indelible part of the thing itself.

It is surprising to find so little evidence for the role of similarity in the process of acquisition. When the child first hears or uses a term such as *hard* to refer to a person, he al-ready possesses its physical meaning, yet apparently he does not recall it at this point. Does this weakness or absence of the similarity function imply that the child would continue to make equally good progress in mastering the language if he had to learn that *hard* meant gentleness in persons, or that it does not matter whether the dual meanings are compatible or incompatible?

The evidence compels us to say that the similarity rela-tion responsible for the emergence of double-function terms in the growth of a language is not active in children's acqui-sition of these terms. In this respect individual mastery fol-lows a course fundamentally different from the history of the language. In one sense this is not surprising, since the child

masters the language of his community, as he does other
cultural products, without knowledge of their past. Therefore
he does not necessarily "recapitulate" the history of the language, and the genetic study does not directly clarify the
historical question mentioned earlier.

The question may be raised whether the children were
perhaps aware of the relations between the dual meanings,
but were unable to formulate them for the experimenter. We
did not find this a problem, and believe that it did not significantly affect the trend of the observations. At no point
did we have the sense that the children were struggling un-
successfully to express what they knew. A related question
concerns the adequacy with which the utterances of the
children were categorized or interpreted. For the most part
the decisions to be made were straightforward. When a ten-
year-old says that a *hard* person is "stubborn, rough, doesn't
give in" we know that he has the psychological sense of the
term; when the same child says that rocks and persons are
hard because neither "can be broken into, you can't get into
the main thing in them," it seems fairly certain that he has
grasped the similarity. Other statements were more difficult
to decide. Let us take a nine-year-old who says that *warm*
persons are "kind and nice." This formulation was considered
adequate; it is overgeneral but well in line with the term's
meaning. This child also stated, when attempting to explain
the dual meaning, that *warm* things and people keep one
warm, adding that the latter do so by hugging and talking.
We were not certain whether the child spoke of the same
thermal property in persons as in things; this answer was
rejected as inadequate. Such uncertainties as arose would
have to be resolved if one were concerned with establishing
a scale, but they did not appreciably influence the trends
that were observed.

The data give evidence of a clear trend, but they do not
tell of the detailed steps responsible for the changes. We need
to understand the conditions responsible for the transition

from the exclusively physical usage, and for the time lag between the presence of dual meanings and the comprehension of their relations. Some observations we made are pertinent to the first question. We saw that at the five- to six-year level children apply the terms to persons in their physical reference. For example, a child explains that her mother is *warm* "because mommy kissed me right here [pointing to her cheek] and made it real warm," or that *warm* people are "warm inside," or that they "make you feel warm." Statements of this kind raise the question whether this step serves as a bridge to the later, distinctively psychological usage, or whether the physical usage has to be superseded if the progress we have described is to occur. Assertions such as that *warm* people are kind because "people usually feel warm if they are kind," provide a bare hint that the bridging procedure may be operative.

Other utterances of the younger children point to a process that has not yet been mentioned. Three- and four-year-olds sometimes said of particular persons that they are *sweet* because they like sweet things, or *soft* because they like soft things. One five-year-old stated that "mommy is *sweet* because she cooks sweet things." These observations, if confirmed, would be evidence of an important effect of contact. It might appear that we have an instance of association by contiguity, but more is involved. Contiguity is a necessary condition for this effect, but most noteworthy is the apparent migration of a quality from thing to person.

SUMMARY

Children's mastery of double-function terms, or terms that name properties of persons and things, shows a regular development with age. Children first use the terms in their reference to objects. When they begin to apply the terms to the psychological properties of persons, they do not realize the relation to the physical reference. Recognition of the double function is last to appear and, as far as we were able to observe, does not occur spontaneously within the age groups studied. In this respect the course of individual development departs from the historical development of the language.

The processes responsible for the trends here observed await further investigation. Such investigation would throw light on the development of cognition of persons.

BIBLIOGRAPHY

Asch, S. (1955), On the Use of Metaphor in the Description of Persons. In *On Expressive Language*, ed. H. Werner. Worcester: Clark University Press, pp. 29-38.
——— (1958), The Metaphor: A Psychological Inquiry. In *Person Perception and Interpersonal Behavior*, ed. R. Tagiuri and L. Petrullo. Stanford: Stanford University Press, pp. 86-94.

The Functions of Perceiving:
New Look Retrospect

JEROME S. BRUNER, Ph.D.

Harvard University

GEORGE S. KLEIN, Ph.D.

New York University

It has been said of adolescence that, though it is inward going, it is not a time of balanced retrospect. It is taken for granted that the so-called New Look in perceptual and cognitive theorizing had its developmental beginnings long before 1946, but the postwar years were the period of its most intense development, certainly in its "search for identity." Yet here we are, at perhaps age thirteen, being asked to write autobiography—a kind of Bar Mitzvah accounting. Adolescence, being a time of conflict, we thought that perhaps the best structure for our accounting might be to examine some of the major sources of stress and antinomy that have plagued the turbulent years of the New Look—or, more properly, the New Looks, for as we have gone about the task of putting these notes together we find that there is indeed a plural and not a singular New Look and that, after all, it is not so new as all that.

What, to begin with, can be said about the degree to which the renewed activity of the so-called New Look has been helpful and to what degree harmful to the progress of work in the field of perception specifically, and in the study of psychological processes generally? Very likely, the most interesting thing historically about the New Look is that it represented a moment of confluence in psychological theory—a response to a desire or a historical force that was anti-separatist in spirit, possibly too much so. To some extent, the antiseparatism stemmed from a need in social psychology and the psychology of personality to recognize the role of perceptual phenomena in guiding action—a development that was a long time growing but slow in finding direct expression in perceptual research. But if it was the case that research began out of an interest in bending perceptual theory to other uses in other fields, it has also been the case that the past decade has witnessed an increasing concern for a better understanding of perceptual processes per se. So while the enthusiastic New Lookers have at times confused the issues and muddied the waters with imperfectly designed and executed research, in the end they may also have contributed materially to the outlook and findings that constitute the field of perceptual research. Our aim is to consider some of these contributions—none of them yet clear, but such is the hazard of writing contemporary history.

We would single out first the manner in which the wooly and residual concept of "set" has been vivified and given substance. Partly as a result of the antidynamic bias of Gestalt theory and partly in reflection of the bias against "internal variables" that characterizes much of American psychology, the concept of "set" and the notions surrounding the word "attention" had been allowed to languish. What seemed most important to research workers who were fundamentally concerned with kinds of perception where stimulus constraints were not seeming to account for all the variance was that perception was highly selective. So work was begun on the effects of need, of interest, of past experience, on the manner of organization of the perceptual field—or, rather, what one saw when one was set in certain ways and, as Julian Hochberg has amusingly remarked, the price of tachistoscopes began to rise. But while it was the case that the very phenomena the New Lookers studied—identification of complex stimulus patterns presented at relatively high speeds or under dim illumination—rigged results so that they magnified the role of variable sets in perception, it was also the case that the same research often pointed to the areas where set factors were of first importance though previously neglected. We make no brief for the various theoretical positions that were put forth by workers in this tradition—hypothesis theories, theories about the role of regulation or of inhibition, and the like—but only remark on the fact that a balance was redressed—and with important consequences.

A similar point can be made about work on other nonstimulus or behavioral determinants in perception—notably past experience. For if it were the case that needs and interests served to program an organism's selectivity of organization and awareness, it was even more the case that past experience had such an effect. It is not a trivial finding that speed of recognition of stimulus materials could be predicted, for example, on the basis of the likelihood of occurrence of such stimuli in the organism's environment—what, elsewhere, one of us has called the surprise-reducing character of perception. But even more strikingly, subsequent research has shown that early sensory experience and deprivation of such experience has a profound effect on the organism's discriminative capacity and on the manner in which the organism's world is structured in terms of perceived relations, equivalence, constancy, etc. While work on early sensory deprivation was inspired by other trends in psychology—notably Hebb's theory of development—it nonetheless tied in closely with the changing outlook in perception brought about by work inspired by the New Look. Indeed, other work also indicated that interruption with the constant bombardment of environmental events has the effect of disrupting the structures so painfully created by the organism's past history.

Perhaps the lesson that has been clearest, where past experience is concerned, is that neither past experience nor the motives and sets that program selectivity influence perception directly, in the sense of providing direct determination of perceptual organization or of selectivity. Rather, they operate by creating structures or "rules of operation" that mediate in a much subtler, indirect fashion to regulate the cognitive activity of the organism. To this point we shall return later. We mention it here to underline one of the mischievous effects of the early work of the New Lookers—the tendency to talk about the effects of needs or past experience or the rest without reference to the complex of mediating mechanisms that are involved. Yet, again there is self-correction in the ways of investigation, for we have seen in the past five years much interesting work at the experimental and theoretical level on the nature of mediators. But more of this in a moment.

Because of the emphasis of New Look perceptual work on selectivity and the rules governing both selectivity of awareness and organization, there is an interesting area of contact between this work and several advances in contemporary biology. The most notable one is in the field of the neurophysiology of perception—even the neurophysiology of sensation. Perhaps the place where this connection is clearest is in the pages of the now-famous Laurentian symposium on consciousness (1954)—or more accurately on the operation of the ascending and descending reticular systems. For two things were apparent in the reports of that symposium and in the work that has followed it. One is the emphasis on the programmed nature of perceptual intake, the other on the role of nonspecific activation as a factor in perceptual organization.

The work from Magoun's laboratory and from Granit's, as well as the work of Galambos and many others, indicates that what registers perceptually—or neurophysiologically—is partly a function of where an organism is directing attention. So that interestingly enough, it was the neurophysiologist who brought the internal variable of attention back into psychology via the back door of physiological research. There has been much less resistance on the part of traditional perceptionists to this backdoor entry by physiologists than there had been to the knocking on the front door by the New Lookers.

In essence, two messages have been contained in the work of the neurophysiologists. The first is that there are cortico-fugal impulses that go down through the reticular formation to program selectivity of intake by way-stations in the sensory system—operating all the way out to peripheral elements like the retinal internuncial fibers or the organ of Corti in the ear. The second is that ascending impulses of a nonspecific type travel up to the cortical areas via the ascending reticular system to serve as boosters or inhibitors of sensory messages, and one can indeed simulate these messages by electrical stimulation, even to the extent of lowering sensory thresholds in tachistoscopic recognition studies by the joint input of a visual stimulus and a jolt to the ascending reticular. Again, the ascending system and its boosting messages seem to be programmed in terms of principles of selectivity that have to do with the general activity or enterprise of the organism at the time of input of the specific stimulus. In general then, though the work of the neurophysiologists has only begun, it would seem as if the model of the nervous system that is now being proposed makes a better fit with the emphasis of the New Look research than with the older conception of a perceptual system completely captive of autochthonous factors programmed once and for all to handle input in terms of certain fixed invariances. But again, when we deal more specifically with the conflicts of the New Look movement, we shall return to this point in discussing the distinction between an emphasis on stimulus domination versus an emphasis on selective programming.

Even the much-maligned research and theorizing on perceptual defense, viewed as a specific instance of interference with or facilitation of activation effects, takes on a more general meaning in the light of these findings in neurophysiology. Indeed, findings like those of Hernandez-Péon and Galambos would indicate that it is a general characteristic of the nervous system, to speak metaphorically, to program out potential inputs that interfere with or distract an organism from the enterprise on which he is working. Why then should we not expect that where there is a built-up avoidance pattern, the same programming out or interference should not occur?

The point that has been made about contact with neurophysiology can be paralleled by one about contact with the work of the ethologists. Certainly the emphasis of Tinbergen on the innate releasing mechanism and its effect on selectivity suggests that the general model of internally regulated programs of perceptual registration holds even for the simplest organisms and that the receptive system is scarcely a matter of passive registration once a traditionally adequate stimulus has impinged. Indeed, the concept of adequate stimulus is something that needs restatement, not just in terms of the capacity for reception of end organs, but in terms of the programmed readiness of the entire receptive system.

But it can also be argued that the ethologists, the neurophysiologists, and the New Lookers, are throwing the picture off balance by elevating ideas about selectivity and programming to the status of the most central concept in perception. Indeed, we believe this is the case, and though we would plead for tolerance toward enthusiasm, we would also remark that there are still many modes of organizing perceptual input that are highly invariant across changes in program and that are not only crucial but highly in need of study.

It seems to us, to take up another point, that there has been a steady increase of insight in the New Look work with respect to an understanding of the perception and judgment of sensory attributes and magnitudes. The early experiment of Bruner and Goodman and the various repetitions were not only marked by technical flaws, but also were hobbled by a conception of need factors "distorting" magnitude judgments—size, weight, brightness, etc. In time, this emphasis was replaced by one that was more relativistic or scalar in nature: that the relevance of a stimulus dimension changes the nature of the scale of judgment imposed on it by the observer—that overestimation and underestimation were matters of relative or comparative judgment, and not a case of distortion of perception from some veridical state. Thus, Bruner and Rodrigues remarked that it was the subjective scalar separation between sizes in a series of objects where size and value were correlated, and not a matter of the absolute subjective sizes of the objects. Tajfel has taken the matter one step further and shown the manner in which imposed value dimensions that correlate or run counter to magnitude changes affect the scale characteristics that develop in judgment. And finally, Klein and his collaborators have shown that the extent of interaction that takes place between a series of magnitudes and a correlated value scale will depend upon the general "flexibility" or "constrictedness" of the perceiver, and that this quality of control is related to certain general cognitive characteristics of the perceiver.

Finally, a word should be said about the reopening of curiosity brought about by the New Look research on the difference between awareness or "report" on the one hand and nonreportable registration on the other. At the very least, we know that input that does not result in reportable awareness when there are no aids to recognition can, with aids to recognition, yield accurate "report" on what is there. Information theory and the work it has generated certainly make that matter clear enough—as in the experiments of Miller, Heise and Lichten, and of Bruner, Miller, and Zimmerman, on the recognition of words presented in noise. With N/2 alternative response categories, a word can be recognized correctly, and with N alternatives, say, recognition in terms of a list of alternatives is close to chance. This is indeed a puzzling finding that tells us that we had better be careful in the N-list case about talking of "chance-recognition performance." Bricker and Chapanis's findings fit this case as well, and we know from their study that subjects can use fragments of the input to help them make a match, as it were, between input and response alternative. Yet, should the number of alternatives be greatly increased, then the match is not possible. Here we come to the issue of underlying cognitive structures and their accessibility for matching with inputs. It is certainly the case that this match may take place later, as in the experiments of Poetzl and Fisher, where unreported parts of a tachistoscopic input appear later in dreams and imagery. The experiments of Klein and his collaborators also indicate that, though one is not able to report the identity of an input, the input may nonetheless affect the nature of what is reported next when a different and supraliminal input is presented. Indeed, the work of Blackwell in America, and of Dixon in England, suggests strongly that the reportability of a stimulus or awareness of a subject depends upon the nature of response alternatives.

The issues have certainly not been straightened out in this troubled area of inquiry, but it is to the credit of the New Lookers that at least they were bold enough to barge in where virgins feared to tread. It is notable, by the way, that some of our purest perceptual virgins have entered the fray after it had been demonstrated that virtue was not automatically to be lost by exposing oneself to the temptations of the unconscious. The less said about subliminal advertising and the clamor it has created, the better—at least at this moment. We have yet to see any evidence about it that mattered terribly much one way or the other.

In sum, then, the New Look has had an activating effect,

a disturbing effect; it has created some useful models; it has got part way through some research that shows signs of being better done; and it has been bold enough to look at problems. It has also been naïve and inept and confusing. Its chief contribution has been to explore the nature of selectivity, but it has also violated its limits. A noisy and brawling adolescent, it has at least had the virtue of not taking much for granted, and in so doing, it has often proceeded without enough attention to the lessons learned by its older siblings and parents.

We turn now to the principal areas of conflict that have plagued the New Lookers and led them into family conflict with other perceptual researchers. We single out three of these: emphasis on autism vs. emphasis upon the programmed nature of perceptual selectivity and organization; the distinction between perception pure and cognition; and finally the relative roles of internally determined selective programs vs. determination by external stimulus events.

AUTISM VS. ADAPTIVE PROGRAMMING

Partly as a result of the early tradition of irrationalism in personality theory and partly out of an impulse to find a simple explanation for complex phenomena, early New Lookers tended to extend the principle of autism into the area of perception: "What looms large in need looms large perceptually," or in extension of the doctrine of primary process, "Perception is a need-satisfying activity." A corollary of this oversimplification was that the effect of need on perception was to distort the percept away from "reality," whatever that might reasonably be expected to be. In brief, the dual principle of some of the earliest work of Murphy, of Sanford, of Bruner, and others, was that (a) the greater the need, the greater its intrusion into and distortion of perception; and (b) distortion went in the direction of warping reality into something approaching wish fulfillment.

It took the zeal of enthusiasts to promulgate that vast (though heuristically useful) oversimplification in the face of the very special conditions that are necessary to produce wish-fulfilling hallucination. In consequence, there was a failure to appreciate the huge effectiveness (not accuracy, necessarily) of perception even under conditions of exigent need. It is not surprising that colleagues who had developed a healthy respect for the stable acuity and finesse of the perceptual system were resistant to the enthusiasts. With time and with the reality-adjusting effect of controversy and corrective research, it soon became apparent that the way in which needs and interests operate is not by any means always or mostly autistic, that the programming of perceptual selectivity was highly stable across changes in need, and that where not stable, it was often geared to requirements that were anything but wish fulfilling. Attention was drawn, for example, to the vigilance-producing effect of need states. It also became evident that a basic rule of set was its predictive expectancy—that thresholds reflected the organism's prediction concerning the transitional and absolute probabilities with which events occurred. Speed of registration or awareness seemed to depend, in sum, upon a subtle programming that governed what inputs would "get in" and how they would be organized.

And so with the effects of need—not on perception per se, but on the nature of the program. Not only needs, but modes of handling them, turned out to be critical, and often in indirect ways. Whether "hot" material was perceived at a lower or higher threshold than psychologically "cool" material depended not so much on need, but on how a person characteristically dealt with his needs. The reality context of the need—what had to be taken into account in gratifying it—had a large part in how the need was permitted to show in behavior; and people differed in their manner of controlling this reality. The degree to which an effect could be discerned at all depended also upon a host of other considerations that entered into the making of a perceptual expectancy—requirements of locomotion, of surprise regulation, of how well practiced the subject was in dealing with inputs such as those used by the experimenter, etc.

But what is amply clear, and it is the subject of the section that follows, is that registration and organization are dependent on a predetermined, though flexible, program—what William James years ago called pre-perception—and such programs seem to vary systematically with many conditions. To argue the contrary on the basis of the results of perceptual experiments where the subject is carefully preset for stability before input is to beg the question, at very least. It does not suffice for the student of apparent movement or differential sensitivity to proclaim, "But who didn't know that!" For if he knows it and fails to appreciate by the effort of research the highly complex presetting that gets him his beautifully clean results, he is guilty of intellectual pound foolishness, of an order to match his exquisite penny wiseness.

We realize that what we have been saying bypasses the question of what Prentice some years ago described as the distinction between functionalism and formalism in perception. The major emphasis of New Look research has been functional, unblushingly so, concerned principally with the functions served by perceiving, the manner in which organization and selectivity serve these, and with the extraperceptual factors that determine function. What has happened over the past decade is a broadening of the conception of function from an overly simple conception of autism to one that recognizes the variable means by which people cope with the givens of experience. This does not mean that formalism as Prentice described it is not a worth-while approach. Rather, it may be that we should celebrate the fact that there are several approaches to perceptual research now flourishing.

PERCEPTION AND COGNITION

Admittedly, one of the difficulties of the New Look has been its loose use of the concept of perception—and our colleagues in neighboring fields do not make usage easier by speaking,

say, of "the perception of national character." Yet it seems
to us not very profitable to circle endlessly the question as it is
usually raised: "Is it *really* perception, or is it inference, judgment, memory, response, or what not?" In fact, the New
Looker has dealt with a somewhat different concept of perception than, say, the student of absolute-brightness thresholds. To caricature the difference, the "perceptual purist" is
interested in studying the most limited and circumscribed attribute of the perceptual experience that he can get hold of
in an experimental setting that will permit him to get a relation between a perceptual response and a stimulus over which
he has rigorous control. He must have a *ceteris paribus* and so
he adopts conventions about "resting state," set, expectancy,
need, past experience, etc. These conventions or fixed param-
eters he then often chooses to forget. The caricature of the
New Looker is based on another source of folly altogether:
he tends to use a stimulus input of a relatively complex kind,
without being able to specify very rigorously its nature, and
then proceeds to vary a great many other conditions that have
little directly to do with conventional descriptions of perception. He often ends up very confused. These are caricatures.
Most of us do not live at such wildly unthoughtful extremes.
But the two extremes perhaps represent our temptations, if
not our practices.

It is impossible to say by *any* criterion that perception in
its purest sense is *not* involved in the final size estimations of
the subjects of the Bruner-Goodman experiment. It is also
plain that there are many other factors interacting with the
purely perceptual. From the first input of light on the subject's eye, through the complex activities that occur before the
subject makes his match and says "Okay, that's it," there are
many interacting processes operating which can be teased
out analytically, to be sure, but which can also be studied in
terms of a final resultant, whether one wants to call that
final resultant a perception or whatever. Eventually, if he is
serious, the student of size estimation will have to tease out

the nature of these processes, both from the point of view of stimulus conditions and behavioral conditions. So, too, the student of the differential threshold. If he is serious, he will have to study the pay-off conditions that affect his phenomenon and all the rest—if ever he is to understand the generality of his effects and not remain a differential-threshold technician.

In the end, the student of the full behavioral context involved in everyday perceiving is bound to set up experiments that involve a wide range of processes over and beyond stimulus input and its variation. For it is precisely in the coming to a decision about the nature of what is present perceptually that past experience and need and the processes of defense and coping come into play. He is doing his research to find out how such processes operate in the making of such decisions for action. To ask him to rule them out of his research in the interest of cleaning up his experiments is as silly as asking the psychophysicist at every turn to replicate his experiments under conditions of inattention or imperious need states, given that his interest is in sensory receptivity under optimal conditions.

In the end, what we are saying is that full explanation of any phenomenon—be it perception or anything else—requires both a close study of the *context* in which the phenomenon occurs, and also of the *intrinsic nature* of the phenomenon itself under idealized conditions. The New Lookers have tended to do the former, the researcher raised in psychophysics and sensory physiology the latter.

It may well turn out that there are some phenomena in perception that are governed entirely by invariant ratios on the retina unaffected by any conditions of judgment or need or the other factors that go into programming perceptual operations, that nothing but these invariants matter. We rather hope so. For these phenomena can then become the last retreat of those who do not want to have their composure disturbed by matters other than those that can be specified as stimulation on the sensory surface of the end organ. And for

the most rabid New Lookers, we wish them a phenomenon
in which the modes of transformation of input stimuli are always overweighed by factors of set and need. For the rest of
us, we think the current confusion is rather healthy, given
how little we really know about the nature of perception in
the large.

SELECTIVITY VS. STIMULUS DOMINANCE

There is a great deal of pseudo controversy here. When a
Gestalt theorist talks about autochthonous factors in perception, when a Gibsonian speaks of the manner in which texture
determines apparent distance or tilt, when a psychophysicist
like Graham speaks of a set of factors in the stimulus input
determining the manner in which brightness or distance or
size will be judged either absolutely or with respect to some
comparison standard, they surely do not intend that there are
no laws of transformation that lead to a conversion of input
into a reportable percept or judgment. It is interesting to look
at what is required to simulate even the simplest forms of perception with a digital computing system. The most striking
thing about the job is that one must set up a program for
handling inputs, a program that governs the way in which
the elementary processes which it controls will operate. Now
it would be a very dumb computer indeed that had only one
rigid order of steps for dealing with input, no provision made
for handling doubtful cases, for example, as to whether this
line is tilted or straight in a tilted background. If one set the
program up that rigidly, then we could properly speak of
complete stimulus determination, for the program would be
such that given the presence of a stimulus pattern at the re-
ceptor, it could behave only in one way—the way dictated
for that program. It seems highly unlikely that such is the
case, and it was certainly never intended by such writers as
Gibson and Hochberg that the proximal stimulus was all,
dictating the nature of the perceptual response save in instances where there was much equivocality, in which case the

program would decide that equivocality was present and signal the system that the time had come for a season in the imaginative sun.

Rather, transformation seems to be all, transformation of inputs by certain interesting rules—for example, that the gradient *lllldddlld* or *llllddddlllldddllddld* both stood for a surface extending into the distance and that the first surface was extending more sharply into the distance than the second. Now, nobody who has ever spent the afternoon in a perceptual laboratory would doubt for a moment that there are such rules of transformation operating in the nervous system—call them rules or structures or schemata or whatever you will. And nobody who had extended his stay in the laboratory for over a week would doubt that one could distinguish between the transformation rules that seem to be highly stable across changes in the state of the organism and across changes in the nature of other characteristics of the stimulus field and those that seem to alter under altered conditions. It seems very foolish indeed to take either the model of the invariant transformations or that of the highly variable ones and propose imperialistically that they are all, and that if certain perceptual phenomena do not conform to them, then, be hanged, they are not perception at all.

Even Gibson's beautiful demonstrations of depth effects produced by texture gradients do not tempt us to go for a walk into his photographs, and yet we know that the rules of transformation he has discovered can be counted on to produce what in painting are called *trompe l'oeil* affects—they are indeed good enough to trick the eye. But we already know enough about the rules governing the organization of the third dimension to know that lots of cues can get used and combined in lots of ways by the nervous system so that there must be some stunning, variable higher-order transformation rules yet to be discovered, and the single determinants of depth, the so-called painter's rules first formulated by Leonardo, do not tell the whole story. The higher order transforms substitute cues for each other, and does all sorts of things to prevent their being a simple correlation between proximal stimulus and report. It is a subtle business and is scarcely "stimulus determination" alone.

That the rules are relatively stable in their operation goes without saying. But that they are also changeable, goes without saying too, for we know that Ivo Kohler's subjects change and develop new rules for dealing with reversed cues by alteration in transformation. We think that this is all that need be said.

In the end, we can only conclude by urging that we wait for the adolescent New Look to become an adult. The real test then will be whether "New Look" still has to be singled out and contrasted with something else. We hope that it will have been absorbed by then, to the enrichment of itself and the host organism—whether the host organism is the study of perception or some more including organism.[1]

BIBLIOGRAPHY

Allport, F. H. (1955), *Theories of Perception and the Concept of Structure.* New York: Wiley.
Blake, R. R. & Ramsey, G. V. (Eds.) (1951), *Perception: An Approach to Personality.* New York: Ronald Press.
Bruner, J. S. (1957), On Perceptual Readiness. *Psychological Review, 64*:123-152.
——— & Krech, D. (Eds.) (1950), *Perception and Personality: A Symposium.* Durham: Duke University Press.
Gardner, R. S., Holzman, P. S., Klein, G. S., Linton, H. & Spence, D. P. (1959), Cognitive Control: A Study of Consistencies in Cognitive Behavior. *Psychological Issues, 1* (4).

---

[1] Comprehensive bibliographies of New Look research can be found in Allport (1955), Blake and Ramsey (1951), Bruner (1957), Bruner and Krech (1950), Gardner et al. (1959), Jenkin (1957), Klein (1956), Tajfel (1957), and Vernon (1952). Because of the ready availability of these sources, no attempt has been made to include specific references to primary sources within the text of this paper.

Jenkin, N. (1957), Affective Processes in Perception. *Psychological Bulletin*, 54:100-127.
Klein, G. S. (1956), Perception, Motives, and Personality: A Clinical Perspective. In: *Psychology of Personality: Six Modern Approaches*, ed. J. L. McCary. New York: Logos Press.
Tajfel, H. (1957), Value and the Perceptual Judgment of Magnitude. *Psychological Review*, 64: 192-204.
Vernon, M. D. (1952), *A Further Study of Visual Perception*. Cambridge: Cambridge University Press.

A Theoretical and Experimental Inquiry into Concrete Values and Value Systems

TAMARA DEMBO, Ph.D.

Clark University

The primary emphasis in this paper is on "concrete values and value systems." The term "concrete" is here used to qualify those values and value systems which are at a given time emotionally important to an individual. Concrete values are distinguished from "abstract" ones, namely, those which he looks at from a distance, without emotional involvement. Concrete

The research reported here is based on work done during the years 1951–1953 while the author was on a USPH Special Research Fellowship in Mental Health. The entire research program was carried out in the Department of Social Relations, Harvard University, under the sponsorship of Dr. Henry A. Murray. I would like to thank Drs. G. W. Allport, H. A. Murray, and T. Parsons for creating a fruitful atmosphere in which this work was undertaken. I would also like to thank Tanja Leshinsky for her aid in the technical analyses of the data, and Victoria Livingston for her criticisms of style and for her help in making the original report an English-sounding one.

values are not intellectual abstractions but functioning units.

In this report I shall first take a few steps toward the conceptualization of values, and then discuss certain methods for the investigation of some value problems as these are formulated within my conceptual framework. In the main, therefore—despite some overlap—the report is divided into two main sections.

CONCEPTUALIZING VALUES

Whereas needs and drives have a more or less established position in psychological theory as sources of energy of behavior, a dynamic construct expressing the essential characteristics of values must still be formulated. One can, in fact, even question whether a conceptualization of values in terms of such dynamic characteristics as forces, tensions, and barriers is the most adequate one to have; perhaps new constructs of a different type must be introduced if one is adequately to grasp the nature of values and determine their place within a person's make-up.

This consideration led me, at the outset, to leave open the question whether a particular constellation of forces should be ascribed to values. I knew too little about those characteristics distinguishing values from needs, drives, and other psychological phenomena easily susceptible to dynamic formulation. I felt that hastily to ascribe definite dynamic properties to values might hinder my receptiveness to other characteristics possibly more fundamental to their nature. In trying to conceptualize values, I came finally to some notions which I should like to discuss here. These notions are, of course, provisional; further work on value problems will be needed to integrate these conceptions within a consistent and comprehensive psychological theory.

My first point is that values are best conceived of as qualities. In our present quantitatively oriented era in psychology, I cannot stress this point too much. Values are qualities of psychological events, their contents as they are experienced. I re-

ject the view which limits the concept of value to a common
characteristic of diverse experiences—that of "positiveness."
There is not one feeling of "positiveness" but diverse ones;
there may be as many as there are experiences. Thus, for example, there are differences in the feelings of positiveness in
such values as "health," "a peaceful world," "wisdom," "a
beautiful home," "being kind." Therefore, I feel we are faced
with the task of analyzing the contents of different experiences, rather than to try to understand a single content, that of
"positiveness." The same holds in regard to "disvalues"—
experiences of diverse negative contents.

If one grants that values are qualities, my second point is
that they are complex qualities; to grasp their nature, then,
one would have to grasp their inner structure, i.e., their components or constituents. Furthermore, in so far as the components of a value may themselves be complex qualities, a
fuller understanding of values would require a determination of the components of components. Just as the physical
world can be broken down into molecules, atoms, electrons,
etc., so too might the world of values be broken down from
larger entities into smaller components.

The third point I wish to make has to do with what I call
"purity" of a value. If—for convenience—one designates those
values elicited from a subject zero-level values, and the components of zero-level values, values on the -1 level,[1] then a
pure value is one which contains no disvalues among its components. Now, I assume that such pure values exist and operate in the individual.[2] I also recognize, however, that values
which are pure in themselves may, under certain circumstances, be regarded by an individual as disvalues, and also
that disvalues may be taken in certain situations as values.
For example, having food is a value, yet a sick person may not

---

[1] The designations -1, -2, etc., are used for components because $+1$, etc., are
used to designate larger structures including zero-level values as elements.

[2] By exist "in the individual" is meant that the person *holds* the belief that
the particular value content is valuable, or, in other words, *accepts* the content
as a value. This study deals mainly with accepted, or held, or believed-in values.

value food when he feels pain, and a religious prohibition may make a person reject an edible object even if he is hungry. Again, though murder is felt by people to be a pure disvalue, to someone under the threat of attack, killing may become a "circumstantial value" and be given the appealing name of "self-defense."

To study how circumstances transform values and disvalues is undeniably important. However, it is at least as important to determine pure noncircumstantial values (and disvalues). Only when one has gained knowledge about pure values can one study systematically how their modification in various life contexts results in circumstantial values (or disvalues).[3]

My problem, therefore, was to find an area where the impact of external circumstances and internal conflict on a subject's values would be reduced to a minimum. With this thought in mind, I decided to investigate an individual's wished-for ideals. How this was done is described below (Experiment I). After ascertaining these wished-for ideals I then sought to determine the components of these values; how this was done is also described below (Experiment II).

In investigating wished-for ideals and the components of such values, I found that there was a remarkable consensuality among individuals of quite diverse ages, backgrounds, occupations, etc.; I also found that there was considerable agreement among individuals as to the components of these values. Moreover, I learned that the components of one value on the zero level often overlapped with the components of other zero-level values. The overlapping of components of different values was of extreme importance and led me to a central issue in the study of values, viz., the issue of the relationship between values, or—more specifically stated—the problem of "value systems."

---

[3] The impact of reality outside the person and conflicting forces within him can modify values he would hold were he free from these pressures. Hindering, conflicting, and imposing circumstances change values and lead to the existence of contrary circumstantial values in different people and cultures.

The expression "system of values" is used not only in psychology and other social sciences, but also in everyday life. However, statements of strict criteria for determining whether values constitute a system are lacking in the literature known to me. I shall advance the following criterion: Values belong to a system in so far as they are not a conglomerate of single entities, but are dependent on each other in such a way that a change in one value affects the other values held.[4] I do not mean that an investigator can see the dependence of one value on another; I mean that the values must be seen as interdependent by the individual who holds them.

The way in which I sought to determine the existence of a subject's system of values is described below (Experiment III).

In terms of our previous designations of elicited values and components of values as being on the zero-level and -1 level, we may regard systems comprised of zero-level values as existing on the $+1$ level. As will be seen, there is more than one system of values on a $+1$ level for a person. Thus the system of values which an individual wishes a child to possess often differs from the system obtaining when an individual is asked concerning values wished for himself.

A number of systems on a $+1$ level must be distinguished from another kind of system which is more abstract, but at the same time more basic than systems existing at the $+1$ level. The nature of this other kind of system will be discussed below.

The next point I wish to make concerns "dealings with values." The values a person accepts are presumed to be interdependent. If one of them is changed or excluded, the person finds that, though he may not wish it, other values are changed. To a certain degree, values are independent of a person's intentions and wishes, much like objects in the physical world which have properties apart from him. In this sense, values accepted by the person are real and not simply the fancies of

---

[4] The concept used here of a dynamic system is the same as used by Köhler (1920), Koffka (1936), and Lewin (1936).

an individual; they are as real as an individual's needs or body parts, which he cannot change at will. Though limited by their properties, a person can handle his needs and his body parts; similarly, he can handle the values which he accepts. For example, he can select values, reject them, approve of them, possess them, etc. The various ways of handling values, I call "dealings with values."[5]

One might think of representing all dealings with values in terms of movements toward a goal; such a treatment would not, however, suffice to characterize the qualitative differences between dealings. As a matter of fact, among the multitude of dealings with values, there seems to be only one kind that can be well described in terms of locomotion to a goal, and these are attempts to possess values; the actual process of possessing values and diverse dealings with possessed values cannot be described in this way.

Not only values but also dealings with values are evaluative in nature. As such, dealings with values will—for a full understanding—have to be analyzed into their components analogously to that which has been done with values per se.

We turn next to the relation between values and disvalues. It hardly needs to be pointed out that sickness, war, and injury are disvalues. Disvalues are in close communication with values. The two areas seem at times to overlap. Frequently subjects in experiments, instead of wishing *for* positive values, made wishes *against* disvalues; e.g., some wished for the absence of physical and mental disease rather than for health. Again, when asked in a subsequent experiment to state disvalues they would wish to be guarded against, some subjects complained, contending that they had already stated these wishes when asked for positive values. The fact that there

---

[5] My notion of "dealings with values" stems from and is closely related to Henry Murray's conception of "vectors." Working on what may be considered "circumstantial values," Murray introduced such vectors as "exploring," "acquiring," "allocating," "constructing," "maintaining," "transmitting," etc., modes of dealing which are applicable also to pure values.

may be confusion between wishing for values and guards against disvalues should not lead to the assumption that values and disvalues can be lumped together. Values in their pure form have positive components; disvalues have negative ones.

In daily life, of course, where choices between disvalues are often forced upon an individual, one evil relative to another one may appear to be a value. If there is no alternative to a choice of one of two disvalues, the lesser disvalue appears relatively valuable. However, since this disvalue, in and of itself, lacks positive content, I shall designate it—when chosen with respect to a greater disvalue—as a quasi value. Thus, given a choice between hurting another person or being hurt oneself—with no way out—a man may choose to hurt the other person; but hurting another, in and of itself, is a disvalue which becomes a better-of-two-evils value, or a quasi value, under certain circumstances. The change of a disvalue into a quasi value does not necessarily mean a change in content. The individual may well be aware of the negative character of the circumstantial quasi value, and regard it as a mere reaction to the impact of adverse circumstances, to what Murray (1938) has termed "press."

There is another possible relationship between values and disvalues. As will be seen, some people believe that to reach a particular value, it is necessary to experience disvalues. They thus consider disvalues as valuable in attaining a value. The idea of salvation through suffering may have its roots in this kind of connection. In these cases, the connection between a disvalue and a value is not seen by the person as something imposed by circumstances. Rather, it is seen as inherent in the possession of the value, in the nature of things, and independent of particular situations. Such connections are another case in point bearing on the reality or independence of values from the individual.

These considerations conclude this first section of the paper. Although I have touched incidentally and cursorily on methodological issues, I have primarily emphasized the conceptualization of values. In the next section, which is primarily devoted to a discussion of methods, I shall—here and there— introduce new theoretical notions, where these seem necessary.

METHODS FOR STUDYING VALUE PROBLEMS

In discussing methodology in this section, I shall relate my discussion to concepts and topics mentioned in the previous section. I will also give, more or less informally, the outcome of applying various methods, indicating what happens typically, as well as what kinds of variations and deviations occur. Throughout, it should be recognized that my primary purpose was theoretical and methodological clarification rather than simply quantitative results.

Before going into a relatively detailed description of each of the methods I have used, I may briefly mention the aims of the various experiments I have undertaken, so as to provide a general orientation for the reader: the first experiment was directed toward the determination of a certain set of zero-level values, viz., those an individual holds for a child close to him; the second experiment was devised to determine the components of such zero-level values; the third experiment was developed for the determination of systems among zero-level values; the fourth experiment was designed to determine zero-level values for oneself and to examine differences between values for the self and values for another person; the fifth experiment was designed to determine zero-level disvalues; the sixth experiment was devised to determine the effects of externally introduced values on the values and value systems held by an individual; the seventh experiment focused on the relationships between a person as agent and the values with which he deals; finally, the eighth experiment was directed toward a determination of the value of disvalues.[6]

---

[6] In designating the experiments as first, second, third, etc., I refer to the order of presentation in this paper, not to the order in which the experiments were actually carried out.

Experiment I: Determining Values on a Zero Level

Despite the relative independence of the realm of wishes from the reality environment, the effect of wishes on the conduct of human beings is not to be underestimated. Wishes are our guides in selecting what to pursue and what to choose. Much of our enjoyment and dissatisfaction is dependent upon the particular wishes we have. What is wished for are accepted values; such accepted values may or may not be possessed.

The general requirement in any psychological experiment with human beings—viz., that the subject be emotionally involved in the task—is especially important in an experiment on wished-for values. One way of inducing a subject to wish seriously is to place him in a situation in which wishing would seem emotionally important to him. Such a situation may be presumed to exist when a subject is asked to make wishes for a child he loves. In such a situation, wishing seems very appropriate to people of all ages and all walks of life and becomes a serious matter. For some, the situation may lead more easily to an emotional involvement if they are told that the wishes will be made to come true through the intervention of a fairy.

The actual procedure I have used is as follows: The subject was met by the experimenter, and thanked for his cooperation. After the subject was seated, the experimenter explained to him that, for convenience, a recorder would be used during the experiment; the recording apparatus was then tested with the subject. After this, the experimenter sat down, and asked the subject two questions in rapid succession: "Are you married?" and "Do you have children?" The answers of the subjects were immediately followed by the instructions. The personal nature of the questions are presumed to have facilitated the emotional involvement of the subjects. The instructions were given immediately after their answers so that the subjects would have no time to follow up some thoughts which the questions themselves might have brought to mind.

This was especially important in those cases in which married subjects could not have children.

The instructions for a subject who was married and did have children were as follows: "At the birth of your next child, there will be a fairy present, and this fairy says you can have seven wishes for your child, wishes which will come true (if you fulfill a condition which is easy to fulfill). What are your seven wishes for the child, for the whole life of the child?"[7]

The phrase in the instructions, here given in parentheses, was said in passing: it was introduced merely to impart a fairy-tale atmosphere to the instructions. The phrase was rarely commented upon by the subject, who usually started at once to think about his wishes. If a subject did ask about the condition, the examiner said, in a tone indicating the relative unimportance of the condition, "Well, I'll just ask you to tell me something later about the wishes."

This procedure was modified somewhat, depending on the subject. Married subjects who answered that they had no children were assured "but you will have," and the experimenter immediately proceeded with the modified instruction, "at the birth of your first child . . . " As mentioned above, the experimenter tried to avoid personal statements on the part of subjects who could not have a child. If, however, a woman interrupted to say that she could not have children, the experimenter took the statement matter-of-factly and asked, "Do you have a sister or brother or a good friend whom you like very much?" Usually getting an affirmative reply, the experimenter continued, "Is he (she) married?" and—assuming an affirmative answer—then went on, "Think of the birth of his (her) next child . . . " The transition to a child of relatives or friends appeared to be accepted willingly by subjects. Subjects who had grown children were asked to make wishes for a grandchild. Single subjects who were for various reasons not expected to marry and have children were asked

---

[7] The choice of seven wishes was arbitrary. Three seemed to me too few, and ten seemed too many.

to make a wish for the child of a favorite relative or friend.
Young people, who still were single, were assured that they
would get married and have children. They were then asked
to make wishes for their first child. Finally, to those subjects
who were children themselves, the experimenter said, "I'll
tell you a story. When you grow up and get married you will
have a child . . . etc."

The experiment on zero-level values was performed with
different groups of subjects and in a variety of ways, e.g., with
individual subjects in the form of interviews, with groups—
the instructions being given by the experimenter, and the
wishes written down by the subjects, etc. Wished-for values
were also elicited informally from people in small social
groups. Conservatively speaking, I performed informal experiments on sixty people; in the controlled experiments, 172
subjects were used—26 examined individually and 146 in
groups.[8] As to the diversity of the subject populations, Catholics, Jews, Protestants and those with no religion were included; the age range was from six to seventy-six; economic
status ranged from lower to upper-upper; educational level
ranged from elementary school to professional training; nationality included American, German, Russian, Norwegian,
Dutch, and Chinese. The subjects also varied in "tempera-
ment" and "ideology."

Now as to the findings: The first point to be made is that,
for the large majority of subjects, the limitation to seven
wishes did not lead to the exclusion of any values which were
regarded as important for the whole life of a child. When the
experimenter asked subjects whether they wished to add more
wishes to the original seven, they usually answered that they
had covered everything in their seven wishes.[9] It may be noted,

---

[8] The 172 subjects also participated in Experiment VIII. The 26 subjects
who participated in individual experiments in Experiment I also participated
in all the other experiments with the exception of Experiments III and VI, in
which 15 subjects participated individually.

[9] In a few cases, a subject added one, two—at most, five—wishes to his
original list of seven. In a few other instances, subjects stopped with two or three
wishes, but when urged to continue, they added others.

in this connection, that subjects were often surprised that seven wishes could cover practically all that was really important and valuable in life.

The second point concerns the surprising agreement among individuals of diverse backgrounds on their zero-level values. There were, of course, values unique to an individual or shared by only a few individuals, but the striking fact is that among the very large range of possible values which could have been selected, different subjects selected the same or similar values. For example, "health" was wished for by about 80 per cent of the subjects; the selection of this value, moreover, seemed to be little, if at all, dependent on such variables as age, sex, economic status, etc.

What are the possible reasons for the relatively limited number of values needed to cover the whole life of a person? Again, how can one account for the wide agreement as to zero-level values among individuals of such diverse backgrounds?

As to the first question, it may be that the experimental instructions set a subject to searching for inclusive values; asked to give wishes for the whole life of a child, and limited to seven wishes, one must cover a lot of ground and not limit oneself to single situations or to short time spans. Whether different instructions, e.g., permitting an indefinite number of wishes, would lead to values of lesser inclusiveness and to the mention of many more than seven values is a topic requiring further investigation.

With regard to the second finding—the high degree of agreement on zero-level values among diverse individuals— I would say that this is due to basic characteristics inherent in human nature. Just as there are a number of basic similarities in body build among men, and needs common to all men, so too may values—pure values not influenced by circumstances—be common to human beings.

In stressing the consensuality as to zero-level values, one should not overlook differences among individuals as to such

values. A few striking individual and group differences may
be mentioned. In some devout Catholics, I found that wishes
for a child were not necessarily limited to his life on earth,
but referred occasionally to his preparedness for the life here-
after; in Jewish adolescents, I found frequent wishes for the
well-being of the parents of the child. Most unusual were the
wished-for values of two subjects, a male student of nineteen
and a female student of seventeen: the boy wished that the
child would grow up to be six-feet-four and have a good voice;
the girl gave as her first wish that the child should die at
birth or soon thereafter. It was later learned that the girl had
been referred to a therapist shortly before she participated in
the experiment.

What are the zero-level values generally wished for a child?
On the basis of my impressions from all of my subjects, I
would say that the values most commonly wished for a child
are "health," "economic security," "knowledge" or "intelligence," and "happy marriage" (or "loving and being loved").
The one detailed analysis I have done—on 56 adolescents
comprising four groups ranging in age from fourteen to seventeen—bears out this impression: of these adolescents, 86 per
cent wished for "health," 70 per cent wished for "economic
security," 66 per cent for "education," and 60 per cent for
"happy marriage."[10] Whether this distribution of zero-level
values for a child would obtain in other groups of subjects
can only be determined empirically. Intensive studies with
other groups—varying in terms of such factors as age, sex,
nationality, economic status, etc.—and experiments made in

----

[10] When I say here that the subjects wished for "health," etc., for the child,
I refer to my classification of wishes formulated in more concrete terms by the
individual. The actual wishes presented by the subjects took the form (in the
case of "health")—"he should have good health," "he should live in good
health," "he should be physically well," etc. Whether or not it is legitimate to
group wishes of somewhat different shades of meaning into one category depends on one's purpose. For a general impression of zero-level values held by
individuals, the above groupings suffice.

different countries with different peoples, would permit us to determine whether there are universally held values.

The fact that different people offer the same values on the zero level gives us the opportunity of determining the nature of −1 level components of the same zero-level value in different people.

Experiment II: Determining Components of Zero-Level Values

In this experiment I sought to apply a method of determining −1 level components of values, and to ascertain the nature of such components, i.e., whether they were all values or included disvalues. Before discussing the method used to induce subjects to analyze values into their components, however, I should like first to make some general remarks about the analysis of qualities.

One can compare two phenomena—objects, ideas, feelings or values—only when they are in some respects qualitatively alike. Qualities thus are primary facts presupposed by any attempt at comparison or quantitative measurement. If one is to measure the essential characteristics of phenomena, one must first determine that the characteristics to be measured are essential, not incidental, that is, one must first answer a qualitative question before quantitative operations may be called into play. It is disturbing that many psychologists glide over problems of qualitative analysis and deal only with those features of events which are easily amenable to quantification, irrespective of the essentiality of those features.

I reject the view that the only studies worthy of the label "scientific" are those concerned with characteristics and properties easily amenable to quantification, those which present charts, tables, and tests of significance. One may be concerned with complex qualities, difficult or impossible to treat quantitatively and still be scientific. For example, a concern with love and hate, happiness and unhappiness, kindness and cruelty, etc., may be scientific without entailing quantitative measurement. To grasp and describe the differences among these values, one requires primarily an analysis of qualities rather than—or at least preparatory to—any measurement operations.

Concerning the analysis of qualities, there is a rather widespread misconception; for many people, such an analysis is equivalent to a detailed description. An analysis of qualities, however, is far more than a description; it is a getting to the core of psychological "matter." Adequate analysis of qualities—the getting to the core—is often hindered by what one might call "the pace of everyday living," and so is the interest of psychologists in these phenomena or it is limited to the aspects which correspond to this pace.

What is the pace of everyday living? It is the speed with which one moves from one thing to another and performs his actions in the environment. This speed is not simply determined by our physical capacities; our purposes also guide our pace or speed of living. We do not always try to run our fastest; we run as fast as we need to run. For this reason, the time we spend on our thoughts and feelings may be relatively limited because a longer time expended would not conform to our purposes. We do not spend time determining the shape of a gate or the type of hinges connecting it to a wall when our goal is to get into a yard; it suffices to get a general impression of a gate.

Now, the analysis of psychological qualities, as I intend this notion, cannot be undertaken in terms of the pace of everyday living. To analyze qualities demands that one get hold of a particular experience and keep this experience—in its full emotional importance—in front of one as long as this is required in order to determine those features which are inherent in the experience. One has to take plenty of time to analyze what qualities (or values) such as "happiness," "love," etc., imply.

Underlying the importance I attribute to the analysis of qualities for the understanding of the qualities themselves is the assumption that our everyday impressions are rooted in the full emotional contents of these impressions; these full contents can only be determined through an analysis of them. Felt as totalities and existing in consciousness without an awareness of the components which constitute them—at our everyday pace—impressions or qualities are ultimately based on these typically unanalyzed, but in fact analyzable components.[11] For an individual really to understand what is inherent in a qualitative experience (e.g., a zero-level value), he must be able to bring into consciousness not only the total impression but also the components which constitute the impression. He must grasp the components of the value, and perhaps their interrelationships. In short, in an analysis of qualities, one gets not a detailed description of impressions, but rather a grasp of those components which lie beyond the curtain of impressions.

I now turn to the method used to induce subjects to analyze their zero-level values, i.e., to determine their components:

The experimenter took the first wish mentioned by a subject in the first experiment—let us use "health" as an example— and said to the subject, "What do you mean by health?" To transpositions of the zero-level value into value-guarding terms, e.g., "absence of disease and crippling," or into definitions, e.g., "proper functioning of the body," the experimenter indicated that such responses were not acceptable. To transpositions, the experimenter replied, "What I am asking for is what is positive about health." To definitions, the experimenter replied by stating, "I am not asking you to define health. I want you to describe to me what health actually means to you. How does it feel to be healthy?" A subject might protest that feelings cannot be described. In such cases, the experimenter assured the subject that many people tend

---

[11] On the Gestalt problem—whether the whole is something other than its parts—I do not feel that a stand has to be taken here. So far, we do not have sufficient knowledge about the components. At some future time this problem might again be raised, after there are enough data to pass a conclusive judgment on it.

to doubt their ability to analyze feelings, but eventually find
that they can do so. Finally, under this sort of questioning and
redirecting, subjects were able to describe feelings, thus bringing out the components of zero-level values. The process was
repeated for each of the zero-level values wished for a child
by subjects.[12]

One illustration of the approach to components may be
given with respect to the value "friendship." Following are
the inquiries for three of the subjects who gave "friendship"
as one of their zero-level values. In the protocols presented
below, the components of the value "friendship" are itali-
cized. It may be noted that some of these components repeat
themselves from one subject to another.[13]

Subject A

E: And what do you mean by friendship?
S: I think a friend is a rare thing, because I set a high standard
for what I think friendship should be, should mean perhaps. Of
course if this standard is never achieved, then the definition is ridiculous. But I mean friendship is just a *true case of love* (C1), which
of course is vague too. I would say taking the whole, the person, and
seeing all of it in its parts, *accepting the whole person* (C2), accepting the
whole as something you feel love for. It's emotional and some of it
is rational, but it is mostly emotional. But yet recognizing the parts,
naturally, and finding it impossible to find a . . . to love each part
separately. To see it all clearly and to *criticize freely and compliment
freely, but loving the whole* (C3).
E: Yes, what do you mean by it?
S: By which term?
E: By the term loving the person.
S: Ah (pause) well, it is an identification of the person.
E: What do you mean by that? In simple words.
S: (Pause).
E: You might be perfectly correct, but I want just . . .

---

[12] This method can be used for components at any —level.
[13] Each symbol (e.g., C1) refers to a component. Where the same component
appears in different subjects, the same symbol is used.

S: Well no, I realized that when I first said it that I didn't know exactly what it meant. I know I have never defined this itself. I have always felt that it is a sort of vague emotion that should exist. I have never been successful in defining it. Well, it is good to be forced to (Laugh).

E: What makes up friendship?

S: Well, it's *enjoying the other's company* (C4) of course, first of all. (Pause) It's a *satisfaction of talking together* (C5) and I also ah—well, it is a satisfaction first of all in knowing that you *can share everything* (C6) with another person. And that requires a *supreme tolerance* (C7) *on the part of both* (C8). That is something that rarely exists I would imagine. As a matter of fact, I think that that is almost the essential part of it. This ah—as I say this ah—tolerance in feature that you perhaps don't agree with, and a strong acceptance of the other. *A willingness to express oneself fully* (C6) and also to *witness the expression of the other self* (C3) and comment on it and criticize it. All *without* the slightest bit of—*slightest bit of embarrassment* (C10). It surely means the fullest expression of every conceivable thought that is conscious in your own mind, every action ever completed. And then only is it the fullest sort of relationship.

E: Anything else?

S: No, I conceive of that as being the absolute greatest satisfaction you can get.

Subject B

E: I see. All right and then you said friends, what did you mean by that?

S: I mean people that *one can help, that one can be helped by* (C11) depending on need. People one can *talk things over with, without embarrassment* (C10).

E: Pardon?

S: Without embarrassment of any kind.

E: Yes.

S: Because ah—you *overlook things in your friends* (C2) that you would raise your eyebrows at with strangers.

E: Yes, what are the characteristics of friendship?

S: (Pause) That is ah—*someone who ah—likes you very much* (C1), *who will do things for you, not out of a sense of compulsion but out of love*

(C12). And of course, if he's a true friend, not a sucker, *you yourself feel the same way to the friend* (C8).

E: It's a mutual relationship.

S: Yes.

E: All right, then you said to like the friend, what did you mean by that?

S: There has to be some characteristic, many characteristics, which ah—which is your share in common with the friend. You like someone, you *rejoice when something good happens to him and are sad when something bad happens to him* (C13). (Pause) And you feel *pleasure in having the person a round just so* (C4).

E: Just so what? What did you say?

S: Just for the sake of the person and friends.

E: Could you say something more?

S: (Pause) Possibly you might feel the *need to help the friend or actually feel frustrated when you don't have an opportunity to help* (C11).

E: You don't have an opportunity to help them.

S: Yes!

E: I see! Anything else?

S: Well, he probably could prefer to do things with your friends rather than with other people.

Subject C

S: Friendships with ah—particular age mates with both sexes, that would be ah spontaneous and ah—thorough and that *would not hinge* let's say *upon ah—a momentary irritation or disagreement or conflict. But would be the more enduring in which a mutual responsiveness was taken for granted, regardless of some particular ah—disagreement let's say over ah—a situation or ideas* (C2). Ah—and so it would be ah—rather *full and free-flowing responsiveness* (implied C10) *on both sides of the friendship* (C8). And so it would be that the child could count on, let's say, his friends being *enthusiastic about his ideas, supporting his ventures* (C14), and vice versa.

E: Hum-ha! But what did you mean by warmth? (Warmth was mentioned by this subject in relation to friendship previous to this excerpt of the record.) Was it one specific thing? Or was it just one of the words that you had?

S: I suppose it was just one of the words to describe it, I can't think of anything, specific thing to say on the warmth, except, I suppose I mean responsiveness and free-flowingness and ah—certainly a certain amount of *affection for the ah—other person* (C1) in relationship, regardless of the other person's intrinsic qualities. Or specific achievements. Ah—you might say—

E: With affection you mean liking.

S: Yes! I mean liking and ah—the kind of liking that goes beneath ah—ah momentary success, failures, experiences of one sort or another. A kind of liking for the sake of the other person just being human and being involved.

Experiment III: Studying Systems of Values

As stated in the first section of this paper the assertion of the existence of a system of values implies that the values in question must be shown to be dependent on each other; what must be demonstrated is that a change, addition or subtraction of one value, affects other values held. I must emphasize that one cannot assert a systematic relation between values solely on the basis of their being held by one individual. What must be shown is that the values are dependent on each other in terms of the relationship of their properties. Furthermore, to assert that a systematic relationship exists between values held by an individual, one must ascertain that the subject experiences the dependency of these values on each other.

The method used to determine whether the zero-level values wished for a child comprised a system was as follows: The experimenter asked the subject to write down his seven wishes and to keep the list in front of him. Then the experimenter said, "The fairy grants you your wishes. But imagine for a moment that your first wish is not granted. Will that affect your second wish? Would the existence of the second wish be possible without the first?" The intention here was to discover if the subject feels that the second value can exist without the presence of the first. To give an example: a subject might have given, as his first wish, "emotional understanding," and, as his second wish, "friendship." In analyzing the two values, the subject might find that emotional understanding was a necessary component of friendship. It would then follow that his second wish could not be granted if his first wish was denied.[14]

If a subject said that the absence of the first value changed the second or precluded it, the experimenter asked why this was so. The inquiry was then repeated with regard to the first and third wishes, the first and fourth, and so on. Then the same procedure was applied to the second value with regard to each of the others in turn. The process was continued until each value had been excluded, and the effect of the exclusion on each remaining value had been ascertained.

This experiment usually took about an hour and a half to perform and the procedure itself was quite tiring for a subject. I often found that pauses interspersed during the experiment—especially when the time for pauses was indicated by the subject—kept the subject involved in the experiment and was conducive to the success of the experiment.

Once again I must mention the unavoidable limitations of the inquiries thus far undertaken with this method. My primary intention was to determine the existence of systems of values and to develop methods for studying such systems. I did not focus on the systems themselves. Once I had determined that the method was adequate to determine whether the dependency of one value on another existed, I shifted to the next theoretical or methodological problem.

Despite these limitations, some remarks can be made concerning systems of values. The relationships between zero-level values may be intrinsic or extrinsic; an intrinsic relationship is said to exist if one value is a necessary prerequisite for another, e.g., as emotional understanding might be for friendship; an extrinsic relation is said to obtain if such is not the case. To illustrate: a person asked whether the absence of

---

[14] If a subject remarked that a fairy could do anything, and hence could grant the second wish without the first, it showed that he was not considering the content of his wishes. The nature of the experiment had then to be further explained to the subject.

"economic security" influences "health" might answer, "Yes, because if you have no money to go to a doctor in time, your health will suffer"; in this instance, it is obvious that economic security (money) is not intrinsically related to health—a lack of economic security is a circumstance which bars taking precautions or getting medicines when health is in danger.

Through the determination of intrinsic relationships, it will eventually be possible to gain information concerning the inner structure and dynamics of value systems. Through the determination of extrinsic relationships among values, we shall be able to ascertain circumstances in the environment which affect the attainment and loss of the possession of values.

I might note here some of the methodological steps which I have found useful in determining the existence of intrinsic relationships among values. I shall state these steps in the form of rules:

1. The zero-level values are elicited from a particular subject, as in Experiment I; this should be done on a piece of paper, leaving sufficient space around each value-name for the components.

2. The components of the zero-level values are determined, as in Experiment II.

3. Indication of the dependencies between zero-level values is then made; this can be done using connecting lines, and inscriptions above such lines may serve to designate the types of influence of one value upon another; the directions of influence may be indicated by arrows.

4. Analyses of the systems of other subjects are then undertaken; this must be done in order to distinguish general from individual characteristics of systems. I must emphasize my belief that no statement about relationships of values is valid on the basis of the analysis of a single system—unless such relationships have been compared with those obtaining in the systems of many other individuals.

These methodological steps, as noted before, pertain to the investigation of intrinsic relationships between values. The investigation of extrinsic relationships would require considerable modifications, and I shall not go into these here.

Although the experiment on value systems showed that the number of relationships within the sets of values differed, among the 15 subjects who were examined in this study, there was only one whose values seemed to him to be completely independent of each other, i.e., the exclusion of any one zero-level value from his set seemed to have no effect on the others. Such an aggregation of zero-level values may reflect some pathology. It seems to me, in this light, that it would be worth while to examine the values held by different clinical groups with regard to their dependence on each other.

Further understanding concerning value systems may be gained through the investigation of several sets of values in one and the same individual. In Part I, I suggested that the same individual may have more than one value system or one set of zero-level values. Assuming that there was some overlap of the values held in the two (or more) sets, it would be possible to determine relationships between the same values as these occur in different sets of zero-level values of the same individual. Statements concerning relationships within the first value system could be validated by studying other sets of values within the person.

Experiment IV: Study of Values for Oneself and the Problem of Multiple Systems of Values in an Individual

The following experiment was performed with some of those subjects who participated in the first experiment. The instructions to these subjects were as follows: "Now there is another fairy, and this fairy says, 'You can have seven wishes again, and they too will come true; this time, however, they are to be wishes for yourself. What would you wish for yourself from now on, for your whole life?' "

In the majority of cases, the wishes made by a subject for himself overlapped only in part with those made for a child; in a few cases there was complete duplication of the two sets of wishes; in rare instances, there was no overlap at all. I would say that complete overlapping is to be expected when a subject tries to remember what he had wished for a child, instead of giving his wishes for himself spontaneously. I believe that most of the subjects did wish anew; and in so doing, they spontaneously mentioned as values for themselves some of those which were also wished for a child.

The fact that in this experiment a number of new values appeared which had not occurred in the initial study seems to me to support my contention that more than one system of values may be held by a single individual. I would, in fact, argue that were the instructions further modified so that one could wish for one's spouse, one's colleague, a teacher, or—to make things more complicated—an enemy, quite different sets of zero-level values would emerge, and consequently different systems could be found.

In general, the character of a set of values depends upon the meaning the recipient of the wishes has for the agent, and also upon the relationship between the agent and the recipient. The distinction between the meaning of one person to another and the relationship between the two can be illustrated by an example. A man can make wishes for his wife as an individual, or for his wife in relation to himself. [15]

The fact that some values recurred in different sets of values held by an individual, i.e., sets of values held for different recipients, also had important implications. If one finds a value occurring in different systems of an individual, and if this value has the same components in these different systems and the same kinds of intrinsic relationships with its components, then we may call the components elements of the value. The relationships among these elements constitute the basic character of that value, in short, the unadulterated value. I assume that all the unadulterated values held by a person

---

[15] The technique of wishing is not only applicable to individuals. One can also make wishes for groups, institutions, events, even for things.

comprise a system; this system is the "more basic system" on level +2 mentioned above. From this basic system, I believe values on the +1 level may be derived by taking into account the meaning of the recipient to the subject, and the nature of the relationship between the subject and the recipient.

One may ask further whether the basic system of one person is the same as that of another. Or more generally, is there a universal system of the same unadulterated values? It is worth while to suggest such a system as a hypothesis so as to give incentive to those investigators who are interested in determining the theoretical structure of value systems.

Let us return now to the value systems at the +1 level. In one sense, whether the values a person accepts are for a child or for himself, they are all his values. One might, therefore, use them as material for the determination of personality characteristics of which the individual is not necessarily conscious. In that case, the wishes for others would have to be interpreted within a theory of projection. In my investigations, although I recognize that all the values accepted by an individual are his, in one sense, I consider an individual's wishes for a child as exactly that—wishes for a child, and not as disguised wishes for the self or as projections.

It is really not surprising that a different system of values is stated by an individual for himself than for a child. In the first place, when wishing for himself, a person wishes in accordance with his picture of himself as an individual set in his ways; a still unborn child, on the other hand, is regarded by many individuals as not fixed—a *tabula rasa*, so to speak— and a person who should be free to develop his own individuality. Many subjects mentioned that they did not want to impose on a child any limitations as to choices of special abilities, occupations, etc., or to have the child molded contrary to the child's desires. In the second place, whereas the subject has already lived part of his life, the still unborn child has his whole life ahead of him; wishes concerning upbringing therefore will typically be made only for the child. In the third place, the subject already may possess some values—e.g., intelligence, higher education—which he feels cannot be taken away from him; a child, on the other hand, neither has nor lacks such qualities, and hence they may be wished for him.

Possession of certain values may influence the wishes one makes for oneself. However, possession of a value does not necessarily preclude its being a desired value. Values possessed may be lost and a person may want to wish for himself continued possession of certain values, e.g., health, economic security. The possibility of losing values raises a problem for investigation: one may wish to study the relationship between values possessed and values wished for in the light of such possibility of loss. Such a study would have to take into account which values, though presently possessed, are susceptible to being lost, and also how realistic a subject is in appraising the possibility of loss. Anxieties about the possible loss of possessed values can be discovered by a simple experiment. After a subject has wished seven values for himself, he may be asked if he possesses any of these values; following this, he is asked whether he will be able to keep these values in the future. Of course, such an experiment can lead to the detection of only those anxieties near the conscious level.

Experiment V: Studying Disvalues

An individual may not only wish to avoid the loss of values; he may also wish to be guarded against disvalues—or to have someone else guarded against disvalues. One may, for example, wish to be spared evil. Now it must be stressed again that a disvalue is not merely the lack of a value. A disvalue has its own content. Pain is not simply the absence of pleasure.

To determine disvalues on the zero level, a procedure analogous to that used in determination of zero-level values was used—wishing for a child. The following instructions were given: "Now there will be another fairy present, and this fairy says, 'You can have seven more wishes for your child; this time they are to be guarding wishes. What would you like your child to be guarded against?" "

A subject asked for "guarding-against" wishes often gave such wishes as restatements of those asked from the first fairy. For example, having asked for economic security in the study of zero-level values, a subject might ask here that the child be guarded against poverty. Such a tendency to transpose values for a child into guards against disvalues might be indicative of the emotional importance of the values in question for the subject: he may play safe by wishing twice for the same thing.

It should be mentioned that in the first experiment subjects sometimes wished for guards against disvalues although they were supposed to wish for values, e.g., instead of asking for peace during the lifetime of the child, they asked for no wars. It may be that for some subjects, the emotional importance of guarding against a disvalue is stronger than that of possessing the benefits of a value. These considerations pose the issue of the relative strengths of values and guards against disvalues— a problem which should be kept in mind for future experimentation.

For the further study of disvalues, e.g., in terms of components of disvalues and systems of disvalues, methods analogous to those used in the study of values may be used (see Experiments II and III, above).[16]

Some relationships between values and disvalues are discussed below. The problem of the relationships between value and disvalue systems is one for the future, that is, if systems of disvalues are found to exist.

Experiment VI: Value Systems and the Acceptance and Rejection of Externally Introduced Values

The experiment discussed here was actually the last of the series to be performed. At the time he participated in this

---

[16] In investigating systems of disvalues, one would have to examine the effects of exclusion as follows: "If the child were not guarded from the first disvalue, would he still be guarded from the second," etc.

experiment, a subject had already been exposed to between five and seven hours—two or three sessions—of experimentation. It had meant hard work. Despite the strain and concentration, however, the subjects (15 juniors at Harvard) were challenged by the new task and were curious about what was coming up. Some of them remarked spontaneously that though the whole experiment had been tiring, they were interested in what was going on; they felt that they had learned a number of things including the fact that one could analyze one's values and get clearer about them.

It is, therefore, not surprising that when the experimenter asked the subject if he would like to know what wishes some other people had made for the child, he was eager to hear them. The experimenter went on, "I have a list of fifty-two wishes which were made for the child; I will read them to you one by one. Will you be kind enough to tell me: first, did you make the same wish for the child or include it in any of your wishes? Second, if you did not, would you like to add the wish to your list? Third, if you add it, is this new wish as important as those you made before?" The subject took up the challenge and, after carefully considering each wish, made his statements on it.

The list of wishes read to the subjects was collected by the experimenter from about a dozen participants in a preliminary experiment. Thus, the list was an empirical one, not one arbitrarily made up by the experimenter. The educational and intellectual level represented in the pilot group was approximately the same as that of the subjects who took part in Experiment VI. [17]

This experiment provided additional information concerning values on the zero level and the components of such values. The wishes from the list which subjects added to their wishes for the child may be considered new values on the zero level. Those which the subjects said were implied in their wishes

---

[17] Examples of these values are: physical superiority, beauty, creativity, intellectual courage, self-fulfillment, to be warm, accepting, intuitive.

may be, at least sometimes, conceived as components of their original zero-level values.

The experiment brings out an interesting methodological point. Whenever it is necessary to elicit the reaction of a subject to a list of values, one runs the risk that such listed values will be just abstractions to him. To make such a list emotionally important to a person, one has to connect it with one of his concrete systems of values, i.e., with a system which is operating at the time of the experiment. Such a connection has to exist throughout the time that the list is presented. That this was accomplished in Experiment VI is shown by the fact that some items on the list which, in the abstract, would appear positive to anybody, were seen, in relation to a functioning system, as either "not necessary" or "not important," and were not added by the subjects.

The results show that in spite of the knowledge that other people considered certain values important for the child—that is, despite social pressure—the subjects were reluctant to add these externally given wishes to their own. This fact is the more surprising as complete freedom was given the subjects to add as many wishes as they wanted, without giving up their own previously made wishes. Subjects regarded many wishes from the list as implied in their own, but rarely added the listed values to their systems.

In general the subjects shied away from major changes in their value systems. It may be that a system functioning within a subject is experienced so strongly by him as a unit that forces work against any change or enlargement of it. The boundary between such a system and new values presented seems to acquire the properties of a barrier. The barrier could be due to forces within the system which resist the acceptance of additional parts. Another possibility is that a subject introduces and supports the barrier from outside the system because of his desire for self-sufficiency, independence, etc. One possibility does not exclude the other. An argument for the second possibility is that though subjects are reluctant to add wishes, they often accept them by saying that they were implied within those they made themselves. Whether the subject actually experiences the new wishes as implied or whether in this way he can include values without forfeiting his feeling of self-sufficiency cannot be decided at present. One should of course also remember that some values on the list may simply not be valued by the subject, at least not as wishes for a child.

These theoretical discussions are presented to provoke interest in the complicated processes comprising the structure and functioning of concrete systems rather than to advance a fully substantiated theory; they should be regarded as inducement for further experimentation. Further, one may ask the subject why he did not add wishes and in this way gain some clues to the reason for his resistance to the inclusion of new parts in his system. It is, for instance, possible that his resistance is due to shame at having to admit that he forgot to mention important values.

Probably forces from outside the system maintain the barrier to a certain extent. However, it seems to me that there is at least some truth to the paradoxical statement that it is not the subjects who form their value systems, but the value systems which determine what the subjects can or cannot do with them. Inherent in this statement is the implication that the properties of a person's value system are independent from his desires—hence the reality of values. It is the same sort of reality that is meant by the independence of a person's needs from his will.[18]

Experiment VII: Studying Beliefs Concerning the Ways in Which Values Come to Be Possessed

In relation to a person, values have at least three possible modes of existence; they may be acknowledged by the per-

---

[18] One is reminded of a person's independence from forms of thought and logic which cannot be changed at will. The structure of a system of values might be as imperative as the conclusion of a syllogism when the premises are given, the same for all men (with the exception of those who show grave disturbances in thought processes).

son; they may be accepted by the person; and they may enter into the possession of a person.

Prior to any other type of relationship between a person and a value, there is the relationship of acknowledgment of the value by the person. A value, existing as "acknowledged," is one which a person believes capable of being desired by someone, even though he himself may not desire it. For example, "economic security" is a value which one might acknowledge without desiring it for oneself or for others.

A value exists as "accepted" in so far as an individual, at a given time, wishes it for himself or for another, i.e., desires to have it in his possession or in the possession of another. An acknowledged value may be, or may become, an accepted value: an accepted value does not, however, have to be possessed. For example, "peace of mind" is a value which most people accept, but few possess.

Finally, a value may exist as "possessed": a possessed value is one which either actually characterizes an individual, e.g., when one is actually intelligent, healthy, etc.; or characterizes the environment in which he lives, e.g., "peaceful world," or characterizes his relations with specific persons or objects in his environment, e.g., "happy marriage."

Now, a change in the existential status of a value, i.e., from one mode of existence to another, comes about either through action initiated by an individual, through outside influence, or through some combination of these factors.[19] Thus, when a person accepts a value (for himself or another), but does not possess it, he may attempt to possess it. In confronting the problem of possession of a value (whether for oneself or for another) one is led to consider whether the possession can come about through one's own action, through outside in-

---

[19] Outside influences producing changes in behavior are treated by Henry Murray (1938) in his concept of "press." The basic and general distinction between influences stemming from the individual and influences stemming from outside the individual (as he experiences them) has been made by Fritz Heider, in many lectures prior to the appearance of his book (1958); Heider's lectures have influenced my considerations of this point.

fluence, or through both. The present experiment was designed to determine how individuals believe one may come into the possession of values accepted, but not yet possessed.

The experimenter proceeded as follows: She asked, regarding each value wished for a child, what would determine its attainment or possession by the child. For example, supposing the first value was "health," the question would be, "What do you think will determine whether the child will be healthy?"

The results clearly show that subjects believed that values wished for a child come into the child's possession in various ways. With regard to some values, they noted that the child would either be born with them or not; if he were not born with them, he could do nothing to get them. Other values might come into possession of the child just through the influence of the parents, e.g., through their mode of bringing up the child, etc. There were certain values for which the child would have to work, if these wished-for values were to come into his possession, and, finally, values the child might acquire just through "good luck."

Thus, one sees that there are various ways in which values, existing as accepted, may enter a new mode of existence, viz., as values possessed. Correspondingly, there are various grantors of values—or to use a less personal term—various "sources" of values. Among the sources leading to the possession of a value, one must of course include the individual himself.

When the source of a value is the individual himself, or his activity in attempting to possess the value, then one may regard the value as a goal-object. Values which come into one's possession in other ways, i.e., without any action on one's own part to secure them, may be regarded as endowments, gifts, etc., but not as goals.

As noted above, one of the sources of values frequently mentioned by subjects was "parents." Parents, through the kind of upbringing they institute, or the kind of home atmosphere they provide, are often believed to contribute to a child's possessing certain values or eventually coming into possession of certain values. Of course, with regard to specific values, there may be disagreements as to their source; in this connection, one may raise certain questions, amenable to experimentation; e.g., "Of which values that they possess do children regard their parents or themselves as a source?" "Do parents and their children agree on the values which have been, can be, and/or should be transmitted from the parents as a source?" Studies bearing on these issues should take into account not only those values of which parents can voluntarily be the source, but also values which may be involuntarily transmitted from parent to child, e.g., healthy disposition, beauty, etc.

The problem of sources of values, and the closely related problem of the responsibility of a grantor for the value transmitted (i.e., the ability of the grantor voluntarily to give or hold back the value) both introduce another important topic which requires investigation, viz., the attitude of the grantor to the recipient because of the values "given," and correspondingly, the attitude of the recipient to the grantor. What relation does a parent have to a child in the light of values he thinks he has given to the child? What relation to the parent or what attitude toward the parent does a child have in the light of values he thinks he has received from the parent? What occurs when there is disagreement between parents and children concerning the source of values which the child possesses, i.e., when the parents believe themselves to be the source and the child regards other grantors as the source? In connection with the problem of sources of values as perceived by different individuals, the studies of Bavelas (1942) and Kalhorn (1944) are directly relevant.

There is one more issue that should be mentioned in connection with the possession of values: this concerns "pride" in values possessed. Pride concerning values possessed does not depend alone, or necessarily, on the effort which a person puts into achieving possession of the value; pride in values possessed is a much more complicated issue. An investigation of people's feelings regarding the loss of values once possessed, and the relation of such feelings to the attitudes of other people toward them after the loss of possession, might give us some clues leading to the clarification of this complex issue of "pride in the possession of values." In this connection, the article by Dembo, Leviton, and Wright (1956) may be mentioned.

Experiment VIII: Studying the Value of Disvalues

Some people believe that in order to possess certain values they must first possess disvalues. In other words, to them suffering seems to be a prerequisite for possession of a value; i.e., they apparently feel an intrinsic connection between the disvalue and the value.

The following experiment was devised to determine the existence of such a special connection between values and disvalues, and to study it. The experimenter proceeded as follows: "Let us return once more to the wishes for the child. I will ask you something very different. (Pause) Would you wish tragedy to your child? By tragedy I mean what is meant by tragedy in everyday life, such things as unhappy love, loss of close people, etc. Would you or would you not wish tragedy to your child? Answer simply yes or no." Several different reactions were observed.

Some subjects looked astonished and said, "Of course not." Others hesitated for a while and then said, "Some tragedies are unavoidable, but I do not wish them for the child; I wish him to overcome them." Still others paused and finally said, "Yes, I do." Quite a number hardly hesitated before they replied, "Yes."

Those subjects who did not wish tragedy were then asked, "Can you imagine that someone might wish tragedy?" Some subjects said they considered such a wish impossible. Others said that the wisher would have to be cruel, terrifically aggressive, sadistic or mentally disturbed. The experimenter continued, "I must tell you that about half the people who are asked this question answer yes. What do you think may be the reason?" Some subjects continued to be baffled and said they had no explanation. Some made a guess, and asked whether the people who wished tragedy thought it was good for the child in some respects, gave new experiences, or what not. Other subjects were able to name reasons which were actually advanced by those people who wished for tragedy.

The subjects who did wish tragedy to the child were asked by the experimenter, "Why do you wish it?" Their answers ran as follows: "Tragedy will bring the depths of experience of life to the child," or "He will understand other people better and will be able really to sympathize with them," or "It makes a better person."

Some of those subjects who did not wish tragedy agreed that possession of certain values, e.g., "depth of experience," necessitated experiencing tragedy. But they felt that the value was not sufficiently important that they would wish tragedy to the child in order for the child to attain depth of experience.

Those people who wished tragedy, and those who did not wish it but named it as a necessary condition for reaching "depth of experience," both agreed that the valued goal could be reached only by locomotion via the disvalue region. The difference between these two types of subjects was not in their perception of the relationship between values and disvalues, but concerned another factor: believing that a particular disvalue-value relationship is a fact, some wished the value anyhow while some others did not.

Since, in this experiment, the subjects were placed in the position of perhaps wishing for disvalues to insure values, I might say something further about wishes. In general, wishes can be conceived as psychological processes supporting those forces which would bring about the content of the wish. Thus, in the present context, wishing for tragedy meant supporting those forces which would bring about tragedy. Some subjects, it appears, were willing to support such forces; others were not[20].

Those subjects who did not wish tragedy and who did not believe that one could reach depth of understanding only through tragedy, obviously saw the disvalue and value as unrelated to each other and, therefore, were not concerned with how the value might be achieved. The other subjects, who did accept the intrinsic connection, were confronted with this issue.

There were finally some subjects who believed that the nature of the relationship between the value and disvalue was dependent upon the individuals involved: some might reach depth of understanding without experiencing tragedy; and some might not attain depth of understanding even with tragedy.

In evaluating the relationship between a disvalue like tragedy and a value such as "depth of experience" or "real sympathy for others," we must keep in mind that there is little empirical information available in the psychological literature as to the dependence (or independence, for that matter) of "understanding" or "sympathy" on experience of tragedy. This is a problem which surely deserves further study. I might note that—if as a criterion of "real sympathy" on the part of a donor one takes the reaction of a recipient—certain findings of Dembo, Leviton, and Wright (1956, p. 60) indicate that an individual may show "real sympathy" without having himself experienced tragedy.

Whatever the case may be, it is important that many people believe—to use a drastic expression—that the way to Heaven is through Hell. For those people, reaching particular values implies suffering as a necessary step toward them. In accepting such a viewpoint, they do not fight or reject disvalues, but sanction and support them.

---

[20] In the sense that support of the forces may or may not have an effect on reality, wishes may be viewed as "real" or "unreal." The wishes of a jury determine a man's fate, but wishes are not horses so poor men can't ride.

The difference between those who believe that the reality of values is such that some can only be reached through dis-values, and those who do not, is of obvious importance in different types of interpersonal relationships. It plays a significant role in the development of the theories of education, punishment, therapy, etc.

In conclusion: this research is not armchair philosophy but down-to-earth psychology of values. It makes us wonder, however, whether Psychology of Values is not at the same time Empirical Philosophy of Values.

BIBLIOGRAPHY

Bavelas, A. (1942), Methods of Investigating Individual and Group Ideology, *Sociometry*, 5:371-377.
Dembo, T.; Leviton, G.; Wright, B. (1956), Adjustment to Misfortune. *Artificial Limbs*, 3 (2):4-62.
Heider, F. (1958), *The Psychology of Interpersonal Relations*. New York: Wiley.
Kalhorn, J. (1944), Values and Sources of Authority among Rural Children. *University of Iowa Studies Child Welfare*, 20 (409):99-151.
Koffka, K. (1936), *Principles of Gestalt Psychology*. London: Kegan Paul.
Köhler, W. (1920), *Die physischen Gestalten in Ruhe und im stationären Zustand*. Erlangen: Braunschweig.
Lewin, K. (1936), *Principles of Topological Psychology*. New York: McGraw-Hill.
Murray, H. (1938), *Explorations in Personality*. New York: Oxford University Press.

Sensoritonic Theory and the Concept of Self-Realization

KURT GOLDSTEIN, M.D.

New School for Social Research

The conception of stimulation as sensoritonic in nature has opened up a new field of experimentation concerning the problem of interaction between organismic and sensory factors; the theoretical formulations and experimental investigations of Werner and Wapner (1952, 1956) have thus contributed essentially to the clarification of the problem of perception.

Their view—and the experimental evidence they advance to support it—to the effect that the perceptual process, whether one considers extero-, proprio-, or interoception, is not purely sensory, but rather sensoritonic in character, is particularly important if one bears in mind that the acceptance of stimulus-response theory is still widespread.

Since I maintain, from my organismic point of view, that any stimulation in any special area involves the whole organism, and that the interaction of sensory and organismic factors is a kind of coming to terms of the organism with the world, I certainly agree with their conceptions, in principle. The many publications of myself and my co-workers (1925, 1928, 1929, 1936, 1939, 1947), particularly Walter Riese, attest to the importance I attribute to tonus phenomena in the understanding of man's behavior and his organization of the world, i.e., to his behavior in space, in time, to his perception, action, and thinking (Goldstein, 1925).

Werner and Wapner, searching for postulates which would make understandable the particular influence of tonus on behavior in special situations, come to the conclusion, on the basis of their experiments, that "perceptual experience varies with variation in the relationship between object-stimuli and on-going state of the organism"; "given a certain impinging stimulus there is no tendency for the pertinent aspect of the organismic state to change," while "given an unchanging stimulus which is in an unstable relation to the existing organismic state, there is a tendency for the organism to change its state so that a stable relationship ensues." These propositions concerning the tendency of the organism to maintain or attain a stable relationship with impinging stimuli would surely gain support from the many observations we have made on patients.

Our experiences with patients, however, suggest that the notion of a tendency toward stability—as important as it is as a general principle for understanding organismic behavior—is not sufficient to account for all of the observations; for example, it is not sufficient to account for why—given the same stimulation and the same modification of the stimulation in pathological individuals—stability may be attained in quite different ways; indeed, in ways antithetical to each other.

From my extensive observations on patients, I came to the conclusion some time ago that an adequate account of all findings requires the consideration of the observed phenomena in terms of their relationship to the total functioning of the organism, especially with regard to the organism's trend toward self-realization.

True enough, the operation of this trend may not be too apparent under experimental conditions: experiments are so executed that the environment, i.e., the rest of the organism, is kept constant. Under these conditions, the tendency toward stability with regard to the stimulated part of the organism may not be influenced by the organism's condition in its totality: the tendency toward stability of the part may appear to be determined solely by what happens in this part.

The situation is different in patients with a local defect, examined under less restricted conditions. Here the tendency toward stability in the part may produce instability in the rest of the organism, which in turn would force the individual to search for another way to achieve stability in the concerned part.

If I understand Werner and Wapner correctly, it was such situations which induced them to assume other factors operating than the sensoritonic one alone, e.g., when they speak about the need "to tie together sensory, conative and cognitive factors contributing to perception" (1956, p. 335). Because I had found that the addition of other factors of equal influence on behavior does not bring us any further in our understanding of behavior, and hence no further in our understanding of stabilization tendencies, I was led to look for an influence of a different kind. It may indeed be more correct to say that I was not led to look for another factor at all, but rather for another point of view—a point of view, in which the phenomena and those factors that seem particularly important for stabilization in special situations are considered in the light of their significance for the stability of the whole organism. I was thus led to the point of view which makes self-realization of the whole organism the basic principle. From this point of view, it would follow that an organism's mode of achieving stability may vary depending on the different relationships which stimulation or defect have with regard to the self-realization of the organism.

I am well aware that the introduction of such a factor as self-realization confronts us with a serious epistemological problem; but I do not think one can avoid this problem if one hopes to understand organismic behavior. It was a feature of my book, *The Organism* (1939), to find some solution to this problem, and thus I finally came to the elaboration of a theory of knowledge in biology. This theory of knowledge, based on an analysis of a great number of investigations of pathological phenomena and the adjustments of individuals to them, proved to be useful also in understanding the different ways in which an organism achieves stability, where a defect cannot be eliminated. I would like to demonstrate this briefly on the basis of some observations of patients.

In some patients, with cerebellar lesions (Goldstein, 1936), one observes a tilting of the body and the head toward the side of the lesion, e.g., in left-sided lesions, to the left side. In other cases, however, with a similar lesion, the head is tilted to the other, the right, side. What determines these deviations and the differences among patients with the same sorts of lesions to the cerebellum? Closer investigation shows that patients of both types behave normally both bodily and mentally—in general—as long as the head and body are tilted. If the patient is forced to bring his head into the previously "normal" erect position, he is not only in danger of falling to the left side, but he feels dizzy, confused, and is hindered in fulfilling a number of bodily and mental performances in a normal manner (1936); if he is allowed to keep his head tilted, he feels well and returns to normality in all these respects (Goldstein, 1947).

To explain this phenomenon, I would like to stress that the patients, in keeping their heads erect, experience a pull to the affected side. This pull corresponds to a tendency of the organism to turn toward stimulation—in this case coming from the outside—and hence, a turning toward the left side (Goldstein, 1939, p. 108); in fact, the organism is, in this situation, so to speak, thrown to the side of stimulation. Normal individuals do not feel this pull deriving from outer stimulation because both sides of the body are stimulated to about the same degree, and hence the pulls to both sides counterbalance each other; an equilibrium is thus established, further guaranteed by the regulative influences of the cerebellum and the frontal lobes so that we normally stand straight without paying attention to our posture. In the patient, however, the pull to the one side is abnormally strong because of the lesion of the cerebellum on that side. Tilting the head leads to the disappearance of the pull. The abnormal position thus represents, so to speak, an *adjustment* of the organism to the defect, and brings about a new order and a new stability. The patient finds that by yielding to the abnormal pull, a better, more constant condition is attained.

Now, why does the other type of patient, suffering from the same kind of defect, hold his head tilted to the opposite side? If one examines these patients carefully, one finds that they have the same defect, but to a much greater degree. There is again a pull in the same direction, but this time it is much stronger. In the first group of cases, the patient merely shows a tendency to fall if he keeps his head upright; in the second group, the patient really falls. Thus, in the second group of patients, stability is affected to a much greater degree, and the patient is more easily thrown into a general disorder, with disturbances in all of his performances (Goldstein, 1936). If a patient of this second group, in his attempt to adjust to the defect, followed the same course as a patient in the first group, i.e., if he yielded to the pull, he would have to assume an extreme position in his attempt to compensate for the stronger pull: he would have to tilt his body. In this position, no balance could be maintained. Such a mode of adjustment to the defect would not bring order, and the normal behavior of the organism as a whole would not be guaranteed. What is observed is that another mode of adjustment takes place, i.e., the pull to the left side is compensated by a *pull to the other side*. This compensatory pull is manifested in the tilting of the head to the right side. By this procedure, equilibrium and a new order are obtained; that this is the case is confirmed by the fact that, under this condition, the patient feels best and manifests normal behavior in all his performances, whereas he immediately falls to the left side if he brings his head into the erect position. This variation in adjustment to a defect, differing only quantitatively in the different cases, reveals that organisms react to disturbances in ways that guarantee self-realization to the greatest possible extent under the prevailing conditions.

I may further exemplify this point by a description of the behavior of patients with a totally different defect, viz., hemianopsia, i.e., blindness of corresponding halves of the retinae in both eyes, due to a lesion of the occipital lobe of the brain. Behavior of these patients in everyday life does not reveal the fact that one half of both retinae is not responsive to stimulation. The patients are subjectively aware of somewhat diminished vision, but they see objects in their entirety, not only half of them. Their visual fields are, it is true, somewhat shrunken, but they are arranged around a center like those of normal people. The region of best vision lies not, as one might assume on the basis of examinations with the perimeter, on the margin corresponding to the location of the fovea in the preserved half of the field, but rather within the field.

I shall not here go into a detailed explanation of the manner in which this new functional fovea (this "pseudo fovea") develops within the intact retina; nor shall I go into the experimentally demonstrated fact of the transformation which takes place in the function of the retina concomitant with the development of the pseudo fovea. For the observed facts, I may refer to the paper by my co-worker, Fuchs (1920) and to a paper of mine (1928). I would chiefly like to emphasize what Jaensch (1909) particularly has shown, namely, that it is only by the building up of the pseudo fovea within the intact retina that perception and recognition are guaranteed. The transformation which takes place is achieved in these patients by a slight shifting of the eyes so that stimuli coming from all sides of the outer world are now reflected in the healthy part of the retinae; this transformation, by which adjustment and stability is achieved, occurs without the patient's being aware of it (Goldstein, 1928).

The above-mentioned shifting of the position of the eyes and the transformation of the function of the retina occur only when the defect is so great that the halves of the retinae do not perceive at all, i.e., if they are totally blind.

Such a shifting (i.e., development of a pseudo fovea) does not occur if vision, even though markedly diminished, is nevertheless present to such a degree that it permits recognition of objects. Even though the vision of such patients with reduced but still existent responsivity may not be as good as in the other cases, it seems that for them the preservation of the normal way of using the visual apparatus is best with regard to the functioning of the total organism. Thus such patients will bear not only quantitative limitations, such as restriction of the visual field, but also deficiencies of a qualitative character, e.g., not seeing a part of an object which lies outside the realm of the intact but restricted visual field. The organism bears all of these impediments if visual recognition—so essential for the total organism—cannot be reached without the shifting of the eyes.

Apparently, what is pertinent in these various situations is not the best possible performance in one special performance field, but rather the best possible activity of the organism as a whole. Here lies the motivation for the specific form of adaptation, and the cause of the differences in adaptation in hemianopsia and hemiamblyopia.

From these illustrations, we see that stabilization with regard to a local defect becomes understandable not through consideration of the stability of functioning of the concerned part alone, but in terms of the tendency of the whole organism to attain a condition so that self-realization is preserved in the best way possible under the given circumstances. In other words, the tendency toward stability seems to mean tendency toward stability of the whole organism.

It should be noted that the two kinds of adjustment to the defect do not represent stability of equal value. In the first kind, i.e., "yielding to the defect," the organism's normal mode of functioning is, in principle, unchanged. This mode of adjustment involves a "more natural" procedure; it occurs more "automatically"; it demands less voluntary activity, and so insures more security. In the second kind of adjustment, the "normal" way of functioning is changed. A more voluntary kind of behavior is necessary, one involving more danger. Therefore, the "normal" procedure will be maintained as long as it is at all possible to carry out the performances essential for the organism as a whole in this way—as long as self-realization can be preserved to the highest possible degree under the circumstances; it therefore necessarily depends upon the demands to which the organism is exposed. Thus, whether the one or the other form of adjustment to the defect takes place, ultimately depends upon which of the forms guarantees a better self-realization.

In conclusion: I have tried to illustrate, on the basis of my experiences with patients, the usefulness of the organismic point of view for the understanding of the phenomena of attaining stability and regaining stability in abnormal conditions. I welcome the opportunity of presenting this viewpoint in a volume in honor of Heinz Werner. I would like my article to be considered an expression of my affirmation of the principle of the sensoritonic basis of perception; I merely would like to add a hint that sensoritonic theory may need expansion in the direction of the organismic theory of behavior.

BIBLIOGRAPHY

Fuchs, W. (1920), Untersuchungen über das Sehen der Hemiano-
piker und Hemiamblyopiker II. (In Gelb, A. and Goldstein, K.:
Psychologische Analysen hirnpathologischer Fälle.) *Zeitschrift
für Psychologie*, *84*:67-169.

Goldstein, K. (1925), Über induzierte Tonusveränderungen. *Deutsche
klinische Wochenschrift*, *4*:294-299.

―――― (1928), Zur Frage der Restitution umschriebener Hirn-
defekte. *Schweizer Archiv für Neurologie und Psychiatrie*, *13*:283-295.

―――― (1929), Zum Problem der Tendenz zum ausgezeichneten
Verhalten. *Deutsche Zeitschrift für Nervenheilkunde*, *109*:1-61.

―――― (1936), The Function of the Cerebellum from a Clinical
Standpoint. *Journal of Nervous and Mental Disease*, *83*:1-12.

―――― (1939), *The Organism*. New York: American Book Company.

―――― (1947), Organismic Approach to the Problem of Motivation.
Annals of the New York Academy of Science, Series II.

Jaensch, E. R., (1909), *Zur Analyse der Gesichtswahrnehmungen*. (*Zeitschrift für Psychologie*, Ergänzungsband 4.) Leipzig: Barth.

Wapner, S. & Werner, H., (1952), Experiments on Sensory-tonic
Field Theory of Perception: V. Effect of Body Status on the
Kinaesthetic Perception of Verticality. *Journal of Experimental
Psychology*, *44*:126-131.

Werner, H. & Wapner, S., (1956), Sensory-tonic Field Theory of
Perception: Basic Concepts and Experiments. *Revista di Psicologia*, *50*:315-337.

Why 'Mama' and 'Papa'?

ROMAN JAKOBSON

*Harvard University and
Massachusetts Institute of Technology*

In Spring 1959, during a linguistic seminar at the Center for
Advanced Study in the Behavioral Sciences, George Peter
Murdock endeavored to verify the alleged tendency of unrelated languages "to develop similar words for father and
mother on the basis of nursery forms." Murdock's (1957)
tables of kinship terms assembled for his "World Ethnographic
Sample" supplied the investigation with 1,072 terms (531 for
mother and 541 for father). The valuable seminar report has
recently been published by Murdock (1959). As the author
concludes, "the purpose of this paper is merely to present the
data, which clearly confirm the hypothesis under test"—a
striking convergence in the structure of these parental kin
terms throughout historically unrelated languages. He asks

whether linguists—"now that the facts are established"—
could not "clarify the theoretical principles that account for
them." In May 26, 1959, at the same seminar, I ventured to
answer Murdock's call, and now I am happy to contribute
those remarks to the book dedicated to *Heinz Werner*.

"The child," H. Werner (1940) stressed, "grows out of his
child's world into an alien world of adults. His behavior is
the result of an interaction between these two worlds." One
could add that likewise the behavior of adults with regard
to the child they nurse and educate is a result of an interaction between both worlds. In particular, the so-called
"baby talk" used by the grownups when speaking with infants is a kind of pidgin, a typical mixed language, where the
addressers try to adjust themselves to the verbal habits of their
addressees and to establish a common code suitable for both
interlocutors in a child-adult dialogue. The socialized and
conventionalized lexical coinages of this baby talk, known
under the name of nursery forms, are deliberately adapted to
the infant's phonemic pattern and to the usual make-up of
his early words; and, on the other hand, they tend to super-
impose upon the child a sharper delimitation and higher stability of word meaning.

Some of such nursery forms overstep the limits of the nurseries, enter into the general usage of the adult society, and
build a specific infantile layer in standard vocabulary. In
particular, adult language usually adopts the nursery forms
designating each of the two mature members of the nuclear
family. Very frequently these intimate, emotional, childishly
tinged words coexist with more general and abstract, exclusively adult parental terms. Thus, for instance, in English,
mama (*mamma, mammy, ma, mom, mommy*) and *papa* (*pap, pappy
pa, pop* or *dada, dad, daddy*) differ in use from the higher terms
mother and *father*; in a similar way, Russian distinguishes *mama*
and *papa* or *t'at'a* from *mat'* (Common Slavic *mati*) and *otec*
(Common Slavic *otĭcĭ*). In Indo-European the intellectualized
parental designations **mātēr* and **pətēr* were built from the

nursery forms with the help of the suffix -*ter*, used for various kin terms. I am inclined to trace to these prototypes not only the cited English nouns and the Slavic *mati* but also the root of the Slavic paternal term *ot*- and similar forms in some other Indo-European languages: cf. Vasmer's (1954) data on Rus. *otec*. The root in question could have lost its initial *p*- through an infantlike elimination of consonantal diversity in **pətēr* when this adult term went down into the nursery.

As an instructive example of the difference in formal and functional properties between the two levels of parental appellations, the use of Bulgarian words *mama* and *majka* 'mother' may be cited. The nursery forms like *mama*, adequately characterized by E. Georgieva (1959) as intermediate between common and proper nouns (*polunaricatelni*, *naricatelno-sobstveni imena*), can be used in standard Bulgarian neither with articles nor with possessive pronouns. The bare *mama* means either 'my, addresser's mother' or 'I, addressee's mother.' As to the term *majka*, it may appear with any "short possessive pronominal form" (*ti, mu, ì, vi, im*) except the first person pronoun *mi*. One's own mother is spoken of in Bulgarian as *mama* or occasionally as *majka* 'mother,' as far as it is clear from context or situation whose *majka* is meant. Finally, in a distancing fashion, the expression *mojata majka* 'the mother of mine' may be used, while the turn *majka mi* 'my mother' is ordinarily avoided. If the parental terms assembled by Murdock could be divided into these two—*mama-papa*, and *mother-father*—classes, his statistical test would yield even more overwhelming results.

Nursery coinages are accepted for a wider circulation in the child-adult verbal intercourse only if they meet the infant's linguistic requirements and thus follow the general line of any interlanguage, as formulated in the indigenous name for Russenorsk, the hybrid tongue of Russian and Norwegian fishermen: *moja på tvoja* 'mine in your way' (Broch, 1927). Those settled nursery forms adopted by speech communities ostensibly reflect the salient features and tendencies of children's speech development and their universal homogeneity. In particular the phonemic range of the intimate parental terms proves to be "severely limited." The principles underlying the successive stages in child's acquisition of language enable us to interpret and clarify the "cross-language parallels" in the structure of such terms throughout the world.

Consonantal clusters appear in no more than 1.1 per cent of the 1,072 parental terms counted by Murdock, and child's speech at its early stages uses no consonantal groups but only combinations of consonants with vowels. Such combinations are nearly constant in the *mama-papa* words, and purely vocalic roots are exceptional: only three among the tabulated instances.

Stops and nasals—briefly, consonants formed by a complete oral closure—predominate in parental terms. According to Murdock's tabulation, stops and nasals approach to 85 per cent of nonsyllabics. The exact ratio cannot be stated, because all nonsibilant fricatives were lumped together with corresponding stops.

Labial and dental—briefly, backward-flanged, or in acoustical terminology, diffuse consonants—prevail over velars and palatals—briefly, forward-flanged (hornlike), acoustically compact consonants. More than 76 per cent of all the terms counted include a labial or dental as opposed to more than 10 per cent with velars and palatals. A more exact computation would ask for a split of Murdock's class of sibilant fricatives into hissing (diffuse) and hushing (compact) consonants.

Wide vowels, especially /a/, are obviously preponderant, but it is impossible to extract numerical data from Murdock's table, because the narrower and wider vowels, within each of the three classes—front, unrounded back, and rounded back—are lumped together, and the relation—/e/:/i/ = /a/:/ə/ = /o/:/u/—which underlies many vocalic patterns, is disregarded.

The contrast between the consonantal presence and vocalic absence of an obstruction in the vocal tract finds its optimal expression when a consonant with a complete oral closure, and especially a backward-flanged consonant with a closure in the front of the oral cavity, is opposed to a forward-flanged vowel with a wide frontal opening. On the acoustical level, vowels differ from consonants by a sharply defined formant structure and a high total energy. The compact vowel displays the maximal energy output, while the diffuse consonant with an oral occlusion represents the maximal reduction in the energy output. Thus nursery names for mother and father, like the earliest meaningful units emerging in infant speech, are based on the polarity between the optimal consonant and the optimal vowel (Jakobson and Halle, 1957).

The principle of maximal contrast accounts for the constituents common to the majority of the *mama-papa* terms. As to the order of these constituents, the sequence "consonant plus vowel" appears to be almost compulsory; yet this question has been omitted in Murdock's test. During the babbling period in the infant's development, many of the uttered syllables consist of a vocalic sound succeeded by a consonantal articulation. The most natural order of sound production is an opening of the mouth followed by its closure. Among Russian interjections, one observes such infantile sound gestures as ['ap] and ['am]; when changed into verbal roots, they are adapted to the Russian phonemic pattern by substituting a fricative velar for the initial aspiration: *xapat'*, *xamat'*, *xamkat'*. As soon as the child moves from his babbling activities to the first acquisition of conventional speech, he at once clings to the model "consonant plus vowel." The sounds assume a phonemic value and thus need to be correctly identified by the listener, and since the best graspable clue in discerning consonants is their transition to the following vowels, the sequence "consonant plus vowel" proves to be the optimal sequence, and therefore it is the only universal variety of the syllable pattern.

Among 436 dentals and palatals, briefly, medial, acoustically acute consonants (the T, N, C and S classes in Murdock's table), there are 159, or 39 per cent, which are followed by a palatal, i.e., acute vowel, while among 507 labials and velars, briefly peripheral, acoustically grave consonants, (Murdock's P, M, K, and η classes) only 88, or 17 per cent, are accompanied by acute vowels. The considerably higher percentage of acute vowels after acute rather than grave consonants reflects an assimilative influence of consonantal tonality upon the tonality of the subsequent vowel, and the same tendency is manifest in the early stage of children's speech. At this stage, vocalic differences do not possess their own phonemic value, and the consonant functions as the only carrier of significative distinctions, the only genuine phoneme. The *mama-papa* terms, like the primary word units in infant language, do not comprise different consonants, and a disyllabic form usually reiterates one and the same consonant. At first child's language is devoid of any hierarchy of linguistic units and obeys the equation: one utterance—one sentence—one word—one morpheme—one phoneme—one distinctive feature. The *mama-papa* pair is a vestige of that stage of one-consonant utterances.

The reduplication of syllables, while passed over in Murdock's test, appears, however, as a favorite device in nursery forms, particularly in parental terms, and in the early word units of infant language. At the transition from babbling to verbal behavior, the reduplication may even serve as a compulsory process, signaling that the uttered sounds do not represent a babble, but a senseful, semantic entity. The patently linguistic essence of such a duplication is quite explicable. In contradistinction to the "wild sounds" of babbling exercises, the phonemes are to be recognizable, distinguishable, identifiable; and in accordance with these requirements, they must be deliberately repeatable. This repetitiveness finds its most concise and succinct expression in, e.g., *papa*. The successive presentations of the same consonantal phonemes, repeatedly supported by the same vowel, improve their intelligibility and contribute to the correctness of message reception (cf. Pollack, 1959).

The most spectacular results of Murdock's test concern the distribution of nasal and oral consonants between maternal and paternal terms: 55 per cent of the words denoting mother and only 15 per cent of those denoting father belong to M, N, and η consonant classes. Thus the traditional assertions that "the mother is usually named with an *m*-form, the father with a *p*, *b*, *t*, or *d*-form" (Lewis, 1951) obtain an instructive statistical corroboration. The origin and the evolution of the *m*-form can easily be traced, if one rejects any, as Lewis says, "mystical" beliefs in the weak *m* "suited to name a woman" or in the "centripetal" connotation of the nasals as opposed to the "centrifugal" meaning of the oral stops, as well as the equally superstitious speculations about the child's "meaningless" syllables, "arbitrarily" interpreted and taught by the grownups to the children "in the nurseries of all countries" (Jespersen, 1922).

Often the sucking activities of a child are accompanied by a slight nasal murmur, the only phonation which can be produced when the lips are pressed to mother's breast or to the feeding bottle and the mouth is full. Later, this phonatory reaction to nursing is reproduced as an anticipatory signal at the mere sight of food and finally as a manifestation of a desire to eat, or more generally, as an expression of discontent and impatient longing for missing food or absent nurser, and any ungranted wish. When the mouth is free from nutrition, the nasal murmur may be supplied with an oral, particularly labial release; it may also obtain an optional vocalic support. Eloquent material on the shape and function of those nasal interjections has been collected by such sagacious observers of infant speech as Grégoire (1937), Leopold (1939), Smoczyński (1955), and others.

Since the mother is, in Grégoire's parlance, *la grande dispensatrice*, most of the infant's longings are addressed to her, and children, being prompted and instigated by the extant nursery words, gradually turn the nasal interjection into a parental term, and adapt its expressive make-up to their regular phonemic pattern. Some investigators, however, for example, Leopold (1947), insist that not seldom this transition from the *m*-interjection to the maternal term proved to be delayed, and one of the two parental terms, *papa* appeared as the first thoroughly designative verbal unit, whereas, for instance, the form *mama* existed in the language of Leopold's daughter, asan interjection only: "it had no intellectual meaning and cannot be considered to be a semantic alternative of *papa*, which was learned with real meaning at 1; 0. *Mama* with the standard meaning was not learned until 1; 3."

The transitional period when *papa* points to the parent present, while *mama* signals a request for the fulfillment of some need or for the absent fulfiller of childish needs, first and foremost but not necessarily for the mother, is attentively described by Grégoire: "Edm. a paru réclamer sa maman, absente ce jour-là, en disant [mam: am: am:]; or, c'est [papa] qu'il émet, lorsqu'il la voit rentrer. . . . . Edm. me voit lui préparer une tartine; il énonce [mamã], et non [papa]." Likewise Smoczyński's children in the middle of their second year, when begging for something from their father, addressed him: [mama ma-ma ma:-ma:-ma:].

The priority of paternal terms with their oral stop, in relation to the maternal terms with nasal, is well founded both on the semantic and on the phonological level. Parsons' (1955) observations on the preoedipal mother-child identity in its plain contradistinction to the father's role give an answer to the question why the first distant, merely deictic, rudimentarily cognitive attitude in child's verbal behavior is embodied in the paternal term, which "heralds just the transition from affective expression to designative language" (Jakobson, 1941), whereas in the maternal term, the purely referential value arises in a later (Parsons would probably suggest— oedipal) stage. It would be interesting to examine whether there is a difference in the settlement of *mama* "with the standard meaning" in the speech development of boys on the one hand and girls on the other. On the phonological level, it may be observed that the optimal consonant-vowel contrast is achieved by the backward-flanged (diffuse), particularly labial stop, confronted with the forward-flanged vowel. The addition of a new, open resonator brings the nasal consonants closer to vowels and thus attenuates the maximal contrast. The phonemic formation of nasal consonants implies the existence of the consonant-vowel contrast, and is a superstructure upon this contrast.

Although the *mama-papa* terms are nursery words, they conform to the developmental character of infant language, and neither their penetration into the national language nor their international diffusion invalidates this basic conformity. Therefore the complete exclusion of "forms resembling *mama* and *papa*" from Murdock's text, "unless comparative data on related languages clearly demonstrated their indigenous origin," seems to be superfluously rigorous.

The captivating test of the eminent anthropologist deserves to be continued and developed. The phonemic relation between the maternal and paternal term should be examined and tabulated. How frequently do both terms belong to the nasal or to the oral class? How often do both of these terms contain a labial or both of them a dental? What are the types of combination between the opposition labial-dental and nasal-oral within the pairs of parental terms? Reinforced, multiform polarizations seem to play here a noticeable role. Cf. such pairs as Russian *mama-t'at'a*, where the feature nasal-oral is combined with the two tonality features—grave-acute and sharp(palatalized)-plain(nonpalatalized). The coincidence of the latter two features creates the optimal contrast of high and low tonality.

Among familial terms the nursery forms are not confined to parental designations, and it would be a tempting task to trace, how the different degrees of relationship designated correspond to the development of the child's language. Thus

Russian *baba* 'grandma' and *d'ad'a* 'uncle' (cf. *papa* and *t'at'a*) introduce the voicing of consonants, a later feature in the phonemic patterning of Russian (and all Slavic) children. The terms *d'ed* 'grandpa' and *t'ot'a* shift from /a/ to other vowels, which belong to the later phonemic acquisitions of children. Nurse is called either *mamka*, a diminutive from *mama*, or *n'an'a* 'nanny,' opposed by its nasals of high tonality (sharp and acute), briefly by a typically diminutive sound symbolism, to *mama* with its nasals of low tonality (plain and grave).

We observe that only seniors in age and function are supplied here with nursery names, and we face the relevant question: for what kinsmen are there such names in a given language or stock of languages? A wide field is open for productive joint work of linguists, anthropologists, and experts in psychology of mental and behavioral development.

BIBLIOGRAPHY

Broch, O. (1927), Russenorsk. *Archiv für slavische Philologie*, 41:209-262.

Georgieva, E. (1959), Mama i majka. *B"lgarski ezik*, 9:287-289.

Grégoire, A. (1937), *L'apprentissage du langage*. Bibliothèque de la Faculté de Philosophie et Lettres de l'Université de Liège, 73.

Jakobson, R. (1941), Kindersprache, Aphasie und allgemeine Lautgesetze. *Uppsala Universitets årsskrift*, 1942:1-83.

———— & Halle, M. (1957), Phonology in Relation to Phonetics. *Manual of Phonetics*, ed. L. Kaiser. Amsterdam: North-Holland Publishing Company, pp. 215-251.

Jespersen, O. (1922), *Language, Its Nature, Development and Origin*. London-New York: Macmillan.

Leopold, W. F. (1939), *Speech Development of a Bilingual Child*, 1: Vocabulary Growth in the First Two Years. Evanston & Chicago: Northwestern University.

———— (1947), *Speech Development of a Bilingual Child*, 2: Sound Learning in the First Two Years. Evanston: Northwestern University.

Lewis, M. M. (1951), *Infant Speech*. New York: Humanities Press; London: Routledge & Kegan Paul.

Murdock, G. P., (1957), World Ethnographic Sample. *American Anthropologist*, *59*:664-687.

───── (1959), Cross-Language Parallels in Parental Kin Terms. *Anthropological Linguistics*, *1* (9):1-5.

Parsons, T. (1955), Family Structure and the Socialization of the Child. *Family Socialization and Interaction Process*, by T. Parsons & R. F. Bales. Glencoe, Ill.: Free Press.

Pollack, I. (1959), Message Repetition and Message Reception. *Journal of the Acoustical Society of America*, *31*:1509-1515.

Smoczyński, P. (1955), Przyswajanie przez dziecko podstaw systemu językowego. *Societas Scientiarum Lodziensis, Sectio 1, no. 19*.

Vasmer, M. (1954), otéc. *Russisches etymologisches Wörterbuch*, *2*:290. Heidelberg: Carl Winter, 1953-1955.

Werner, H. (1940), *Comparative Psychology of Mental Development*. New York: International Universities Press, 2nd rev. ed., 1957.

Selector-Integrator Mechanisms in Behavior

NORMAN R. F. MAIER, Ph.D.

University of Michigan

Psychological theorizing would be essentially simplified if the measurement of the responses (or output) and the measurement of the stimulus (or input) told the whole story. However, the organism itself makes its own unique contribution to both the stimulus and the response, and continues to be a source of confusion. This confusion becomes apparent when one measures ability by means of performance. Since the only measure of ability is through this approach, indirect methods must be used to separate ability from performance. These indirect approaches often lack refinement and may be questioned, yet it would be unfortunate to overlook a distinction merely because it could not be proved to a critical audience. Nevertheless, the strict scientist could conceivably discourage a researcher from making qualitative distinctions by requiring him to furnish conclusive evidence for them. The burden of proof, according to the law of parsimony, seems to rest with the person who makes the qualitative distinctions.

The number of basic mechanisms or qualitative distinctions that psychology must make or the number of evolutionary steps that it must postulate has been determined by nature. It is the scientist's job to make qualitative distinctions where they do indeed occur and to make quantitative measures where these are relevant. Progress in science depends not upon the simplicity or the complexity of its theories but rather upon whether the theories make distinctions of the proper kind.

Since performance is measurable, what are some of the problems regarding the inference of ability? Certainly the ability to perform may differ from the performance. To guard against this source of error one can state that ability to perform on a given occasion depends upon the performance on that occasion, but does this statement advance our knowledge? An ability can conceivably remain constant, but the ability to express it may vary. When a violinist's performances vary, does he lose and gain ability or does only his performance vary?

It seems that there are many factors that influence performance, and ability is but one among others. Motivation, morale, fatigue, and adjustment are examples of a few of them. It is recognized that performance cannot exceed ability (except in so far as chance plays a part), but that ability may exceed performance. This means that the loss of an ability cannot be assumed merely because it is inaccessible under certain circumstances. However, an ability may be inferred if it can be brought to expression. This suggests that progress may more readily be made if many ways for producing behavior are studied. Researches that limit behavior are most likely to overlook latent abilities. It also suggests that performance be

studied under a variety of conditions so as to separate variations in ability from variations in performance.

Let us examine some samples of specific data to clarify
problem areas in which present psychological concepts fail
to be helpful in understanding variations in behavior. Research by Zucker (1943) raises a problem in point. He found
that delinquent and nondelinquent populations of children
completed the items in a story-completion test differently.
Seventy-five per cent of the solutions of delinquents were
characterized by having nonconstructive endings, whereas
only 24 per cent of the nondelinquents completed their stories
in this manner.

What are the implications of these findings? It might be
argued that the learning or biological make-up of these two
populations of children were different or it might be assumed
that they performed differently and were of like make-up.

Further light is thrown on this question by an experiment
by Edwards (1954). He used the same story-completion tests
as Zucker, but instead of using delinquent and nondelinquent
populations, he used sixth-grade school children in a role-
playing situation. Three groups were compared. One group
was given a role which described the home picture as one of
being rejected by the parents; a second group was given the
role which described the home as being warm and accepting;
and the third group was uninstructed, and therefore the
children were left to assume their own real life roles. However, the school was located in a depressed area, which was a
source of an actual delinquent population.

Story completions of a nonconstructive or delinquent
variety showed different percentages for these three groups.
The results were as follows: 76 per cent for the rejected group;
32 per cent for the accepted group; and 67 per cent for the
control group.

It may be assumed in this instance that the three populations had similar behavior make-ups since the division of the
groups was random. It also follows, since the roles supplied

were unrelated to the stories, that no specific learnings were
given. The difference in behavior, therefore, must be attributed to some performance factor other than the difference in
ability. The role instructions, which may have set up a kind
of "feeling," evidently determined the types of behaviors that
would be expressed and organized in a given situation. This
suggests that delinquent and constructive behaviors need not
be specifically learned. Each individual has adequate constructive and nonconstructive behaviors available for expression, so that the actual behavior expressed is a sample revealed on a given occasion. Since Edward's findings so accurately duplicate those of Zucker, the importance of some
selection process becomes very apparent. This statement does
not preclude the possibility that learning may supplement
the degree of ability and create some basic differences in
children reared under different conditions.

From the above analysis it follows that individual differences
in behavior must be viewed in two ways: (a) differences due
to the variation in ability, and (b) differences in behavior
samples shown on a given occasion.

The value of this distinction also becomes apparent from
an analysis of three experiments on variability, conducted by
Krechevsky (1937). He compared normal and brain-injured
rats on three different measures of variability, and although
the results were clear-cut in each instance, each led to a
different conclusion.

In the first experiment he used a checkerboard maze, which
offered 20 routes to food, all of equal length and all rewarded.
In this free type of situation the rat could confine its runs to
one or several routes. He found that normal rats averaged 5.46
routes in 15 runs, whereas the brain-injured rats averaged
3.00 routes. This raised the question of the nature of the effect
of the brain injury. Has the ability to show variable behavior
been reduced in the animal or has the operation affected the
performance process? Suppose the operation alters the need
to show variable behavior. In such event, operated rats

would show less variable behavior in a free situation than normals since such behavior would be less need satisfying for them.

Krechevsky's second study throws some light on this matter. He taught normal and operated rats two routes to food. One route was varied from time to time; the other was kept constant and was somewhat shorter. No errors could be made on either route since there were no blind alleys. In the test situation the animal was confronted with a choice between the two routes. It was found that normal rats took the variable route 57.1 per cent of the time, whereas operated rats took it 34.3 per cent of the time.

In this instance the operated rats chose the efficient (shorter) route, and one might conclude that they were of superior ability. But was this the reason for the choice? They may have avoided the variable route because it offered difficulty or they may have selected the constant path because they disliked variability.

The interpretation that the operated rats were wise and chose the shorter path was eliminated by Krechevsky's control experiment in which he used both a long and a short path, but eliminated the variability. With variability removed, normal rats lost their preference for the long path since their choices of it went from 57.1 to 47.0 per cent. Operated rats, however, increased their choices for the long path from 34.3 to 41.3 per cent. In this instance the normal rats seem the wiser, but the scores approach similarity because variability influenced normal and operated rats in the opposite ways. It seems that operated rats avoid variable situations, but is this due to lack of ability or is it a difference in preference?

To determine whether the operation affected the basic ability, we must have a situation that makes a variable path desirable. Can operated rats cope with variable situations if the matter of selection due to preference is eliminated?

Krechevsky's third experiment supplies the answer to this question. In this experiment he made the variable path

shorter than the constant path. In Table 1 the results of the
different test conditions are summarized. The last line of the
table shows that this change in the length of paths had little
effect on the normal rats. They selected the variable path
55.0 per cent of the time, which is about the same as the
previous 57.1 per cent obtained when it was the longer path.
In choosing between the two paths about an equal number of
times, normal rats found a further way to express a desire
or a need to vary behavior: they increased their variability by
frequently alternating between the two routes on successive
trips.

TABLE 1

Choice Between a Variable and a Constant Path

| | Per Cent Variable Path is Chosen by | |
| | Normal | Operated |
TEST	Rats	Rats
Experiment 2A		
Longer Variable Path		
vs. shorter Constant Path	57.1	34.3
Experiment 2B		
Longer Path Not Varied		
vs. shorter Constant Path	47.0	41.3
Experiment 3		
Shorter Variable Path		
vs. longer Constant Path	55.0	51.3

Making the variable path the shorter of the two, however,
markedly influenced the performance of operated rats. They
now chose the variable path 51.3 per cent of the time instead
of the former 34.3 per cent. The shorter length of the path,
therefore, offset the disadvantage of variability.

These data clearly indicate that the ability to show variable
behavior can be brought to expression in operated rats. It
must be concluded, therefore, that this ability is not destroyed

by operation. If only adaptive ability had been considered, the first experiment would have suggested that operated rats were inferior to normals, the second experiment would have shown them to be superior, and the third would have shown them to be equal.

The results are consistent with each other, however, if we interpret them to mean that brain operations changed the animals with respect to the mechanisms that determine the expression of variable behavior. Apparently normal rats prefer variable situations, whereas operated rats prefer constant situations, and this difference in preference causes them to behave differently under certain conditions.

Possibly an even more dramatic example of the pitfalls inherent in the process of inferring ability from performance is provided by the recent work of McCleary (1959). He found that cats with bilateral lesions in the area of the subcallosal cortex returned promptly to a food trough at which they had just received severe electric shocks to the mouth. Normal cats under similar circumstances did not return for a matter of days even though it was their sole source of food. It would be tempting to conclude that the lesion had interfered with the animals' ability to become frightened of the food trough. A control experiment, however, demonstrated that the ability to acquire a fear was perfectly intact. In a standard shock-avoidance task the operated animals learned an avoidance response as promptly as did the normals. The author concluded that the brain lesion interfered with normal emotional behavior or did not, depending on the performance required of the animal.

ABILITY VS. PERFORMANCE

In order to cope with some of the problems raised when the differences between the ability to behave and performance are not clearly differentiated, it may be well to make this basic distinction at the outset rather than cope with it late in the theorizing process. Thus the ability to behave may be thought of as an organism's behavior potential. This represents the behavior repertoire. Every animal has the ability to express a variety of behaviors, but on a given occasion only certain of these many latent behaviors are expressed. Instead of assuming that the stimulus is the only factor that initiates behavior, and thereby making the stimulus a part of the behavior description, it will be assumed here that other possibilities for initiating behaviors exist. These initiators may be either in the external world or in the organism itself. The processes that determine the behaviors that are brought to expression will be regarded as selector-integrator mechanisms. The name implies not only that certain behaviors are selected from alternative possibilities, but also that the parts of behavior are integrated or organized into some pattern.

Viewed in this manner the behavior repertoire may be thought of as analogous to the cells of a memory drum of a computer. The selector mechanism would be the particular program which would make a specific selection from among stored information. The information may be stored in the form of simple behavior segments or memories, or as complex built-in behavior sequences or systems of meanings. The latter would be analogous to subroutines stored in a computer. The selection obtained from the program would represent the elements or sequences of behavior expressed on a given occasion. Furthermore, the behaviors selected could be organized by the program into a specified sequence or configuration to provide a desired output. This aspect of the programming process would be analogous to the integrative function of the selector-integrator mechanism in behavior. Thus the organization of the behavior pattern would be determined by the way the parts were stored as well as by the way they were integrated at the time of expression. It can be seen that stored learned sequences might be helpful on some occasions, but might be a disadvantage and need breaking up on other occasions.

Whether or not the analogy is fully accurate, it does make

the essential separation: it distinguishes between (a) the behavior repertoire or ability; and (b) a selection-integration process, which selects and integrates a sample from the repertoire to produce performance. Although some theories of motivation make a similar distinction, it will be seen that this similarity ceases when a variety of selector-integrator mechanisms are introduced.

Returning to the facts about delinquency already mentioned, it becomes apparent that delinquent and constructive behavior need not assume different behavior repertoires. As a matter of fact, delinquency seems to be a phenomenon of the selector-integrator mechanism. The same is true of variable behavior in rats. It is incorrect to interpret Krechevsky's results as due to a change in the behavior repertoire. Rather the results readily fall into place if it is assumed that the brain injury has altered the selector-integrator mechanism.

Having made the basic distinction between two aspects of behavior, the next step is to examine each of them more carefully and make distinctions within these aspects. These qualitative distinctions should be made at the initial stages of theorizing since the developmental process may be different for each process. If certain processes fail to be basically different, they can be combined with others. The assumption of too many qualitative differences, therefore, can always be corrected, but the assumption that qualitative differences are not present, when they do in fact exist, makes all research based upon this false assumption valueless.

THE BEHAVIOR REPERTOIRE

The arousal of instinctive patterns or the selection of a habit from a family hierarchy (Hull, 1935) would be the function of the selector-integrator mechanisms. An organism's behavior repertoire may be assumed to consist of the abilities obtained from maturation and through learning. Thus bodily structures, sensory capacity, and neural connections (influenced by heredity and growing conditions) plus the changes

produced by learning would establish the functional linkages
or patterns that would be available for expression. This much
is not unique and is consistent with the conceptualization in
most theories.

In addition to the functional linkages, which tie segments of
behavior together (association formation), it is also necessary
to include a closely related process—that of retention or memory. Learning is a function of the ease with which associative
connections are formed, whereas retention depends upon the
durability of these linkages. Lashley (1929) has shown retention (as measured by relearning) to be differently related
to brain injury than original learning. Since the measurement of retention utilizes relearning scores, one would expect
the element of learning to be present in both measures. Despite
this fact, the ability to retain and the ability to learn have
been found to be only moderately correlated.

Unlearning also is different from forgetting. Buytendijk
(1931) found brain-operated rats equal to normals in learning
a position response, but when he required them to reverse
their habits, the operated rats were clearly handicapped.
Maier (1932a, 1932b) found that lesions which had marked
effects on a test measuring the ability to reorganize experience had no effect on the formation of a simple association.
It is permissible to postulate basic differences, since there is no
evidence showing that learning, retention, and unlearning
merely are different aspects of the same process.

It would appear that the ability to form behavior units
would influence the behavior repertoire in an additive way,
but that the ability to disassociate or to break up learned
patterns would be a different process and its function would
be to make for greater flexibility and ease in the reorganiza-
tions of experience. If we assume that creativity is more than
learning, and that solutions to problems sometimes may be
new integrations rather than whole units transferred from
other situations, the concept of elasticity becomes as essential to the behavior repertoire as does the concept of learning.

In general, learning has been treated as if it were an asset to adjustment. It seems, however, that its possible disadvantages should also be recognized. Frequently, parts of learned patterns are desired, while the whole pattern would be a detriment. This disadvantage was found to be apparent in problem-solving situations, in that subjects persist in following habitual lines of thinking (Maier, 1930, 1931b, 1945). However, once this condition is recognized, it becomes evident in other situations. For example, speech sounds in a particular language are specific combinations. Since a different language requires other basic combinations, it is difficult for an adult to lose his accent; a child, however, readily learns to speak a new language without an accent. On the other hand, adults who speak many languages have little accent, perhaps because their basic speech sounds are fragmented through the learning of several languages.

Basic research supporting this hypothesis is not lacking. Padilla (1930) found chicks unable to acquire the normal pecking movements when kept in darkness for two weeks. It appeared that the reflexes associated with pecking had become combined with feeding from a medicine dropper, and these combinations interfered with the learning of normal pecking because the initial elements were no longer available. However, shorter periods in darkness had been found to be an asset to the acquisition of pecking because of the increased maturity (Shepard and Breed, 1913; Bird, 1925; and Moseley, 1925).

Since individuals differ in their aptitudes for acquiring learning, it is to be expected that the ability to disassociate or fragment behavior segments will also be an aptitude that will show variations between individuals. For this reason flexibility is an appropriate part of the behavior repertoire, even though it may not reveal itself as clearly as does habit formation.

TYPES OF SELECTOR-INTEGRATOR MECHANISMS

In considering the methods by which behavior is selected from a given behavior repertoire, psychological processes formerly regarded as unrelated become grouped together. Most of these processes, being well known, need not be discussed in detail. However, an attempt will be made to describe them with reference to the functional meanings that emerge when they are treated as selector-integrator mechanisms.

Locus, Intensity, and Form of the Stimulus

The most primitive type of behavior selection is determined by the *location* of the stimulus. The response of an amoeba, for example, depends upon where it is stimulated; i.e., different behaviors can be elicited from its repertoire merely by stimulating its various parts. The *intensity* of the stimulus also acts selectively. Generally speaking, mild stimulation activates approach behavior, whereas strong stimulation activates withdrawal.

This relationship between approach and withdrawal, as a function of stimulus intensity, seems to be preserved throughout the animal kingdom. Not only does the direction of movement of the amoeba depend on stimulus intensity, but whether or not a dog will show fear of or approach the hand depends upon how quickly the hand is moved. The fear behavior shown by goslings when the hawk flies overhead, as contrasted with their preparing for feeding when the mother approaches, seems to depend upon rate of change in stimulation. The build of the hawk is such as to produce rapid change in the visual field, whereas the long neck and slim body of the goose yields a more gradual change.

As organisms increase in complexity of bodily make-up, stimulation effects spread, first to adjacent regions; later, with the development of conductive tissues, more remote parts of the body are included in the behavior. The *location* of the stimulus thus becomes less decisive and the *form* of stimulation becomes a critical selector as one proceeds up the evolutionary ladder. The highest development of this type is associated with the appearance and refinement of sense organs. Through the development of sense organs, the environment becomes capable of selecting different behaviors from an organism merely by stimulating it with different forms of energy.

Although the size of an animal's repertoire of behavior also increases as the selector mechanisms evolve and improve, it is clear that the behavior expressed will be selective, depending upon the stimulus conditions. The development of this type of control over behavior is unique in that it is entirely external to the animal.

Stimulus Set and Attention

Even in the simplest animals the behavior expressed includes more than the influence of the stimulus. In the amoeba the same stimulus has different effects, depending upon the movement pattern in progress at the time. Thus, if the amoeba is moving in a particular direction, this temporary "anterior end" is dominant over other portions of the body (Maier and Schneirla, 1935). As soon as an activity pattern is established a physiological gradient is in evidence, and this condition in the organism influences the behavior that a particular stimulus can produce at a given time. This physiological gradient is perhaps the most primitive kind of set.

Such terms as stimulus set, mental set, and expectations refer to conditions in the organism that alter the way an organism will respond to stimulation. In general, this type of influence over behavior has been neglected in research, particularly in that on lower animals, so that much of the comparative evidence depends on observational data.

While studying delayed reactions Tinklepaugh (1928) described some unusual behavior in a monkey. Although a monkey normally will eat lettuce, he refused it when the experimenter fooled him by causing him to expect a banana. In this experiment Tinklepaugh pretended to place a slice of banana under a cup, but palmed the banana and substituted the lettuce instead. When the monkey turned up the cup and found lettuce he became excited and refused to eat the lettuce. Apparently the behavior elicited was influenced by an expectation or stimulus set.

Hull (1935) introduced a provision for the influence of expectation in order to show how behavior described by Maier (1929) as reasoning in rats might be reduced to S-R theory. Hull thus attempted to account for the appearance of a new adaptive response by making it a selection from the "family of habits." This approach tends to minimize the importance of the set by making it a part of the habit strength and thus a part of the behavior repertoire.

The phenomenon of attention is similar to a set or expectation in that it represents a condition of the organism that influences receptivity or responsiveness to stimulation of a particular kind. The influence of attention in reducing reaction time, increasing sensitivity for one stimulus and excluding others, increasing discrimination, etc., are well-known phenomena. Although the phenomenon of attention played a prominent part in the history of psychology, modern theory has neglected it. However, recent research by Hernandez-Péon, Scherrer, and Jouvet (1956) has provided empirical evidence that the nervous system is organized in such a way that stimuli irrelevant to the objects being attended to are not permitted to stimulate the cortex. When the cat in this instance was attending visually (and presumably olfactorily) to the mice in the bottle, the clicks stimulating its ear were prevented from intruding on the cortical representation of the stimulus. In attention, then, the nervous system is organized to be sensitive to certain stimuli and to suppress irrelevant ones.

Usually the term attention has been applied to human beings only, it being assumed that attention is a condition of awareness and that introspection was needed for its study. However, Maier (1930) demonstrated that the performance of rats in a difficult problem situation was best (a) in new test situations; (b) on the first four as against the last four trials of the day; (c) when changes in the situation were made; and (d) after several days' rest. The results of each of these conditions are in conflict with what one would predict from learning, but each involves a factor (novelty or change) that leads to obtaining attention. Thus an animal frequently violates a principle of learning when the behavior selected is influenced by attention. Frank (1932) found herself unable to duplicate her own data, in a study of normal, underfed and rachitic rats, when she repeated the experiment in another laboratory. The various inconsistencies in her data, however, became reconciled when the findings were analyzed in terms of different distractors offered in the two laboratories. Consideration of both motivation and distraction led to the correct predictions regarding the subsequent analyses of her data. Depending upon the way distraction and motivation interacted in selecting behavior from the three groups of rats, the same experimental conditions caused the three groups of rats to behave differently. Analyzed in terms of learning ability alone, these findings are entirely ambiguous.

The specific natures of stimulus set and of the attention mechanism are unknown and it is quite possible that their evolution has a varied history. However, both set and attention seem to select the stimuli and put the organism in readiness for its response. In this sense attention is closely related to perception, but the laws of attention (Pillsbury, 1908) and the laws of perception (Koffka, 1935) are quite different.

Perception

The way an individual organizes sensory data determines not only what is learned (Maier, 1939b) but also which of several possible behaviors will be expressed. Kuo (1930) clearly demonstrated that cats when shocked in the presence of rats may learn to fear (a) rats, (b) the shock-box, or (c) a rat in the shock-box. Thus the learning is not a function of the relationship in the environment, but of the relationship that a given organism perceives. In a similar manner the behavior selected for expression is influenced not merely by the stimulus situation, but by the way the sensory data are organized by the individual. For example, if a person hears a noise which he interprets as that produced by someone clicking his false teeth, he may show irritation; whereas if he perceives the same noise as caused by a faulty radiator, he may be able to dismiss it entirely. Situations perceived as threatening release one kind of behavior, while those perceived as supportive release another kind.

The concept of equivalent stimuli developed by Klüver (1933) holds that a given response will be elicited by a variety of situations. Stimulus conditions that elicit the same response are said to be equivalent with respect to that response, whereas stimulus conditions that fail to elicit a given response are said to be nonequivalent. The concept of equivalence in stimuli is not merely a matter of stimulus generalization, but is one of perceptual organization. Klüver pointed out that an animal might readily discriminate between the stimuli it found to be equivalent.

Because animals show wide individual differences in the stimuli they find to be equivalent, it follows that the influence of *transfer of training* and the *concepts* aroused by a given situation will be an individual matter. The researches of Lashley (1938), Maier (1939b, 1941), and Wapner (1944) demonstrated that, even in the rat, the stimuli essential for arousing a previously trained response varied greatly from one individual to another. These researches revealed that two rats responding similarly in a training situation might react quite differently to presentations of the same set of new stimuli. Maier (1941) and Wapner (1944) demonstrated further that brain injury increased the range of equivalent stimuli by causing the animal to be less responsive to differences than formerly. Thus operated rats expressed their learned response in a greater number of situations. Retesting the rats with the same battery of new stimulus combinations had an opposite effect and made rats more discriminating. Hence, extra exposure made the learned response less accessible. These findings support the view that perceptual organization determines the behaviors that will be selected from an animal's repertoire.

The work of Koffka (1935), Werner (1940), Werner and Wapner (1949, 1954), Wapner and Werner (1957), and Witkin, Lewis, Hertzman, Machover, Meissner, and Wapner (1954) demonstrates that the laws governing perceptual organization not only differ from those of learning but are less likely to include concepts related to reinforcement and more likely to include concepts related to the individual and the total stimulus situation. Thus it is important to make a basic distinction between the functions of perception and functions of learning. When learning is considered a part of the behavior repertoire and perception is regarded as a selector-integrator mechanism, an exceptionally sharp separation between them results. This separation, however, does *not* preclude the possibility that perceptions are learned and that responses associated with them will be aroused by a particular perception. However, it does mean that a well-learned response will cease to be available if something occurs to change the perception in a recall situation. Gottschaldt (1926) caused recognition failures to occur in well-learned responses by embedding stimuli in such a fashion that different perceptual organizations were formed during the recall period. Methods for altering perception are more varied and extensive than those for altering associations, and the part played by each must be differentiated when a distinction between the behavior repertoire and the behavior sample selected for expression is made.

Needs and the Motivation Process

Needs, like attention, refer to a condition of the organism, but the condition is a physiological one, especially with respect to such basic needs as hunger, thirst, sex, and the maternal one. A hungry animal is sensitive to food in its en-

vironment and will locate it when a well-fed animal will fail
to react to food cues. I have repeatedly observed that rats
who are on their way to a known food position will hop over
food placed on an elevated path. However, rats that are exploring a series of paths will never miss such a piece of food.
If hurried, an exploring animal will stop suddenly and back
up to the food it has passed over. Thus hunger and stimulus-
set seem to combine in that hunger increases sensitivity to
food, while set limits the sensitivity to a specific expectation.

Hungry men think and dream of food as Guetzkow and
Bowman (1946) have shown. Hunger also initiates organized
behavior sequences, even though an activity such as restless-
ness may be random. If an animal has learned the location of
food, certain learned responses will be selected from its behavior repertoire. In such instances the animal will not only
go to the locations where food has formerly been found (i.e.,
express reinforced habits) but will systematically explore a
general region. This "hunting pattern" is both typical and
clearly distinctive in that such behavior is recognized by other
animals. Thus the prey flees when the lion is hungry and is
on the hunt, but grazes undisturbed when the lion takes a
leisurely stroll.

Hunger, therefore, not only selects stimuli from the organism's environment, but selectively releases and integrates
a number of different responses so that the behavior shows
variety, though variety of a select nature.

Thirst, maternal and sex needs serve a similar function, although each is unique in its selectivity of stimuli. In this respect
each need becomes a separate selector mechanism. However,
for the present, it seems appropriate to group physiological
needs together in accordance with prevalent theory.

Social needs function in a manner similar to the physiological ones, but in this instance it is difficult to locate the
stimulating condition or organ. Many of these needs are of an
acquired (learned) nature, such as a boy's need for a bicycle.
In such cases it would be reasonable to assume that the loca-

tion of the need was in the brain. Nevertheless, a boy with a need for a bicycle is selective in his observations, and his behaviors are clearly oriented toward obtaining the bicycle. Like all need conditions, social needs select goal-oriented behaviors.

It will be apparent that acquiring a need involves a different kind of learning than acquiring a conditioned response or gaining an education. If responses are learned through reinforcement, it is obvious that the boy who has no bicycle has the strongest need, and yet it is the neighbor boy with a bicycle who experiences the reinforcement. Social pressure, the mere observation of what others have, is one of the important ways in which needs are acquired. A boy who acquires a need for a bicycle may undergo a great behavior change, not because his behavior repertoire has been altered, but because this acquired need selects from his repertoire specific behaviors previously present but unexpressed.

Attitudes

Attitudes represent relatively permanent sets which selectively influence the responses elicited—by determining the facts that are observed, as well as by influencing the interpretations with which these observed facts are invested. When defined as selectors of stimuli, attitudes are similar to attention in that they determine what is observed. Thus an unfavorable attitude toward a racial group causes its faults to be observed and hence reacted to, whereas a favorable attitude causes its best behaviors to be seen. Maier and Lansky (1957) have shown that even in a role-playing situation, persons exposed to the same facts will select and react, primarily, to those facts which are consistent with the attitude supplied. Likewise, interpretations of facts and organizations of behavior are guided by an attitude.

A person holding an unfavorable attitude toward Negroes would be similar to a person who had been instructed to pay attention to all of the undesirable things Negroes did. The difference would be that, generally speaking, the acts of attention are constantly changing and are subject to shifting interests as well as to changes in the intensity of stimulation; whereas attitudes are relatively constant and less dependent upon stimulus intensity.

A second difference between attitude and attention is the emotional involvement or feeling that accompanies attitudes. Liking or disliking are characteristic emotional accompaniments of attitudes, while attention is primarily a cognitive function; although it must be pointed out that autonomic responses are associated with stages of attention. It is generally recognized that attitudes, particularly unfavorable ones, represent emotional sets, whereas attention is more a function of intelligence. Often the two selective conditions accompany one another—in that the attitude determines the kinds of stimuli on which attention will be focused.

Direction in Thinking

The controversy over whether the ideas recalled during productive thinking are more than random and more than a function of the strength of associative bonds is an old one. Psychologists who held that there were thought processes that could not be reduced to the laws of recall suggested various kinds of selective factors. For Selz (1913) the "determining tendency" served a selective function, for Wertheimer (1925) the reorganization function was a kind of closure, and for Köhler (1929) the sensefulness of the behavior was the product of insight. My concept "direction in thinking" (Maier, 1930, 1931a) performs a similar function, but combines the selective function of the determining tendency with the integrative function of Wertheimer's closure.

The string problem (Maier, 1931b), which requires the tying together of the ends of two strings hanging from the ceiling, illustrates the selective function of a "direction" in problem solving. When the two strings are far enough apart so that the subject cannot reach one while holding onto the other, he may envisage his difficulty to be either of the following:

1. My arm is too short.
2. The strings are too short.
3. The end of the first string won't stay in the middle while I go to get the second one.
4. The second string won't come to me while I hold on to the first one.

Each of these difficulties is associated with a general selective function or a direction in thinking. This direction greatly determines both (a) what is perceived in the environment, and (b) the ideas or thoughts that are recalled. The first difficulty mentioned above causes sticks, poles, and objects with handles to be readily perceived; while mental images of such objects and experiences having to do with extending the reach are recalled. The second difficulty causes strings, window-shade cords, and belts to be noticed; while various ideas having to do with lengthening a string are recalled. The third difficulty inclines the person to think of chairs that might be moved between the strings so that one of the strings could be tied to it; while impractical methods of anchoring one cord in the center are tried out. The fourth difficulty causes electric fans to be noticed or requested; at the same time, such activities as opening a window to permit a breeze to blow the one cord toward the center while the other is carried there may be performed.

These selective perceptions and recalls indicate that the activities expressed are neither random nor based upon strength of associative connections because the direction not only selects relevant objects and memories but also violates the principles of recall based upon association. The research of Lewin (1926) on nonsense syllables clearly showed that a strong association between a pair of nonsense syllables could be inhibited readily by merely instructing the subject to rhyme each syllable as it was exposed.

Very close to the concept of direction is that of "hypothesis" in behavior developed by Krechevsky (1932). He found that rats in a discrimination-problem situation are following a system rather than making random choices. Thus they may make some reactions to brightness, then a series of reactions to position, followed by a sequence of alternations, etc. Even in the rat, it appears that a selective mechanism was needed to account for the lack of randomness in trial-and-error behavior.

Although an attitude and a direction in thinking are similar in that they both influence perceptions and recall, there are basic differences. Attitudes, as already suggested, involve emotions, whereas directions in thinking exert primarily a cognitive influence. Furthermore, directions are more subject to change and can be altered by instruction (Maier, 1933); whereas attitudes, by comparison, are rigid when viewed rationally. Then too, directions in thinking are largely influenced by the perception of the difficulty or immediate situation, whereas attitudes usually have a longer history and hence are brought to the situation rather than derived from it.

An Obstacle as a Problem Situation

A problem exists when a response to a given situation is blocked. Ordinarily a hungry animal responds to food by approaching it and eating. However, when an obstacle blocks the approach, variable behavior comes to expression. Thorndike (1898) described such behavior as "random trial and error", whereas Adams (1929) found an element of selectivity and insightfulness in the behavior expressed; but both recognized the characteristic of variability in the behavior. A somewhat higher status was accorded to "trial-and-error" behavior when Dewey (1910) described problem solving as "mental trial and error." In this manner Thorndike's simple mechanism was generalized to the thinking process of man. The fact that Dewey's model of thinking also emphasized the point that the person, when confronted with a problem, goes from one idea to another is, however, of importance since variability still emerges as the dominant characteristic of problem-solving behavior.

Variability is a biologically sound mechanism for problem solving, since it is apparent that when a given sample of behavior is inadequate another sample may be effective. In brief, a problem stimulates an animal to run through his repertoire of behavior. If the solution is included in this repertoire, the problem is solved.

Direction in thinking may shorten this process by confining the variability to certain areas in the behavior repertoire. Thus, in the case of the string problem, variability may be restricted to trying out different ways in which to increase the reach of the arm. However, variability also may operate so that the directions in thinking are varied. Sherburne (1940) found that superior problem solvers varied their directions in thinking, whereas less capable individuals tended to confine their variability within a single direction.

Variability, it appears, may be restricted or range widely but still serve no other purpose than that of selecting latent solutions from a repertoire stored in the animal. However, what Wertheimer (1945) calls reorganization, and what I have called the combination of parts of isolated experiences, further increases the scope of the variability process. One may think of *reproductive* thinking as the application of an old solution to a new problem situation, and of *productive* thinking as yielding a solution made up of parts of several old solutions or ideas.

In productive thinking the combination of elements results in a new integration or product. For this to be accomplished, old combinations must be broken down and new integrations formulated. For example, when the materials in the string problem are so limited that none of them can be used for extending the reach, when ways to lengthen the cord are impossible, and when things for anchoring the string do not exist, the problem remains insoluble as long as only these directions are explored. If only a pair of pliers is available, none of the above approaches is feasible. However, one of the strings can be transformed into a pendulum, so that the swinging string will then come to the problem solver while he is holding the other string. In this instance the pliers change their function and become a weight; the string, which previously dragged on the floor and was too long, must be shortened; and pendulums, which formerly served as timing devices, become methods for getting objects to come to the problem solver. That such experiences are already in an individual's repertoire can be argued. The controversy as to whether there is such a thing as creative problem solving is characterized by this kind of argument. Although I have reported experimental evidence elsewhere (Maier, 1929, 1938, 1940, 1945) in support of this developing of new integrations, for our present purposes this point is irrelevant. If new combinations do in fact occur in problem situations, the principle of variability is operating. The creative person continually varies the way he breaks up experiences and forms recombinations so that variability is present in the thinking of an inventor as well as in the problem solving of a chicken. The inventor and the chicken differ, however, with respect to their repertoires, their directions of thinking, the plasticity of their nervous systems, their ability to break down past learning, and in their behavioral equipment.

A problem situation does not indefinitely initiate variability, however. With repeated failure and a depletion of possible variable responses, substitute goals or escape may take the animal out of the problem. If these opportunities are not available, if the need for the incentive is great, or if pressure forces the animal to obtain a solution to a problem, the situation may become a frustrating condition.

Operationally, a frustrating situation and a problem situation are alike, although they may differ in the degree to which failures and pressures are involved. The behaviors, however, are qualitatively different, indicating that a change takes place in the organism. Thus a problem may frustrate one individual while initiating problem-solving behavior in another. This is why stressful situations divide behaviors into two basic classes: problem-solving responses and frustrated responses (Maier, 1946; Jenkins, 1957).

An Obstacle as a Frustrating Agent

The transition from problem-solving behavior to frustrated behavior is rather sharp and apparently depends upon the tolerance or frustration threshold of the individual. Increasing either the degree or the period of stress noticeably increases the number of individuals exhibiting frustrated behavior. (See Maier and Klee, 1943; Maier and Feldman, 1948; Marquart, 1948; and Shimoyama, 1957.)

Three types of behavior have been experimentally linked with frustration. Dollard, Doob, Miller, Mowrer, and Sears (1939) have demonstrated experimentally that frustration leads to *aggression*. Individuals who previously showed cooperative behavior will show hostile and destructive behavior if kept in the same situation for periods of time. The research of Barker, Dembo, and Lewin (1941) linked frustration with *regression*. Their studies revealed that the play of children will regress and become less mature when frustration is induced. For example, a five-year-old child may be able to play with a toy as a normal five-year-old or as a three-year-old, depending upon whether or not he is frustrated.

The third type of frustrated behavior was investigated by Maier and his students. My book (1949) brought together a series of studies showing that frustration leads to rigidity or *abnormal fixation*. The same animals that were capable of showing variable behavior on other occasions became rigid and inflexible under stress. Patrick (1934) and Marquart (1948) have shown similar results in their researches with human subjects.

The condition of frustration, therefore, is known to be responsible for the expression of behavior having the characteristics of aggression, regression, and fixation. Perhaps there are others, not yet experimentally isolated. The characteristic of *resignation* seems to be one of these. However, enough is known to make the state of frustration in the organism an important selector and integrator of behavior.

The characteristics of aggression, regression, and fixation may be combined in a single act or they may be revealed separately. Although the behavior expressed under frustration may show variations, as yet not fully understood, the characteristics are distinctive enough to contrast markedly with those expressed when the organism is in a problem-solving condition, where the goal to be achieved is central to the selection of behavior.

Further studies on the selective factors operating during frustration are needed so that predictions as to the specific acts to be expressed can be made. Thus, a delinquent child may show aggression, but whether the behavior takes the form of vandalism, fighting, or stealing is not differentiated by such a term. An additional concept, that of availability (Maier and Ellen, 1959) seems to determine the specific form that aggression will take. If a child who is a member of a gang feels hostile, the suggestion of a gang leader might cause the whole group to express their hostilities in a specific manner. Regression, which often occurs in conjunction with aggression, renders the individual suggestible, while the leader's suggestion makes the specific act available.

Although aggression, regression, and abnormal fixation need to be further explored, it is obvious that they are clearly associated with frustration. Much of frustrated behavior combines all of these characteristics, but they obviously vary greatly in proportion. To some extent the behavior repertoire may be a factor in determining the type of behavior expressed by a frustrated individual, and certainly the principle of availability would be a factor in the selection and integration of the specific acts selected (Maier and Ellen, 1959). Since the *behavior in progress* at the time of frustration is that which is most available, a gentle response may turn into a destructive act; it may become rigid or ritualistic, or it may become immature when the condition of frustration replaces that of problem solving. These changes can take place without there being any change in the behavior repertoire.

RESEARCH NEEDS

Of the selector-integrator mechanisms described in this paper some are located in the environment, while others represent a condition of the organism. The dimensions of the stimulus as selectors are the mechanisms most closely associated with the environment, while stimulus-set, attention, need, and direction in thinking are completely in the organism. Perception and the obstacle situations represent a combination of organismic and environmental influence. Perception is an individual matter in that the same stimuli may be organized differently, yet the environment also plays a part in that such external factors as proximity, closure, continuity of lines, etc., influence perceptual organization. Since an obstacle in the situation may initiate either problem-solving behavior or frustrated behavior, the resulting selection is an individual contribution. Nevertheless, in that the obstacle is in the environment, this aspect of the mechanism is external to the individual.

Whether or not the eight selector mechanisms can be reduced by combining some of them or whether further distinctions are needed is a question that can best be answered through research. Certainly, however, when different laws are needed to describe an influence on behavior expression, the distinctions should be maintained.

In the light of our present knowledge it seems unwise to arrange the selector-integrator mechanisms in any evolutionary order. Each mechanism, as well as each aspect of the behavior repertoire, seems to range from the simple to the complex. Perhaps our understanding of the developmental process would be increased if this process could also be viewed within the limited framework constituted by each selector-integrator mechanism and by each portion of the behavior repertoire. This approach would necessitate an increase in the number of qualitative distinctions, but might well eventuate in a greater consistency of quantitative findings.

The reader will undoubtedly have observed that the selecting aspect of the selector-integrator mechanism has been more adequately treated than the integrating aspect. This suggests a possible deficiency in our research coverage.

Prevalent theory treats the organization of behavior as if it were built into the organism. Reflex integration has been quite adequately explained by the way neural connections and thresholds are arranged (Fulton, 1926). Coghill (1929) correlated neural development and the behavior changes of the developing salamander from the head-flexion stage through the coil and "S" stages to swimming movements, thereby demonstrating that the integration of innate behavior is built into the organism.

Learning theorists followed the same lead and assumed that the behavior pattern expressed was a learned one. Learned responses were initially conceptualized as chains of associative bonds, but through the Gestalt influence behavior was likened to patterns of action. There appears to be a basic validity in assuming that the organization of behavior can be traced to the behavior repertoire, but is this the complete answer?

The feeding response of the amoeba varies when it engulfs a particle of food, depending upon the stimulus conditions. The amoeba does not run through a sequence of movements as does a squirrel burying a nut on a table; going through the full sequence of the movements from digging to covering, but accomplishing nothing. Such "blind" behaviors may occur, but are these typical?

Schneirla's researches (1941, 1952) on the army ant show how colony behavior is integrated around stimuli supplied while a behavior sequence is in progress. Comparable studies are needed on higher animals to show both the contributions made by the environmental and by the various internal conditions of the organism to the particular integration revealed on a given occasion. It is clear from Schneirla's studies that the behavior brought to expression by the selector-integrator mechanisms is organized in accordance with conditions as they exist at a given time.

It is well known that when a cat pulls a string to escape from a problem box, it does not always accomplish this with the same set of movements. Pulling the string may be done in a different way each time. Variations include the use of either the right or left paw, and the teeth. Guthrie and Horton (1946) contend that these variations represent different learnings and point to their own research in which the learned pattern is highly specific. Their problem box utilized a post that had to be tilted in order to free the confined animal. Since cats do not run into objects, the only way the correct response could be discovered by them was through accident. It was found that cats solved the problem by backing into the post and that these backing responses were highly specific. Their unique findings can be explained by assuming that the cat is unaware of what it is doing when it accidentally backs into the post, and so it can only learn a "blind" act. The Guthrie-Horton situation restricted the learning of the accomplishment and consequently forced the animal to learn a kinesthetic act which of necessity is specific.

When strings are to be pulled the cat does not avoid them as it does a post. Instead it manipulates them and so it can observe what it is doing. Thus the cat's behavior can be oriented toward the pulling of the string rather than guided by specific movements controlled by kinesthetic cues. Pulling strings can be done in a variety of ways and each way of pulling them seems to be organized at the time of expression. No disorganized mixtures of previous responses seem to appear and the behavior adapts itself to changing conditions. Successes and failures in getting hold of the string supply a "feedback" which influences the performance.

What is called "goal-oriented behavior" is activity that is
directed toward some end, and various means are used to
achieve this end. If the concept of selector-integrator mechanisms as an approach to behavior is a sound one, it also follows
that each of the means to an end has some integration, and
it would appear that the nature of the goal plays a prominent
part in this integration. Thus I should like to postulate the
existence of equivalent behaviors as well as equivalent stimuli.
Behaviors that accomplish the same objective would therefore be regarded as equivalent, with a given animal expressing
new samples of behavior in its attempts to achieve the same
goal.

Evidence in support of this view is not entirely lacking.
Animals that have run through a maze will do so after cerebellar injuries (Lashley and McCarthy, 1926). Such injuries
destroy the equilibrium and prevent normal locomotion, but
the rats still take the correct pathways although they roll and
drag themselves along. These movements, expressed for the
first time, are not random but are organized to yield a particular end result.

Both Brunswik (1943) and Tolman (1955) have recognized
the fact that the same end may be accomplished by different
behaviors. They suggest that performance be defined in terms
of the accomplishment rather than the pattern of movements,
since the latter cannot be predicted. Thus learning would be
measured by *what* the behavior accomplished rather than by
how something was accomplished. This change in definition,
however, does not escape the necessity of explaining how the
integrated behavior pattern that appears spontaneously comes
to expression.

Mary Henle (1956) drew attention to a large area of activity
that has apparently been generally overlooked. She points
out that motivational theories fail to deal with the many
activities that are carried on in the goal region. She distinguishes between "satisfaction and release of tension in the
case of goal striving as contrasted in many cases with regret

when it becomes necessary to terminate activity in the goal region." The continued enjoyment of friends or the pleasure of a ride in the country represent activities that are continued because they are enjoyed, but need not lead to some further goal. These activities not only are selected, but they are integrated and organized into functional patterns not previously laid down. Sets, attitudes, needs, problems or obstacles, and stimulation all enter into the selection and integration of such behavior.

If response integration is viewed as a special problem, it opens a field for investigation corresponding to that of sensory integration or perception. At one time it was thought that perceptual organization was largely a matter of the sense organs and of learning. Modern perception theory, as already indicated, includes personality variables and makes each perceptual experience an integrated unit. The study of response integration may lead to equally rich findings.

SUMMARY

The behavior theory suggested is characterized by the postulation of a clear-cut distinction between the *ability* to behave and the *actual* behavior that is expressed on a given occasion. It is assumed: (1) that an organism has a store of potential behaviors which constitute its behavior repertoire; and (2) that a number of selector-integrator mechanisms operate to determine which of these potential behaviors will be expressed, and thus constitute the organism's performance at a given time. The analogy of the computer is suggested—in that the behavior repertoire is analogous to the stored data, whereas the selector-integrator mechanisms are analogous to the programs which the computer follows. Behavior then becomes analogous to the output of the computer. Thus the behavior that constitutes performance is dependent upon both the repertoire and the selector mechanism in much the same way that the product of the computer is dependent upon both its stored data and its program.

The behavior repertoire includes (1) the influence of heredity and growth (so-called innate elements and sequences of behavior); (2) learning (consisting of patterns, memories, habit sequences, and skills); and (3) the ability to unlearn or to break up learned patterns to make elements of these patterns available (primarily essential to problem solving).

Eight selector-integrator mechanisms, which may operate at the same time to select and organize behavior, are differentiated. These are (1) the locus, intensity, and form of the stimulus; (2) stimulus set and attention; (3) perception; (4) attitudes; (5) needs; (6) direction in thinking; (7) the obstacle as a problem; and (8) the obstacle as a frustration instigator.

Although motivation is traditionally regarded as the mechanism that brings behavior to expression, it is apparent from the above-mentioned selector integrators that motivation is only one of eight possible mechanisms. The viewpoint that it takes a stimulus to trigger off a response is also represented, but only as one of the eight mechanisms determining the sample of behavior expressed. At this time, it seems that eight mechanisms are necessary to account for the performance problems raised. Perhaps this number can eventually be reduced, but it is also possible that additional ones will be needed. The number of different mechanisms postulated is of secondary concern. The important point is that a break has been made from the limitations imposed by the current use of a minimum number of mechanisms. The law of parsimony is valid only when it is invoked to choose between equally adequate theories; it does not favor the simple explanation when simplicity alone is its major virtue.

This reorganization of psychological concepts introduces some changes in functional meanings and also modifies the relative importance of the various contributors to behavior. Behavior now becomes a sample selected and integrated from the general repertoire of an animal at a given time. It is possible that this approach will expose a variety of ways in which growth and evolution proceed, if development is viewed from the standpoint of (a) the acquisition of the behavior repertoire, and (b) the refinements of the selector-integrator mechanisms. The developmental approach may be the best way to demonstrate the presence of qualitative distinctions among the various selector-integrator mechanisms and among the factors that contribute to the behavior repertoire.

Areas deficient in research naturally come to light when a field of study is viewed from a different perspective. The need to know more about the ability to escape the restrictions imposed by learning is one problem raised in considering the constitution of the behavior repertoire. Thus far, traditional approaches have made innate and learned patterns of behavior the subject of investigation, but they have not dealt with the way these interfere with the emergence of new behavior. The ability to disassociate and to fragment linkages may be as important as the ability to form associations.

Although the selector-integrator mechanisms mentioned have been the subject of numerous investigations, they have not been studied as parallel or interacting determiners of performance. The integrative aspect of these mechanisms seems to be the most neglected subject.

It is suggested that the concept of *equivalence* in behavior be introduced in order to group together the various behavior patterns that achieve the same results. This concept is the complement of the concept of equivalent stimuli, which groups together various stimuli that elicit the same response.

The traditional view, that the organization of behavior is controlled by the behavior repertoire, seems to be only partly correct. It appears that much of behavior is integrated at the time of expression, somewhat as sensory data are spontaneously organized in perceptions. One can perceive only one of several possible perceptual organizations at a given time (i.e., figure-ground reversals), and it seems that only one, of several possible patterns of movement, will make its appearance at a given time. The one behavior pattern which is expressed, however, makes its appearance as an organized whole, having a clearly apparent function, adapted to changing circumstances. Study of the spontaneous integration of behavior may conceivably lead to a set of principles of behavioral organization comparable to the principles of perception.

The writer is indebted to Dr. L. R. Hoffman and Miss Melba Colgrove for their critical comments and suggestions.

BIBLIOGRAPHY

Adams, D. K. (1929), Experimental Studies of Adaptive Behavior in Cats. *Comparative Psychology Monographs*, *6*:1-168.
Barker, R.; Dembo, T.; and Lewin, K. (1941), *Frustration and Regression: An Experiment with Young Children*. Iowa City: University of Iowa Press.
Bird, C. (1925), The Relative Importance of Maturation and Habit in the Development of an Instinct. *Pedagogical Seminary*, *32*:68-91.
Brunswik, E. (1943), Organismic Achievement and Environmental Probability. *Psychological Review*, *50*:255-272.
Buytendijk, F. J. (1931), Le cerveau et l'intelligence. *Journal de Psychologie*, *28*:345-371.
Coghill, G. E. (1929), *Anatomy and the Problem of Behavior*. New York: Macmillan.
Dewey, J. (1910), *How We Think*. Boston: Heath.
Dollard J.; Doob, L. W.; Miller, N. E.; Mowrer, O. H.; and Sears, R. R. (1939), *Frustration and Aggression*. New Haven: Yale University Press.
Edwards, W. (1954), Unpublished research reported by N. R. F. Maier in *The Kentucky Symposium*. New York: Wiley, pp. 54-65.
Frank, M. (1932), The Effects of a Rickets-Producing Diet on the Learning Ability of White Rats. *Journal of Comparative Psychology*, *13*:87-105.
Fulton, J. F. (1926), *Muscular Contraction and the Reflex Control of Movement*. Baltimore: Williams & Wilkins.
Gottschaldt, K. (1926), Über den Einfluss der Erfahrung auf die Wahrnehmung von Figuren. *Psychologische Forschung*, *8*:261-317; *12*:1-87.

Guetzkow, H. S. and Bowman, P. H. (1946), *Men and Hunger*. Elgin, Ill.: Brethren Publishing House.

Guthrie, E. R. and Horton, G. P. (1946), *Cats in a Puzzle Box*. New York: Rinehart.

Henle, M. (1956), On Activity in the Goal Region. *Psychological Review*, *63*:299-302.

Hernandez-Péon, R.; Scherrer, H.; and Jouvet, M. (1956), Modification of Electric Activity in Cochlear Nucleus During "Attention" in Unanesthetized Cats. *Science*, *123*:331-332.

Hull, C. L. (1935), The Mechanism of the Assembly of Behavior Segments in Novel Combinations Suitable for Problem Solution. *Psychological Review*, *42*:219-245.

Jenkins, R. L. (1957), Motivation and Frustration in Delinquency. *American Journal of Orthopsychiatry*, *27*:528-537.

Klüver, H. (1933), *Behavior Mechanisms in Monkeys*. Chicago: University of Chicago Press.

Koffka, K. (1935), *Principles of Gestalt Psychology*. New York: Harcourt, Brace.

Köhler, W. (1929), *Gestalt Psychology*. New York: Horace Liveright.

Krechevsky, I. (1932), "Hypotheses" versus "Chance" in the Pre-solution Period in Sensory Discrimination. *University of California Publications in Psychology*, *6*: 27-44.

—— (1937), Brain Mechanisms and Variability: Part I. Variability Within a Means-End-Readiness. Part II. Variability When No Learning is Involved. Part III. Limitations of the Effect of Cortical Injury Upon Variability. *Journal of Comparative Psychology*, *23*:121-138; 139-163; 351-364.

Kuo, Z. Y. (1930), The Genesis of the Cat's Response to the Rat. *Journal of Comparative Psychology*, *11*:1-35.

Lashley, K. S. (1929), *Brain Mechanisms in Intelligence*. Chicago: University of Chicago Press.

—— (1938), The Mechanism of Vision: XV. Preliminary Studies of the Rat's Capacity for Detail Vision. *Journal of General Psychology*, *38*:123-193.

—— and McCarthy, D. A. (1926), The Survival of the Maze Habit After Cerebellar Injuries. *Journal of Comparative Psychology*, *6*:423-433.

Lewin, K. (1926), Vorsatz, Wille und Bedürfnis. *Psychologische Forschung*, *7*:330-385.

Maier, N. R. F. (1929), Reasoning in White Rats. *Comparative Psychology Monographs*, *6*:1-93.

—— (1930), Reasoning in Humans: I. On Direction. *Journal of Comparative Psychologv*, *10*:115-143.

—— (1931a), Reasoning and Learning. *Psychological Review*, *38*:332-346.

—— (1931b), Reasoning in Humans: II. The Solution of a Problem and Its Appearance in Consciousness. *Journal of Comparative Psychology*, *12*:181-194.

—— (1932a), The Effect of Cerebral Destruction on Reasoning and Learning in Rats. *Journal of Comparative Neurology*, *54*:45-75.

—— (1932b), Cortical Destruction of the Posterior Part of the Brain and Its Effect on Reasoning in Rats. *Journal of Comparative Neurology*, *56*:179-214.

—— (1933), An Aspect of Human Reasoning. *British Journal of Psychology* (*General Section*), *24*:144-155.

—— (1938), A Further Analysis of Reasoning in Rats: II. The Integration of Four Separate Experiences in Problem Solving. *Comparative Psychology Monographs*, *15*:1-43.

—— (1939a), The Specific Processes Constituting the Learning Function. *Psychological Review*, *46*:241-252.

—— (1939b), Qualitative Differences in the Learning of Rats in a Discrimination Situation. *Journal of Comparative Psychology*, *27*:289-328.

—— (1940), The Behavior Mechanisms Concerned with Problem Solving. *Psychological Review*, *47*:43-58.

—— (1941), The Effect of Cortical Injuries on Equivalence Reactions in Rats. *Journal of Comparative Psychology*, *32*:165-189.

—— (1945), Reasoning in Humans: III. The Mechanisms of Equivalent Stimuli and of Reasoning. *Journal of Experimental Psychology*, *35*:349-360.

—— (1946), *Psychology in Industry*. Boston: Houghton, Mifflin.

—— (1949), *Frustration: The Study of Behavior Without a Goal*. New York: McGraw-Hill.

—— (1954), The Premature Crystallization of Learning Theory. In *The Kentucky Symposium: Learning Theory, Personality Theory, and Clinical Research*. New York: Wiley, pp. 54-65.

—— and Ellen, P. (1959), The Integrative Value of Concepts in Frustration Theory. *Journal of Consulting Psvchologv*, *23*:195-206.

───── and Feldman, R. S. (1948), Studies of Abnormal Behavior in the Rat: XXII. Strength of Fixation and Duration of Frustration. *Journal of Comparative and Physiological Psychology, 41*: 348-363.

───── and Klee, J. B. (1943), Studies of Abnormal Behavior in the Rat: XII. The Pattern of Punishment and Its Relation to Abnormal Fixations. *Journal of Experimental Psychology, 32*:377-398.

───── and Lansky, L. M. (1957), Effect of Attitude on Selection of Facts. *Personnel Psychology, 10*:293-303.

───── and Schneirla, T. C. (1935), *Principles of Animal Psychology*, New York: McGraw-Hill.

Marquart, D. I. (1948), The Pattern of Punishment and Its Relation to Abnormal Fixation in Adult Human Subjects. *Journal of General Psychology, 39*:107-144.

McCleary, R. A. (1959), The Influence of Sub-collosal Lesions on Fear-Motivated Behavior in Cats. Unpublished manuscript.

Moseley, D. (1925), The Accuracy of the Pecking Response in Chicks. *Journal of Comparative Psychology, 5*:75-97.

Padilla, S. G. (1930), Further Studies on the Delayed Pecking of Chickens. Doctorate Dissertation, University of Michigan.

Patrick, J. K. (1934), Studies in Rational Behavior and Emotional Excitement: II. The Effect of Emotional Excitement on Rational Behavior of Human Subjects. *Journal of Comparative Psychology, 18*: 153-195.

Pillsbury, W. B. (1908), *Attention*. New York: Macmillan.

Schneirla, T. C. (1941), Social Organization in Insects as Related to Individual Function. *Psychological Review, 48*:465-486.

───── (1952), Sexual Broods and the Production of Young Queens in Two Species of Army Ants. *Zoologica, 37*:5-37.

Selz, O. (1913), *Über die Gesetze des geordneten Denkverlaufs*. Stuttgart: W. Spemann.

Shepard, J. F. and Breed, F. S. (1913), Maturation and Use in the Development of an Instinct. *Journal of Animal Behavior, 3*:274-285.

Sherburne, B. J. (1940), Qualitative Differences in the Solution of a Problem Involving Reasoning. Doctorate Dissertation, University of Michigan.

Shimoyama, T. (1957), Studies of Abnormal Fixation in the Rat.

I. Effects of Frequency of Punishment in the Insoluble Situation. *Japanese Journal of Psychology*, *28*:203-209.

Thorndike, E. L. (1898), Animal Intelligence; An Experimental Study of the Associative Process in Animals. *Psychological Review Monographs*, *2*:1-109.

Tinklepaugh, O. L. (1928), An Experimental Study of Representative Factors in Monkeys. *Journal of Comparative Psychology*, *8*:197-236.

Tolman, E. C. (1955), Principles of Performance. *Psychological Review*, *62*:315-326.

Wapner, S. (1944), The Differential Effects of Cortical Injury and Retesting on Equivalence Reactions in the Rat. *Psychological Monographs*, *57*:1-59.

—— and Werner, H. (1957), *Perceptual Development: An Investigation within the Framework of Sensory-Tonic Field Theory*. Worcester: Clark University Press.

Werner, H. (1940), *Comparative Psychology of Mental Development*, 3rd ed. New York: International Universities Press, 1957.

—— and Wapner, S. (1949), Sensory-Tonic Field Theory of Perception. *Journal of Personality*, *18*:88-107.

—— —— (1952), Toward a General Theory of Perception. *Psychological Review*, *59*:324-338.

—— —— (1954), Studies in Physiognomic Perception. I. Effect of Configurational Dynamics and Meaning-Induced Sets on the Position of the Apparent Median Plane. *Journal of Psychology*, *38*:51-65.

Wertheimer, M. (1925), *Drei Abhandlungen zur Gestalttheorie*. Erlangen: Verlag der Philosophischen Akademie.

—— (1945), *Productive Thinking*. New York: Harper.

Witkin, H. A.; Lewis, H. B.; Hertzman, M.; Machover, K.; Meissner, P. B.; and Wapner, S. (1954), *Personality Through Perception*. New York: Harper.

Zucker, H. (1943), The Emotional Attachment of Children to Their Parents as Related to Behavior and Delinquency. *Journal of Psychology*, *15*:31-40.

Resistance to Being Rubricized

ABRAHAM H. MASLOW, Ph.D.

Brandeis University

"Resistance" in the Freudian conceptual system refers to the maintenance of repressions. But Schachtel (1947) has already shown that difficulties in the coming to consciousness of ideas may have other sources than repression. Some kinds of awareness which were possible for the child may be said simply to have been "forgotten" in the course of growing up. I, too, have attempted to make a differentiation between the weaker resistance to unconscious primary-process cognitions and the very much stronger resistance to forbidden impulses, drives or wishes (1959). These developments, and others, indicate that it may be desirable to expand the concept "resistance" to mean approximately "difficulties in achieving insight for *whatever* reason" (excluding of course constitutional incapacity, e.g., feeblemindedness, reduction to the concrete, gender differences, and perhaps even constitutional determinants of the Sheldon type).

The thesis of this note is that another source of "resistance" in the therapeutic situation can be a healthy distaste by the patient for being rubricized or casually classified, i.e., for being deprived of his individuality, his uniqueness, his differences from all others, his special identity.

I have previously (1954, Chapter 14) described rubricizing as a cheap form of cognizing, i.e., really a form of *not*-cognizing, a quick, easy cataloguing whose function is to make unnecessary the effort required by more careful, idiographic perceiving or thinking. To place a person in a system takes less energy than to know him in his own right, since in the former instance, all that has to be perceived is that one abstracted characteristic which indicates his belongingness in a class, e.g., babies, waiters, Swedes, schizophrenics, females, generals, nurses, etc. What is stressed in rubricizing is the category in which the person belongs, of which he is a sample, *not* the person as such—similarities rather than differences.

In this same publication, the very important fact was noted that being rubricized is generally offensive to the person rubricized, since it denies his individuality or pays no attention to his personhood, to his differential, unique identity. William James's famous statement makes the point clear:

> The first thing the intellect does with an object is to class it with something else. But any object that is infinitely important to us and awakens our devotion feels to us also as if it must be *sui generis* and unique. Probably a crab would be filled with a sense of personal outrage if it could hear us class it without ado or apology as a crustacean, and thus dispose of it. "I am no such thing," it would say; "I am *myself, myself* alone" [1902, p. 10].

One illustrative example of the resentment elicited by being rubricized may be cited from a current study by the author on conceptions of masculinity and femininity in Mexico and in the U. S. A. Most American women, after their first adjustment to Mexico, find it very pleasant to be valued so highly as females, to create a turmoil of whistling and sighing wherever they go, to be sought out eagerly by men of all ages, to be regarded as beautiful and as valuable. For many American women, ambivalent as they often are about their femininity, this can be a very satisfying and therapeutic experience, making them feel more female, more ready to enjoy femininity, which in turn makes them often *look* more feminine.

But as time goes on, they (some of them, at least) find this less pleasing. They discover that *any* woman is valuable to the Mexican male, that there seems to be little discrimination between old and young women, beautiful and not beautiful, intelligent and not intelligent. Furthermore, they find that in contrast with the young American male (who, as one girl put it, "gets so traumatized when you refuse to go out with him that he has to go to his psychiatrist"), the Mexican male takes a refusal very calmly, *too* calmly. He does not seem to mind and quickly turns to another woman. But this means then to a specific woman that *she*, she herself, as a person, is not specially valuable to him, and that all his efforts were directed toward a *woman*, not toward *her*, which implies that one woman is about as good as another, and that she is interchangeable with others. She discovers that *she* is not valuable; it is the class "woman" that is valuable. And finally she may feel insulted rather than flattered, since she wants to be valued as a person, for *herself*, rather than for her gender. Of course, femalehood is prepotent over personhood, i.e., it calls for prior gratification, yet its gratification brings the claims of personhood into the foreground of the motivational economy. Enduring romantic love, monogamy, and the self-actualization of women are all made possible by regard for a particular person rather than for the class, "woman."

Another very common example of the resentment to being rubricized is the rage so commonly aroused in adolescents when they are told, "Oh that's just a stage you're going through. You'll grow out of it eventually." What is tragic and real and unique to the child cannot be laughed at even though it has happened and will happen to millions of others.

One final illustration: a psychiatrist terminated a very brief and hurried first interview with a prospective patient by saying, "Your troubles are roughly those characteristic of your age." The potential patient became very angry and later reported feeling "brushed off" and insulted. She felt as if she had been treated like a child: "I am *not* a specimen. I'm *me*, not anybody else."

Considerations of this sort can also help us to expand our notion of resistance in classical psychoanalysis. Because resistance is customarily treated as *only* a defense of the neurosis, as a resistance to getting well or to perceiving unpleasant truths, it is therefore often treated as something undesirable, something to overcome and to analyze away. But as the examples above have indicated, what has been treated as sickness *may* sometimes be health, or at least not sickness. The therapist's difficulties with his patients, their refusal to accept an interpretation, their anger and fighting back, their stubbornness, almost surely, in *some* cases, arises from a refusal to be rubricized. Such resistance may therefore be seen as an assertion of and protection of personal uniqueness, identity or selfhood against attack or neglect. Such reactions not only maintain the dignity of the individual; they also serve to protect him against bad psychotherapy, textbook interpretation, "wild analysis", overintellectual or premature interpretations or explanations, meaningless abstractions or conceptualizations, all of which imply to the patient a lack of respect.

Novices at therapy in their eagerness to cure quickly, "textbook boys" who memorize a conceptual system and then conceive of therapy as no more than passing out concepts, theorists without clinical experience, the undergraduate or graduate student in psychology who has just memorized Fenichel and is willing to tell everyone in the dormitory what category he belongs in—these are the rubricizers against whom patients have to protect themselves. These are the ones who pass out easily and quickly, perhaps even on first contact, such statements as "You are an anal character" or "You're just trying to dominate everyone" or "You want me to sleep with you" or "You really want your father to give you a baby," etc.[1] To call the legitimate self-protective reaction against such rubricizing "resistance" in the classical sense is then just another example of the misuse of a concept.

Fortunately, there are indications of a reaction against rubricizing among those responsible for the treatment of people. One sees this in the general turning away from taxonomical, "Kraepelinian," or "state hospital" psychiatry by enlightened therapists. The main effort, sometimes the *only* effort, used to be diagnosis, i.e., placing the individual within a class. But experience has taught that diagnosis is more a legal and administrative necessity than a therapeutic one. Now, even in psychiatric hospitals, it has become increasingly recognized that nobody is a textbook patient; diagnostic statements in staff meetings are getting longer, richer, more complex, less a simple labeling.

The patient, it is now realized, must be approached as a single, unique person rather than as a member of a class— that is, if the main purpose is psychotherapy. Understanding a person is not the same as classifying or rubricizing him. And understanding a person is the *sine qua non* for therapy.

SUMMARY

Human beings often resent being rubricized, which can be seen by them as a denial of their individuality (self, identity).

---

[1] This tendency to rubricize (instead of using concrete, idiographic, patient-centered experience-language) almost certainly tends to get stronger, even in the very best therapists, when they are ill, tired, preoccupied, anxious, not interested, disrespectful of the patient, in a hurry, etc. It may therefore also serve as an aid in the psychoanalyst's ongoing self-analysis of the countertransference.

They may be expected to react by reaffirming their identity
in the various ways open to them. In psychotherapy, such
reactions must be sympathetically understood as affirma-
tions of personal dignity, which in *any* case is under severe
assault in some forms of therapy. Either such self-protective
reactions ought not to be called "resistance" (in the sense of a
sickness-protecting maneuver), or else the concept "resistance" must be expanded to include many kinds of difficulty
in achieving awareness. It is furthermore pointed out that
such resistances are extremely valuable protectors against
bad psychotherapy.[2]

BIBLIOGRAPHY

James, W. (1902), *The Varieties of Religious Experience.* New York:
    Modern Library Edition, 1942.
Maslow, A. H. (1954), *Motivation and Personality.* New York: Harper.
────── (1959), Creativity in Self-Actualizing People. In *Creativity
    and its Cultivation,* ed. H. H. Anderson. New York: Harper.
Schachtel, E. (1947), On Memory and Childhood Amnesia. *Psy-
    chiatry, 10*:1-26.

─────────

[2] This paper can also be read as a contribution to the general problem of
communication between therapist and patient. The good therapist faces the
task of putting his nomothetic knowledge to idiographic uses. The conceptual
framework with which he works and which may be experientially rich and
meaningful for him is useless for the patient in its conceptual form. Insight
therapy consists not only of uncovering, experiencing, and categorizing unconscious materials. It is also largely a job of pulling together under a concept
all sorts of fully conscious but unnamed and therefore unconnected subjective
experiences, or even, more simply, giving a name to an unnamed experience.
The patient may have the "Aha" experience upon true insight, e.g., "My God!
I've really hated my mother all the time that I thought I loved her!" But he
may also have it without reference to any unconscious materials, e.g., "So *that's*
what you mean by anxiety!" (referring to such and such experiences in the
stomach, the throat, the legs, the heart of which he has been perfectly aware
but has never named). Such considerations should be helpful also in the training of therapists.

Organism and Quantity

A Study of Organic Structure as a Quantitative Problem

GARDNER MURPHY, Ph.D.

Menninger Foundation

UNDER WHAT CONDITIONS DO QUALITIES BECOME QUANTITIES?

One of the great theoretical and systematic contributions of Heinz Werner is his theory of development. Historically similar theories have been enunciated by Herbert Spencer and by J. Hughlings Jackson. A tribute to Heinz Werner today takes the form of pursuing some of the issues raised in the great tradition: Spencer-Jackson-Werner. Werner's rich and beautiful system must be read for its own sake. Other systems which bear any resemblance to it may also, like the present one, deviate a point and stimulate further investigation.

A modern version of Herbert Spencer's theory of cosmic evolution might run somewhat as follows: From the primordial and unique quality comes a group of differentiated qualities distinguishable from one another and from the parent quality, each being in its own right unique yet classifiable in terms of its resemblances to and differences from other qualities. Differentiation involves, in short, temporal and spatial patterning of the derivative qualities. Spatial and temporal patterning are matters of quantity. They cannot be described except in terms of Cartesian coordinate systems plus time measurements or, in the modern fashion, in terms of four-dimensional time-space formulations. Having commenced with one quality, we now have a variety of qualities separable from one another, their mutual relationships being stated quantitatively. In the beginning there was quality, but the process of evolution gives quality plus quantity.

It is not enough to say that the qualities derived from a primordial unique quality stand merely in spatial and temporal relation to one another. The fact that they represent differentiation means that their similarities and differences permit quantitative statement. Qualitative differences in physics and chemistry are almost universally capable of statement in terms of quantitative differences. It appears probable that all resemble other qualities only by virtue of having something in common with them. The skin of a mulatto differs from the skin of a full-blood Negro or a full-blood white man in a qualitative manner. Yet the spinning of a color wheel above the skin will permit an absolute quantitative differentiation of all possible types of black-white racial mixture in skin color. It appears probable that all qualities derived from the primordial unique quality differ from one another in a manner which can be stated mathematically. Resemblance, hence all classification, involves quantitative procedure.

There appear to remain certain qualitative variations which cannot be stated in quantitative terms. Granted that qualities bear temporal and spatial relations to other qualities, and granted that their resemblances may be stated quantitatively, there appears to be something distinct in each quality. Is this merely because analysis is incomplete, as in those cases in chemistry in which the qualitative difference between two atoms is merely a crude way of expressing what we know to be a quantitative difference?[1] Or is quality a *primordial datum* in cosmic structure?

The answer to this question has been sought in metaphysics and in the physical sciences. While in no way anxious to deny the validity of the methods pursued in metaphysics and in the physical sciences, I suspect that the problem as stated is exclusively psychological, and might lead to the preparation of experiments which would solve it.

A group of faint stars close together in their apparent position in the sidereal globe is sometimes seen as a single star. Let the group be observed through a field glass or low-power telescope; the star assumes a fuzzy appearance suggesting not a point of light but a blur. Let an eye-piece with higher power be introduced; and the light will appear to coagulate in a number of specific spots. In the beginning was a unique quality—a white star. Under low power came the beginning of differentiation, the unique quality tending, so to speak, to generate diverse qualities. The fuzzy appearance has its own spatial extent, and its characteristic hue, brilliance, and saturation. Under high power, all this has changed. There now appear a number of distinct qualities, each localized in time-space, each bearing time-space relations to the others, and each displaying a unique quality differing from that of the others and from the parent star which the naked eye perceived.

Now let us select one of these stars which the high-power glass has revealed, and let us proceed to spectroscopic analysis. We find that even this unique quality is physically divisible into other qualities; and a geometrically and physically satisfying conception may be formed of a binary star whose

---

[1] The functional qualitative differences in *behavior* of molecules or atoms are really quantitative, being simply questions of time-space.

two components differ in certain properties: mass, distance from common center of gravity, angular momentum, etc. Up until the moment when we introduced the spectroscope, we suggested that the act of perception enjoys varying powers of disentangling the physical world. The eye indeed is an optical instrument. The eye or the other sense organs may under certain conditions reveal a physical entity as a bare quality; under other conditions, as a spatial pattern containing qualitatively distinct elements. When, however, conceptual thinking is added to perceptual grasp on the data of the physical world, we find that even the residual qualities which result from the finest *perceptual* analysis are capable of further *conceptual* analysis. This last state of analysis is always purely quantitative. What we call a quality is simply a name for an *incompletely analyzed perceptual datum*. A large part of the realm of visual and auditory sense perception is already describable in terms of equations (such as those given by Talbot, Hecht, Emmert). In the analysis of olfactory phenomena, we are passing now from the first to the second stage of observation. We have begun to note resemblances between odors and to classify them in tentative ways. The next stage will carry us to quantitative statements regarding the points of identity and difference between odors, and we shall then have completed the problem in so far as the student of perception is concerned with it. The fourth stage, that of showing what lies behind the unique and indivisible elements of olfactory experiences, will necessarily lead to the conceptual and mathematical.

It might be objected that we are falling into the "psychologist's fallacy," so vigorously and effectively attacked by William James (1890, p. 196). We should indeed be falling into this fallacy if we argued that the abstractions to which the conceptual method leads us *"constitute"* *the sensations or the data of the perception*, but we are far from making such an assertion. On the contrary, our assertion is that the qualities of experience as immediately apprehended are derived from other less specific qualities and that they themselves *disappear* at a time when their essence has been analyzed and found to be dependent upon a space-time pattern. At any moment, introspective technique may discover a new way of approaching that which is now unique, exactly as reflector telescopes found a new way of bursting asunder qualitatively unique stellar objects. We shall not maintain that we were originally mistaken in calling a phenomenon what we did call it; we shall not say that the redness was not really red or the shrillness really shrill. From our new introspective point of view we shall say that the datum previously reported, which was a quality when it was reported, is now, according to our new observation, *replaced* by a quantitative pattern seen in time-space terms. Exactly as the qualitatively unique atoms have become merely different patterns of quantitatively described units, so what are now psychologically unique qualities will give way to quantitative patterns. The term "specific quality" might be used to define a certain stage in a temporal progression from the primordial unique quality to a later state of quantitative patterning of ultimately distinct particles.

An instance of what is meant by proceeding to a deeper level of analysis in the study of a specific quality is an experiment determining the conditions under which softness and hardness are felt. It would be ridiculous to maintain that softness is, in itself, a composite experience, or that it is made up of something other than softness. It certainly is not partially constituted by warmth or spatial extent. It is just as specific a quality as the pure middle C of an ideal tuning fork. Under experimental conditions, however, Sullivan (1927) proved it possible to vary three major physical factors upon which three aspects of this experience depend, namely, (a) variation in the intensity of pressure throughout the stimulated area; (b) presence of well-defined boundary lines; (c) coldness. By varying these three physical variables which by themselves would give a variety of different sensations, it is possible to produce specific qualities: soft and hard. It would be meaningless to maintain that the subject was originally mistaken in reporting hardness and that he should have reported even pressure, well-defined boundaries, coldness. Actually, however, he discovers by varying the stimuli that he can identify separately the three groups of sensations. When he has done this, elements of spatial and temporal order begin to appear.

The hypothesis presented is that as more and more refined control in external manipulation and in introspective discrimination is developed, even the most specific and homogeneous of our qualities of experience will *give place* to (not be "equated with") spatial and temporal patterns. If this can be carried to infinity, it might indeed lead us to spatial and temporal patterns in which there would appear no individual differences at a lower level, the quantitative differences consisting merely in different spatial and temporal patterns formed by the same elements, all of which in themselves would be of identical character.

Whether any such ultimate reduction of all quality to quantity will ever be achieved is an idle guess. Similar questions in physics have hardly begun to be tackled. Who knows whether the *particles* of today will all turn out to be composed of the same kind of ultimate stuff? One might round out a theory by postulating that we shall arrive at such a destination, but this would serve no purpose. Our concern is with the demonstration that the term quality in psychology and in all studies of organisms is a way-station term indicating that we are on our journey: the train is headed in a quantitative direction. At each new station old baggage of qualities is thrown out. The process may go on indefinitely. The term "qualitative" defines that part of the baggage of the infant's mind which has not yet been replaced by spatial and temporal patterns. That it *should* be replaced is not our contention, nor are we concerned to show which particular qualities are the next ones likely to be replaced by quantities. And as fast as old qualities are lost, new ones will appear.

ORGANIC SYSTEMS

In current protests against "atomism," it is customary to insist that the whole is more than the sum of its parts. Usually this statement is found to mean that the way in which the parts are assembled is in itself a significant datum. As thus stated, it is not clear why the modes of relationship which the parts exhibit toward one another are not in a true sense "parts" of the whole. Since it is so frequently difficult to tell what aspects of a datum are "entities" and what aspects are "relations" between entities, it appears overbold to set up a rigid criterion as to the parts to be defined, insisting that the modes of relationship are in no sense "parts" of a whole.

To take a simple case, suppose a geometrical situation such that the lines which bound a prism be regarded as among the "elements" which compose it. Yet the distances between various points—for example, the distances between points on the two parallel surfaces—may be conceived as lines. Thus the *relation* which a point on one surface bears to a point on another surface is a line, which is surely a "*part*" of the whole in the same sense in which any other lines in the figure are "parts." It is a commonplace to note in contemporary studies of perception (as was in fact noted a hundred years ago) that the spatial relations in an optical presentation are as immediately and directly perceived as the supposed points from which light comes. In gauging a distance with the eye, for example, the relations of objects seen are surely a part of the immediately given situation just as are the colors of the object seen. If, then, in their attack upon atomism, psychologists say that the whole is more than the sum of its parts and then proceed to explain that they mean merely to insist that *relations between the parts also exist*, they have merely added to the number of parts.

Sometimes an antiatomism argument is offered in a somewhat more cogent way through contending that a pattern or a mode of organization is itself a "system" rather than a sum of elements. A system is an interacting group of elements.

In such modes of expression an organization or a "form" is offered as an indivisible and unique entity, the analysis of which is absurd or unthinkable. Suppose that if certain points *ABC* are given, an equilateral triangle may be drawn by constructing the lines *AB, BC* and *AC.* The unique quality of equilateralness is the "form" which the parts must assume in order to constitute the whole. In three-dimensional space the definition of the form of a tetrahedron or cylinder is such that to speak of subdivision or fragmentation of the form would be meaningless. Actually, however, the fragmentation is possible if we think in quantitative terms. There are in the world of space no distinct and indivisible forms or modes of organization. There is an infinite variety of modes of organization, each of which shows its complexity by differing from other modes in *one or more respects.* To define what is meant by an equilateral triangle requires a series of steps, each of which is distinct from the others. To define a tetrahedron or a cylinder necessitates following certain specific geometrical rules, each of which may appear in a large number of different contexts.

To use an illustration from three-dimentional space: a sculptor may make the nose of a portrait figure as long or as short as he likes, as wide or as narrow as he likes, its bridge as high or as low as he likes. There is an infinity of possibilities in each one of three directions. In so far as the term organization or form is used to define things in space, it yields to exactly that type of analytic dissection which it was supposed capable of resisting.

One method of defining an atomistic procedure, as contrasted with a totalistic or phenomenological procedure, is in terms of the randomness of the order in which parts are assembled. It might be stated, for example, that the adding of a column of figures represents the ideal situation for the atomist because the numbers will give the same sum in whatever order they are added.

Let us see what can be done with this conception. Let us

think for a moment of geometrical objects as generated by points in motion. We proceed to an "operational" geometry. If we desire to generate a cylinder, we start with a point which moves in a straight line for a distance r from the point of origin o to the terminus a. The point a now moves clockwise at a fixed distance r from o so as to generate a circle. The circle now moves along an axis determined by o and perpendicular to the plane of the circle. But the cylinder may be generated in an infinite number of other ways. It is just as "good" for a sculptor to start with an irregular piece of stone and chip or hew his way as he likes, making a long cylinder with ragged ends which is then to be smoothed off, or two planes perfectly parallel to one another but separated by an irregular curved surface which needs to be finished more finely in order to constitute a cylinder. The steps may be taken in an infinite number of orders. Organization, even in the realm of living matter, may also be achieved by a great variety of different routes. Bergson and Driesch, who might be thought of as the last to accept an atomistic view of life, expressly emphasize the point that the same organic pattern may be reached by an infinite number of different paths. It is clear that additive concepts (which contain some of the most objectionable features of atomism in general) appear whenever one attempts to define the structure of a geometrical object, while studies in embryology and comparative anatomy (Whyte, 1951) show that additive concepts obtain even in complex living structures.

The elements in our "operational geometry" are not necessarily homogeneous. It is not urged that the rotation of a line r around the point o be regarded as made up of elements which are *like* the elements that make up the process of moving the circle along the line perpendicular to itself. This would be nonsense. We suggest only that when the necessary steps have been defined, be they three or three hundred, *they may be taken in any order*. There are, to be sure, many biological systems which could *not* have developed except in fixed orders, but where we are attempting merely to point out limits in the sweeping generalizations of organicists, we have a right to emphasize prominent exceptions. Actually, groups of analogous organs strikingly similar arising in different orders from different contexts are biological commonplaces.

The same is true of temporal patterns. A melody may be altered by varying the intervals between tones, or the duration of tones, or in other ways. The term "organization" is simply a convenient way of saying "the sum of a number of distinct quantitative differences between points of reference." We refer, of course, to a scientific, not to an aesthetic, or any other normative approach. Far from being the final stroke by which atomism is to be dislodged from science, organization is a strictly additive concept. It is the clearest clue to the inevitable atomism intrinsic in every procedure which is pursued in a quantitative spirit.

The term "system" is, however, sometimes used in a still more complex sense. Let us imagine a system *ABCDE* such that *A* influences *B* and *D*, *B* influences *A*, *D*, and *E*, *C* influences *A* and *D*, *D* influences *B* and *E*, while *E* influences only *A*. Arrows indicate ascertained functional dependence. Let us assume now a condition of balance, in other words, a static system in which continuous influences of the sort described are exerted. The statistical exclusion of specific influences by the method of partial correlations is invalid in such a case. We remove, for example, the influence of *A*, but in so doing, partially mangle *B*, so that our statement that

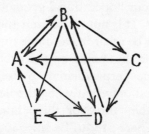

Figure 1

such and such causal relations would hold in the system *if A were absent* lacks meaning. The system is a system, and must be regarded in its totality.

What, in this case, do the arrows mean? Each arrow points to a specific relation, a functional dependence which in most cases may be looked upon naïvely in cause-effect terms. In such a pattern it will be evident that the system of forces is really the *sum* of a number of distinct causal forces. It is true that the method of partial correlations is invalid for their disentangling, but it is not true that each cause is interwoven or fused with the rest. On the contrary, the case as stated presupposes a genuine influence exerted independently along the line of each arrow.

We must distinguish between the numerical values of *ABCDE* themselves and the numerical values which indicate the potency of the *forces* operating along the paths of the arrows. Suppose, for example, that *ABCDE* be the endocrine system of an imaginary mammal. No gland functions in isolation. It is influenced by one or more other glands. The influences, however, are specific, not confused. The influence of the thyroid upon the thymus and pituitary may coexist with the influence of the adrenals and gonads upon the thymus. In each case, no matter how refined the analysis, we shall discover that the blood carries at any given time stimulating or inhibiting influences from each gland to each other gland which is involved in the system of causal relations shown by the arrows.

Let us now introduce the time factor. If at any given time the influence from *A* to *B* is removed, while all other influences remain, the influence of *D* upon other glands will soon be changed and in a short time the entire system will be reorganized. This will not, however, mean that a less "atomistic" structure has resulted. On the contrary, new influences now exist, put together in a new way. It takes a certain time for any change in one gland to bring about its full effect upon the other glands. At any time, however, in the process of readjustment, the arrows in the figure should show the influence exerted by each gland on each other gland, and if necessary it should be possible to devise patterns to show the rate of change in such glandular influences.

The issue will be clearer if we refer to endocrine surgery. The removal of a gland may cause a far-reaching readjustment in other glandular functions. Yet at every point in the readjustment the activity of each gland represents the resultant of all the forces acting upon it; and at every point inhibiting and stimulating effects may be added algebraically. In some cases the effect of stimulation and inhibition may not appear to be added algebraically, but the present theory would suppose, as glandular evidence in fact suggests, that we are concerned with the disturbing influences of another gland or group of glands which complicate the picture. The instances of positive results achieved by gland surgery, and by such methods of gland treatment as the hypodermic administration of thyroxin, suggest that biological resultants, when measurable, resemble geometrical resultants, simply because in the last analysis chemical processes may be treated according to the same system of mathematics which the student of geometry or algebra uses. These "atomistic" systems of thought are applicable to chemistry and biology for the same fundamental reason. If a biological organic system differed fundamentally in its atomism from a chemical organic system such as one has in a benzene ring, the clinical and experimental methods of modern medicine would long since have been forced to resort to an entirely different sort of mathematics.

The influence exerted by one element upon another may be conceived as an arrow, as in the diagram above (Fig. 1). These arrows will be referred to as "*paths of influence*." In the case of the endocrine system, gland A exerts an influence upon gland B, and the blood stream is the path along which the influence works. Considered mathematically, paths of influence can be described in terms of functions. If the activity of gland *A* increases the activity of gland *B*, activity of *B* is a function of activity of *A*. The correlation of the activity of *B* with that of *A* need not be linear. Fortunately, as in the study of the influence of the adrenals upon the digestive hormones and the liver, the time relations are reasonably well known and it is feasible to state the paths of influence mathematically as functions. This is not, however, primarily an essay in mathematics, and the phrase "paths of influence" will be used instead of the word "functions" because it will be easier on this basis to visualize the schema, remembering that *A* and *B* are different points in space and that a real influence is exerted in finite time along a path from one to the other.

There is a fundamental inadequacy in the above discussion, in that the system *ABCDE* has been supposed to be self-contained. The geometer has the right to construct self-contained systems, but the biologist and psychologist have no such right. A more accurate delineation of the problem would make use of the following figure (Fig. 2).

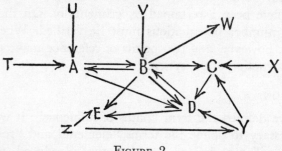

FIGURE 2

The endocrine organs or any other organs which may profitably be discussed in this connection receive influences from outside of the group of organs under discussion. The endocrines are affected by other bodily structures and of course by the oxygen and carbon dioxide pressure, the humidity, and other factors in the world outside. The arrows indicate the dependence of each of these centers of activity upon causal influences derived from outside the system. It will make no difference whether these "outside" factors be *outside the body* or *within it*. It is sufficient that they are *outside the pattern or system* the essence of which we wish to examine. The numerical values of the influences exerted between any two endocrine organs will depend not only upon changes going on in the other endocrines, but upon extrasystemic factors. It is clear then that the conception of an *organism* as a self-contained system is without mathematical meaning (von Bertalanffy, 1952). The interaction between the different glands at a given time is determined partly by the characteristics of the glands themselves, partly by influences received from other glands, and partly by more remote influences from outside the system.

A clear example of the present mode of thinking appears in L. J. Henderson's (1930) nomogram of the blood. Six measurable influences are defined, the interaction of which constitutes a coherent mathematical pattern. Any four of the numerical values desired may be obtained from any two which have been ascertained experimentally. On this basis, a large number of equations must be verified. When once verified, however, any two points of reference make possible the construction of the system.

RELATIONS

We have defined the term "paths of influence"; it will next be necessary to define the terms "element" and "relation." "Elements" are defined as phenomena reduced to their simplest forms so that they are qualitatively homogeneous and quantitatively indivisible.

The term "relation" is one of the most abused of those with which the psychologist must deal. Much anguish has attended the Gestalt declaration regarding the importance of the interrelations of aspects of experiences. Logicians have had endless trouble with the term "relation." I quote but one illustration of the lexicographer's difficulty in telling what a relation is: "The character of a plurality of things; a fact concerning two or more things, especially and more properly when it is regarded as a predicate of one of the things connecting it with the others; the condition of being such and such with regard to something else" (*Century Dictionary*, 1906, p. 318). I propose to use the term relation in a simpler sense: "A relation is the difference between two numerical values, each of which defines the amount of anything possessed by the two things measured." The term will not be used in the sense of any sort of qualitative similarity as such, nor with any finalistic meaning such as would be involved in discussing "the relation of the citizen to the state." Absolute differences can be measured only when two things are measured in the same units. Relations will always be metrical.

A few illustrations will suffice. If one thing is over another, the relation is one of up and down. My hand, for example, is eleven inches above the table. The relation of the hand to the table is plus 11. The relation of the table to the hand is minus 11. Upness and downness refer now to absolute numerical values in terms of a chosen unit, and may vary in value from zero to plus or minus infinity. The relation of the outdoor to the indoor temperature will mean the number of degrees between the two. The relation of income to expenditure will mean not a ratio such as 4/3, but the absolute amount in terms of our chosen unit, such as the dollar. A great many forms of mathematical conceptions which are ordinarily discussed from a slightly different point of view can be subsumed under the present scheme. The relation of "perpendicularity," for example, which obtains between two lines, is simply a relation of 90, when the unit is the degree, and one line is conceived to rotate about the point of intersection. The numerical values are, to be sure, meaningless except as abstractions from a nexus of phenomena which also possess quality (see p. 183); numerical values must refer consistently to data of a given quality. One does not set two degrees centigrade equal to two inches.

The term "organization" will refer to a *group of relations considered as coexisting*. Obviously, however, the organization is not merely a single numerical value. The relations (numeral values) must be regarded as *continuing to exist along with the numerical sum* which together they yield. The term sum does, however, bring out the fact that the relations may be put together in any order. In a certain sense, the relations, though all quantitative and yielding a quantitative sum, must be regarded as having another kind of existence beyond the existence as part of the sum. The same is true, of course, in the simplest problem in arithmetic. When we say that $2 \times 3 = 6 \times 1$, obviously more is intended than that $6 = 6$. In the ordinary situation in arithmetic, the quantitative parts remain. It is only *as sums* that the left and right sides of the equation are equal. In every other respect than as sums, they may differ. The problem is the same in measuring organic systems.

Considered as sums, equations can tell all there is in an organic system; but considered as anything other than sums, they cannot do so. Patterns may be forced into the form of equations, and this is one legitimate meaning of the numerical values inherent in equations; but it is only one of their meanings. A student of organic systems is concerned with addition; there are, however, many other problems with which he may be concerned. All problems in the mathematics of organic systems are therefore additive problems, but the rules invoked in addition are flexible; and it is through this flexibility that the biologist and psychologist makes legitimate use of organismic (or organicist or Gestaltist) doctrines.

From other considerations it is equally clear that the numerical sum of the data on the left and right sides of an equation are of no special significance in organismic theory. The units are frequently arbitrary. The solution of equations would come out in some such form as $152 = 152$. The choice of axes from which relations are measured is usually arbitrary. In most of our present biological and psychological problems we have to choose arbitrary axes; and if this be so, it is not the sum of the items on each side of the equation but rather the processes involved in combining various numerical values (like the "operational geometry" above) which constitute the heart of our problem.

A brief rebuttal of some of the major propositions just advanced may be attempted here, that the opposition may have a chance to make some of its objections articulate.

The point may be made that relations do not do any real *work*. They are simply numbers; they cannot guide what is going on. They are merely quantities discovered, lying, so to speak, in the midst of material events within the organism. The elements and the paths of influence between elements determine everything. To this must be replied that we can never speak of elements in quantitative language without making numbers, in a certain sense, "do work," and there is no reason why numbers which define relations should be less capable of accomplishing anything than other numbers. Moreover, in discussing endocrine imbalance and other instances in which the relation between two glands is the cause of some biological or psychological disturbance, it is clear that neither the numerical value of one gland's activity nor that of another gland's activity, but quite strictly the relation between the two, does the effective work. There is neither theoretical nor empirical justification for the denial that relations, as well as other quantities, are efficient causes. We are inclined to agree that there is no sense in discussing whether quantities exist in and by themselves and apart from matter (in Plato's sense of the term); but as known to the biologist and psychologist they are certainly just as real and just as important parts of a datum as are the qualities of the datum.

Another objection is that a relation has been defined so as to suggest a bridge between two numerical values. This notion of a bridge involves a supposition regarding organic structure. This seems to be an admission that relations do more than merely make contact between two related things. They integrate or unify the separate elements. The reply is that from the point of view of the outside observer who is still in the qualitative stage of observation (see p. 183) this may appear to be the case, and that from one level of description it is a perfectly fair way to describe the matter, but at a further level of analysis the bridge will, so to speak, tumble down and all we shall have is a number defining the distance between the two river banks. Spatial and temporal patterns will replace unanalyzed wholeness.

Finally, this objection will be raised against the way in which we are describing elements, relations, and paths of influence as "atoms" in a process of analysis: Is not an atom an *indivisible* thing and do not our quantitative definitions defeat our purpose since any quantity is capable of *subdivision*? But we are using the term atom in a somewhat different sense. A quantity as such has no organization. It is simply a quantity which is so defined as to be greater than some and less than other quantities. At any given moment an organic system is expressed in the numerical values of elements, relations, and paths of influence; the changes in time are, as we saw, likewise "atomistic." The quantity is taken as an atom in the sense that it *functions as that whole quantity* collaborating with some other whole quantity in producing a third or fourth quantity, and so on. In Figure 3 below, the letters *a, b, c, d,* and *e,* and the lines of influence shown by the arrows as well as the relations between each two elements are atoms, that is, numbers to be manipulated exactly as they stand rather than regarded as capable of subdivision. Being simply numbers, there is no qualitative differentiation between their parts. In this sense of the term, the organic system is composed of atoms. *The relations and paths of influence are atoms in the same sense in which the elements are atoms.* There do not have to be "relations between relations" or other forms of infinite regression: *Differentiation, in Spencer's or Werner's sense, is movement from a homogeneous quality to a group of quantifiable elements, relations, and paths of influence, and integration is the assemblage of the differential elements into a new system, retaining the parts but utilizing the possibilities for new lines of influence between elements and groups of elements.*

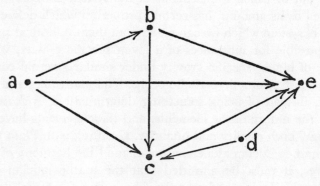

FIGURE 3

Believers in Plato's absolute mathematical patterns will object that the efficacy of the work done by the various elements in the pattern depends entirely upon the mathematical character of the constellation. The elements are permitted to "do the work," but their hands are guided, so to speak, by a mathematical principle.[2] Points *a*, *b*, and *c* are able to do the work of an organic system only if the numerical values assigned to them or to the interaction[3] between them be so and so. Paths described by points can be ellipses, parabolas or hyperbolas only if such and such quantitative statements regarding their relations be posited. The points in themselves do not, so to speak, know in what direction to go. They are mere potentiality, mere meaningless elements, the shaping of which into a system depends upon the real work done by the mathematical equations.

An opposite objection will be raised by "mechanist" fol-

---

[2] So, too, followers of Aristotle will of course insist that potentiality inhering in the elements can become actuality only by virtue of real *forms*.

[3] Interaction in R. A. Fisher's sense is too complex a problem for the present essay.

lowers of Democritus, who will call for study of the part
played by the material units in the life of an organic system.
Granted that the equation is always present, the kind of *material* out of which the elements of the system are composed,
as well as its amount, has certain properties which define the
type of system which we can make from them. Elliptical paths
are possible for substances of a given specific gravity, while
those of higher specific gravity under similar external conditions must assume hyperbolic orbits. The mathematics of the
orbit, instead of being something determinative, is *derivative*
from the nature of the elements, and these elements have, as
we saw, both quality and quantity. Granting with Plato that
the mathematician alone can understand the harmony of the
spheres, it must be admitted that the mathematician can
achieve his understanding only if he knows the actual properties of the material bodies of which a system is composed;
e.g., the properties of an animal's proteins define the kind of
mathematics which will give insight in the understanding of
any creature's life. The properties of the whole, whether it be
a whole organ or a whole animal, are thus always properties
derivative from the material elements of the system.

But if this be true, why should the mathematician be con-
sulted at all? If his laws are secondary, if the mathematical
equation is, so to speak, written by the tissues of the body, why
regard the role of quantitative analysis as of any fundamental
consequence in the pursuit of biological truth? The answer lies
in the fact that the elements themselves have, as we saw,
numerical values of various sorts, numerical values defining
the various attributes of molecular structure, electromagnetic
properties, etc. These are numerical attributes of the elements
of the system. The numerical attributes are the most important
of all the attributes.

But to return to our own position: No work is done by
numbers alone or by equations alone. The organic system
contains elements, the attributes of which may be measured.
The equations have no meaning except in terms of actual

numerical differences between real values discovered in the observation of the system. The elements, acting not singly but together, each influencing the other along one or more "paths of influence," tell what the numerical attributes of the system as a whole must be.

Are material elements more "real," then, than relations? Being known to science as "pointer readings," they are numbers. Relations are also numbers. The elements, the relations, and the paths of influence are equally real, equally substantial, and equally measurable. On this basis, then, we have the formal definition of an organic system in which, to use Aristotle's terminology, forms are as real as matter, or, to use Northrop's (1931) terminology, a "functional" view of nature as contrasted with either a physical or a mathematical view. It is only the system which is organized; the separate relations are no more organized than the elements are.

FROM PHYSICAL TO PSYCHOLOGICAL

Though I should be willing to define all of the above-mentioned analysis in application to simple biological systems on the assumption that numbers must be treated as "real," I am inclined to consider the argument simpler and more convincing for the world of immediate experience as studied by the psychologist, particularly the world of spatial perception. Psychological space is real; it is three-dimensional; it is measurable; it is open to experimental manipulation. Psychological space is the space in which happenings seem to occur. It is this psychological, this immediately given space with which we are dealing in all the typical studies with the stereoscope, motion picture camera, illusions of reversible perspective, and so on. The experimental work of students of space perception is grist to our mill; it is with this in mind that the present discussion of psychological atomism is undertaken.

In rejection of Gestalt theory on this point, and in rejection of the finality of phenomenology, I urge that a radical desire to avoid the definition of elements and relations often constitutes a movement from the *third level of perception* (see p. 202) to the *second level*, or even back to the first. We know from a thousand records of the mystics and the poets that it is possible to annihilate elements and relations when they have once been separated from a given total. Psychologically the fact is interesting that we wish to find ourselves in the un-analyzed wholeness or the unique quality in which there seem to be no parts. Let it be granted that regression to the second level of observation, or the first, is often valuable. There is al-so much to be learned through methods which push analysis to its limits.

There are two approaches which the psychologist may take when confronted with the question whether the conscious sys-tem as the individual himself knows it, his stream of thought, is to be considered quantitatively. The first is to insist that each mental element or structure must correspond to some physiological element or structure and to carry over the en-tire preceding argument about organic systems into the do-main of the conscious system. This would not mean one-to-one correspondence between psychological elements and physiological elements, since, as we have seen, what is ele-mentary at one stage of analysis is found to be a composite when analysis has progressed further. If we should achieve a one-to-one correspondence between the physiological and the psychological at eleven o'clock some morning, we should probably discover at two o'clock that afternoon that the physiological element was in fact a composite while the psy-chological element still remained elementary.

For any given, relatively closed system like a perceptual field there is probably a corresponding brain pattern. But it will be necessary to discover the mathematics of each psycho-logical pattern in itself, not go at it by analogy based on the patterns found in physiology. To be sure, the latter patterns may often give useful hypotheses. The facts of cone and rod vision suggest, for example, interesting hypotheses about the organization of visual fields for the light-adapted and the dark-adapted eye. A great many of the simpler laws of perception are certainly clarified by mathematical study of the properties of nervous tissue in the manner of Sherrington, Adrian, or Lashley. These physiological laws, however, are clues, never more. Our attempt to transfer specific physiological patterns into psychology may succeed in some cases of isomorphism, but psychological systems do not have to be clearly reduced to physiological systems to pass muster as empirically real.

But is the logic applied to the measurement of organic systems applicable also to phenomenal fields?

Taking the visual field as a highly organized system, we discover many instances in which the data suggest the same sort of mathematical analysis which we have already undertaken, and in which analysis of the numerical results suggests an identity, if not in the equations, at least in the *basic principles* involved in physiology and in psychology. The laws of color contrast or color constancy, for example, are clear instances in which the properties of the elements reported are, when taken at their face value, determined by the properties of systems and in which apparently no element exists by its own right. Closer scrutiny shows, however, that the same visual field of which this antielementarist declaration is made will permit, as the Gestaltists have emphasized, a "phenomenal analysis" in which a host of true elements will be discovered. The elements thus discovered will indeed appear to be "dependent upon" the system, as we saw in the case of physiological systems. This means that each element appears in a context of "paths of influence" exerted by each other element, the paths of influence being capable of experimental analysis and quantitative treatment. The confusion which arises when one says that there are no real elements in the visual field is the same confusion which follows when one says, quite truly, that no part of the body ever functions "in isolation." The trouble is to distinguish between elements and *lines of influence;* the latter are as fundamental as the former. Each element in the visual field corresponds roughly to the lines appearing in Figure 1 (p. 188). Each letter has a numerical value which depends upon the system, yet the system depends upon the elements, while the mathematics of the system as a whole is a derivative of the properties of the elements and of their spatial location. The points *A, B, C, D, E* do not represent *unvarying elements*, but elements defined for a *specific situation*. In the visual field the objects discovered by phenomenal analysis are specific qualities capable of being replaced from moment to moment by other specific qualities. Qualities seem to change constantly within the visual field; even such qualities as hue and brilliance. In the same way, when objects in the visual field change qualitatively and when it seems that there are no true elements, it is necessary to set up a more refined procedure in which the specific quality may be seen to be a derivative of more purely elementary entities, *quantitatively patterned in psychological time and usually also in psychological space*. The qualities will be shown to be reducible to *composites*, while the paths of influence will prove to be true atoms.

Yet it is important to distinguish between the sense in which the above-mentioned logic of the organism applies to conscious states and the sense in which it does not apply. Paths of influence within conscious states such as the perceptual field can often be ascertained or even measured, and the various elements such as patches of color within such a perceptual field may be measured with respect to such characteristics as saturation and brilliance. The logic of interdependence as described above seems pertinent here. It seems true to say that the most highly organized perceptual field can be really understood in the language of atomism. It is true that each colored particle in a mosaic depends upon the whole system of paths of influence; but after completing such analysis of elements and of paths of influence, *we should be able to describe the integrated whole—Werner's third level of description—in terms of the paths of influence which connect the elements or the clusters of elements (subwholes) within the total.*

Yet we must make clear in what sense we may *not* speak of the logic of organization as applicable to the conscious field. For any such argument as the present, it is necessary to remain noncommittal about the relations of mental to physical states. If we should assume any theory of mind-body relation, we should commit ourselves to metaphysics and make the utility of the present conception for research purposes practically nil. We prefer to assume in a naïve manner that conscious states accompany physiological states and that the elements and patterns of the conscious field express what is going on in the body. Within a phenomenal field (e.g., a perceptual field), parts and wholes "depend" upon one another and act as systems exactly as the body as a whole does, and both systems exhibit elements, relations, and paths of influence. Until detailed knowledge of brain physiology is at hand, it seems unlikely that mathematical formulations will be found which apply equally well to conscious fields and to physiological fields; but they are being sought and may soon be found.

An element can be completely described if its qualities are named. Since the apparent *quantitative* aspects of elements cannot help being relations in the sense in which we are here using our terms, an ideal analysis should give each element a single quality so as to make it homogeneous, and this quality must differ from all other qualities. Since, however, qualities of any given element also resemble in some way the qualities of other elements, the question of reducing qualitative similarity to quantitative terms arises. If two qualities are similar, a linear scale may be found upon which the two are found to stand near together. The present argument regards this quantitative statement of similarity as an artifact. [4] The statement that two feelings are similar can be reduced to quantitative terms if necessary, but the similarity is not genuinely a matter of linear distance; it is a qualitative continuum, like the experienced spectrum. It will therefore be strictly true that all

---

[4] But see S. S. Stevens (1959).

elements possess specific qualities, that all relations are quantities. Similarity is not a true property of the *quantitative structure of the system*. The dynamics of the system are to be understood in terms of the specific qualities, the relations between them, and the paths of influence.

Biological and psychological systems not only conform to the atomistic pattern laid down by the old as well as the new mechanics; they are likely to require mathematical restatement as modern physics reconstructs its concept of mechanics. Psychological systems also have the advantage that we can usually observe things as wholes before we observe them as constellations of parts; that we can, if we wish, go back again after carrying through the analysis and see how the thing looks in its entirety. The psychologist, in the light of his genetic problem relating to the development of perception, can state the nature of the changes which lead from the specific quality which we call a whole to the elements which have been analyzed out (p. 183), and state under what conditions the elements may again disappear and be lost as the whole is contemplated.

A good statement of the Gestalt view is that wholes and parts bear not an "external relation" in the sense in which the two banks of a river are related when the river is spanned by a bridge, but that they bear a relation *defined by a system as a whole* as in simultaneous color contrast. The field of optics is rich in instances in which two or more phenomenal objects appear to reinforce or inhibit one another.

PERSONALITY STRUCTURE

There is no sphere of psychology in which there is more frequent reference to the conception of wholeness than the field of personality study. Justly protesting against studies which attempt to define and measure traits *without reference to their context* in the individual make-up, psychologists have tended to refer to the "personality as a whole." The result has been a continuation of the confusion against which we have tried to protest. If it is misleading to dissect and independently discuss the traits of personality as if they existed in a vacuum, it is likewise misleading to define wholeness without reference to the observable phases of personality and the observable relations that exist between these phases; they must have some existence as *parts* if they are to be described. If our general analysis is sound, personality at any given moment is constituted of specific tendencies and an elaborate nexus of relations between these tendencies. Similarly, when the time dimension is introduced, personality is dynamically regarded as a shift in behavior tendencies. The general logic of parts, paths of influence, and organic systems would appear to be identical with that which we have already considered.

This general statement, however, must, in order to be useful, be implemented by reference to a specific definition of *personality integration;* that is to say, a mechanism by which traits as known and measured can be defined with reference to one another and to the total. Such a definition appears to involve three steps.

First, any given trait or behavior tendency is not only a response but is a stimulus to other responses. Any act serves to maintain other activities. *A* and *B*, two definable and "independent" acts, mutually reinforce, balance, or sustain one another. Integration, then, means that each act serves to cause, to facilitate, or to maintain some other definite activity. This can easily be stated, if desired, in terms of "*paths* of influence" whenever empirical data make clear what the actual influence is.

Second, when acts are antagonistic, one inhibits or raises the threshold for another. Such a response may be designated "dissociation;" from another point of view it may be called "repression." The only thing of importance for our purposes is that the paths of influence involve negative rather than positive effects.

Third, when the time dimension is introduced, any activity leads to other acts occurring later in time. These may engender a third set of acts, or they may, of course, act back upon the first. Personality may, quite literally, constitute a shifting field of activity in which each act determines in part the occurrence of other simultaneous acts and the proneness of the individual to later acts of any specified type. The personality as a whole is a name for the interrelation of activities considered both simultaneously and successively.

If this is correct for the dynamic system of the entire behavior activity, it appears also to be sound for the subjective unity of the personality as known to itself; that is, the sense of individual unity. This is indeed a perceptual field differing in no fundamental respect from other perceptual fields considered earlier in this essay.

It is worth while to note again that the present view presupposes that there are two diametrically opposed kinds of Gestalt psychology, one of which asserts that parts must always be seen in terms of integration or architectural totality, the other of which denies that there are any parts. As before, the present view coincides entirely with the former position, regarding it as incompatible with the latter position. The term integration as used in personality study would appear to mean the system of mutual reinforcements and inhibitions obtaining either within a behavioral system or a subjective system, and except for its complexity would present no special problems not encountered in the study of any life process. *Werner's three steps are deeply embedded in the reality known to science*, and all three are subject to the type of analysis used here. This does not mean that he must accept our formulation. It means only that we gratefully acknowledge the fundamental importance of the developmental issues which he so wisely defined.

SUMMARY

We have attempted in the foregoing to indicate that physical systems can be defined in terms of elements, their relations and the paths of influence obtaining between them. These mathematical conceptions seem sufficient in the description of physical systems and justify neither holism nor the belief that parts must be defined in terms of wholes. Wholes must indeed be confronted directly and treated as something different from the separate elements appearing within them, but it is logically a disservice to use the whole as an explanation for elements or of relations between them.

In psychological systems it might appear at first sight that the compelling logic is of a different sort. It is, however, necessary to identify elements within psychological systems and then to define their context and their paths of influence, just as in the case of physical systems. The psychological system is subject to the same logic, for the reason that we are dealing with a universally logical necessity arising from our constitution as human beings and its relation to the structure of the known world. Difference in subject matter does not force upon us different means of defining and interrelating experiences.

Surely Gestalt psychology has demonstrated the futility of any constancy hypothesis which would necessitate rigid linkage of physiological response and simple physical stimuli. There are, nevertheless, identifiable elements in the physiological and in the psychological series and, exactly as in the physical system, these elements in living systems must be defined in terms of identifiable properties if they are to be knowable. A given psychological element can occur in more than one system (cf. the constancies). It may of course arise as a result of different stimulus contexts. But if it is not identifiable across the barriers that separate one psychological field from another, if it is not knowable, classifiable, and recognizable as the same, no procedure based on the study of integration from simple to complex can be worked out. Both logically and empirically, psychological systems must be formed of elements. Again both logic and experiment point the way to the study of the relations between elements, e.g., in the field of perception, and to the supreme importance of studying the paths of influence, as they serve to structure the visual field.

This might, in a later essay, guide the development of our thought to the structural problems found at Werner's *third* level, the *integrative* level of experience. It is conceivable that the "paths of influence" existing at the *second* level, when more deeply channeled, or when carrying a richer freight of internal traffic within the system, may carry us over to firmer integrations of elements. If so, the quantitative method of structural analysis considered here would apply also to Werner's third level.

BIBLIOGRAPHY

Century Dictionary and Cyclopedia (1906), Vol. 6. New York: Century.
Henderson, L. J. (1930), *Blood: A Study in General Physiology*. New Haven: Yale University Press.
James, W. (1890), *Principles of Psychology*, Vol. 1. New York: Holt.
Northrop, F. S. C. (1931), *Science and First Principles*. New York: Macmillan.
Spencer, H. (1920), *First Principles*, 6th ed. New York: Appleton.
Stevens, S. S. (1959), Quantification of Sensation. *Daedalus*, *88*:606-621.
Sullivan, A. H. (1927), The Cutaneous Perception of Softness and Hardness. *Journal of Experimental Psychology*, *10*:447-462.
Taylor, J. (Ed.) (1958), *Selected Writings of John Hughlings Jackson*. New York: Basic Books.
von Bertalanffy, L. (1952), *Problems of Life: An Evaluation of Modern Biological Thought*. London: Watts.
Whyte, L. L. (Ed.) (1951), *Aspects of Form*. London: Lund.

Psychoanalysis as a Developmental Psychology

DAVID RAPAPORT, Ph.D.

Austen Riggs Center

For this occasion I have set myself the task of exploring some of the basic concepts of psychoanalysis as a developmental psychology. I will attempt to do three things: first, to demonstrate that the core of psychoanalysis as a developmental psychology is the concept of instinctual drives and drive-restraining factors; second, to clarify the relation between instinctual drives and experience; and finally, to reconsider the developmental relation between archaic and ordered forms of thought. For each of these topics I will present a brief survey

Revision of an address given September 21, 1957, at the presentation of the Freud statue by the American Psychoanalytic Association to Clark University, to commemorate Freud's only visit and lectures in this country.

This study was made possible by the Ford Foundation's grant in support of research at the Austen Riggs Center.

of the outstanding relevant theories and discoveries of present-day nonpsychoanalytic developmental psychology. These surveys will be brief and my choice of examples perforce arbitrary; and, although some of the examples are still controversial, I shall not attempt to enter on these controversies here to justify my choice.

Paradoxically, the significance of ego psychology, which is a relatively recent branch of psychoanalysis, for psychoanalysis as a developmental psychology is (due to the work of Hartmann and particularly Erikson) better understood than the significance of some concepts which have a much longer history in psychoanalysis. I will discuss today some of these older concepts and only where they require it will I touch on ego psychology.

First, however, a few words concerning the concept of development and developmental psychology. In speaking of developmental psychology I refer to those investigations and theories which Werner (1926) surveyed, and not to the "child study" and "child development" movement and investigations fashionable in the 1930's and '40's.

Paul Weiss (1939) characterized development as a process of autonomous and progressive differentiation of the somatic organizations which are required for the functioning of the organism, and considered the process to be "determined by *intrinsic* developmental factors quite unrelated to actual functioning" (p. 569). His formulation implies that the development of behavior as seen by the student of organic (as against psychological) development is, on the whole, independent of experience. Weiss writes:

> . . . we must concede to the behavioral system the capacity of being later, secondarily, elaborated into greater detail, higher efficiency, and finer adjustments under the guidance of its actual operation. In order to rate these improvements correctly, one must keep in mind that they compare with the groundwork of organization as the interior decoration of a building compares with its construction [p. 570].

Developmental psychology as a rule uses the term "maturation" to describe those "intrinsic factors" which are prior to and independent of experience, and the term "development" to refer both to these and to their interaction with experience. In the past, attention has only too often been distracted from the role of "intrinsic factors" in human behavior by the fact that in human development these intrinsic factors are more flexible than they are in the development of lower organisms, and by the fact that their interaction with experience is far more extensive than what is observed in organic development. In the period when behaviorism dominated psychology, the role of experience in development was the focus of interest, and little effort was devoted to the search for maturational factors in human behavior other than those involved in somatic development. Freud's and Heinz Werner's (1926) developmental psychologies did not conform to the trend of this period. Werner searched for the common characteristics of developmental changes, regardless of their experiential content, and defined developmental psychology as follows:

> . . . a discipline which investigates the characteristics common to any behavior in the process of progression or regression, in order to establish both the common pattern of each developmental level and the relationship between these levels, that is, the direction of mental development [1957].

Clearly his quest was for intrinsic maturational factors.

As for psychoanalysis as a developmental psychology, it is my purpose to demonstrate that its central achievement was the disentangling of an intrinsic maturational factor from the tangle of the progressive changes apparently wrought by experience. I consider such a demonstration the more important since it is this central achievement of Freud's which has been abandoned by all the so-called neo-Freudian schools, whose theories, without exception, lack such an intrinsic factor.

THE CONCEPT OF DRIVE AS THE CORE OF FREUD'S DE-
VELOPMENTAL THEORY

I shall first briefly sketch Freud's discovery of an intrinsic maturational factor, in order to lay the groundwork for the discussion of this factor and of Freud's genetic method.

Freud's initial discoveries and theory (Breuer and Freud,
1895; Freud, 1893-96) were not developmental. His discoveries of traumatic experiences, the unconscious memories
and dammed-up affects pertaining to them, and his explanation of these[1] established connections only between experience
and subsequent behavior, and involved no intrinsic maturational factors. Hartmann and Kris (1945) characterized such
connections as anamnestic, but not genetic in their sense or
developmental in our sense.[2] The meaning of these discoveries
changed radically when Freud (1897)[3] found that his patients'
reports of seduction in infancy referred not to real experiences
but to childhood fantasies. The study of these fantasies brought
into view something whose impact on behavior is equal to, or
even greater than, the impact of external reality. Freud's
(1900) account of this factor made internal, psychological
reality the subject matter of science for the first time.

Freud conceived of these fantasies as wish fulfillments of
instinctual drives, particularly sexual drives, and he generalized this conception into the central proposition of psychoanalytic theory, that innate, progressively maturing, unconscious instinctual drives underlie the conscious and experiential determiners of behavior. With this conception of instinc-

---

[1] Defense against re-experiencing the traumatic situation, e.g., sexual seduction.

[2] "The genetic approach in psychoanalysis does not deal only with anamnestic
data, nor does it intend to show only 'how the past is contained in the present.'
Genetic propositions describe why, in past situations of conflict, a specific solution was adopted; why the one was retained and the other dropped, and what
causal relation exists between these solutions and later developments" (Hartmann and Kris, 1945, p. 17).

[3] This date refers to Draft M (pp. 202-205) and Draft N (pp. 207-210) in
Freud (1887-1902).

tual drives, Freud postulated an *intrinsic* maturational factor independent of prior experience, and thus went beyond the anamnestic relationship between behavior and antecedent experience. The theory of the phases of libido development, which is so often regarded as the core of Freud's developmental theory (1905), is simply the specific theory of the development of this particular instinctual drive, which, considered by itself, can be construed as the progressive alteration of the libidinal drive by experience (see Kardiner, 1939, 1945; and Sullivan, 1953). The significance of the theory of instinctual drives for developmental psychology becomes particularly clear if we contrast this theory with associationist and conditioning theories, the pure forms of which attempt to explain behavior solely in terms of antecedent experience, that is, in terms of learning not organized by and around intrinsic maturational factors.[4]

The method by which Freud arrived at his concept of instinctual drives is also fundamental to his developmental psychology, because it is by that method that he also arrived at the conception of the relation between the intrinsic maturational ("constitutional") and the experiential ("accidental") factors in the determination of behavior. He formulated this relation as follows:

> It is not easy to estimate the relative efficacy of constitutional and accidental factors. . . . The constitutional factor must await experiences before it can make itself felt; the accidental factor must have a constitutional basis in order to come into operation. To cover the majority of cases we can picture . . . 'a complemental

---

[4] Some of the reinforcement theorists (e.g., Miller, Dollard, Mowrer) tend to assume that their learning (conditioning) theories are compatible with the psychoanalytic theory and provide it with a learning theory—which it does indeed sorely need. The fact that they have a drive concept seems to suggest that these learning theories are compatible with psychoanalysis. But this is a fallacy: their drive concept is not an intrinsic maturational factor. Moreover, while a psychoanalytic ego psychology has shown (see pp. 216-217, 240ff. below) that not all behavior can be explained by tension reduction (reinforcement) alone, the sole central principle of these theories is tension reduction. For a discussion of these points, see Rapaport (1952, 1953a).

series', in which the diminishing intensity of one factor is balanced by the increasing intensity of the other [1905, pp. 239-240].

The method—Hartmann and Kris (1945) termed it "the genetic approach"—consists of starting out with a given behavior and situation, and tracing a series of antecedent behaviors, all of which were attempts to solve the same problem posed by the mounting intensity of an instinctual drive, in various situations and at various stages of development. The further back in such a series one goes, the more the relative significance of the experiential (accidental) factors recedes, and the more the instinctual drive (the intrinsic maturational factor) and the specific developmental phase in which the problem originally arose and in which the pattern for its ultimate solution was set, become dominant.

The usefulness of the genetic approach for developmental psychology seems to be limited by the fact that the evidence for its validity comes mainly from the psychoanalytic situation, where the method is complicated by *interpretations*. Freud was aware of these limitations, and wrote:

> The direct observation of children has the disadvantage of working upon data which are easily misunderstandable; psycho-analysis is made difficult by the fact that it can only reach its data, as well as its conclusions, after long detours. But by co-operation the two methods can attain a satisfactory degree of certainty in their findings [1905, p. 201].

In the last decades persistent attempts have been made to carry out what Freud suggested here (Anna Freud and Burlingham, 1943, 1944; Anna Freud and Dann, 1951; Spitz, 1946a, 1946b, 1949; Leitch, 1948; Leitch and Escalona, 1949; Escalona et al., 1952; Kris, 1951, 1955; Benjamin, 1959; P. H. Wolff, 1959; Coleman, Kris, and Provence, 1953; and others). Yet the limitations of the method may not be as formidable as they seem when we consider that Freud developed the genetic approach when he was still using the cathartic technique which involves no interpretations. Be that as it may, the significance of the genetic approach for developmental psychology is not only that it is a method which traces an intrinsic maturational factor—instinctual drive—underlying behavior, but also that it traces the development of a complex unit, namely, "behavior as a problem solution," rather than the development of isolated organs, functions, or abilities. Because the genetic approach can trace the developmental course of complex behaviors, it enabled psychoanalysis to bring the study of personality development within the scope of developmental psychology, a feat not even attempted by any other developmental theory.

The discussion of the instinctual drives as intrinsic maturational factors would be incomplete if I did not mention another closely related discovery of Freud's: the intrinsic factors that restrain instinctual drives. I will discuss these more fully in the last part of this paper, but I want to indicate here that it is this concept that enables psychoanalysis to account for both tension discharge and tension maintenance without explaining either as the consequence of environmental influences alone.

The central role of conflict in psychopathology was one of Freud's early discoveries, and it confronted him with the question, What are the conflicting factors? at a time when he still explained behavior by antecedent experience alone (Breuer and Freud, 1895), and had not yet arrived at his conception of the instinctual drive. Both of the factors which he designated then as the components of the conflict he conceived of as originating in experience: the affect elicited by experience[5] and the defense mechanisms resulting from environmental necessity. But when the instinctual drive as an intrinsic maturational factor took the place of affect as one of the factors in the conflict (1900), the question, What is the

---

[5] At this time Freud's (1900, pp. 468, 582) view of affects rested on the James-Lange theory.

nature of the other factor? arose again. In regard to this factor
Freud wavered: in 1900 and 1911 he believed that it was experiential in nature, while in 1905 and 1914 he saw it as a
manifestation of another intrinsic maturational factor. I will
quote here only Freud's earliest statement of the latter view,
without discussing the ramifications of this conception in present-day psychoanalytic ego psychology:

> It is during [the] . . . period of total or only partial latency that
> are built up the mental forces which are later to impede the course
> of the sexual instinct and, like dams, restrict its flow—disgust, feel-
> ings of shame and the claims of aesthetic and moral ideals. One gets
> an impression from civilized children that the construction of these
> dams is a product of education, and no doubt education has much
> to do with it. But in reality this development is organically deter-
> mined and fixed by heredity, and it can occasionally occur with-
> out any help at all from education [1905, pp. 177-178].[6]

Freud's ego psychology, which he began to develop in "The
Unconscious" (1915b), and continued in 1923, 1926, 1932,
and 1937, increasingly implied such an intrinsic restraining
factor among the other intrinsic factors in ego development.
Anna Freud's (1936) work on defenses, Hartmann's (1939) on
adaptation, and Erikson's (1939, 1940) on psychosocial development made this factor more explicit. Finally, Hartmann,
Kris, and Loewenstein (1946) arrived at the explicit recognition that the ego in general (and this implies those of its
functions which restrain instinctual drives) cannot be derived
from the conflict between instinctual drives and reality. They
concluded therefore that the assumption that the ego differentiates from the id under the impact of reality is untenable and
must be replaced by the assumption that both id and ego
differentiate from a common undifferentiated matrix. They
further concluded that the ego enters the conflict between id
and environment as an independent agent rooted in, among
other things, both restraining and adaptive intrinsic matura-

---

[6] For a parallel statement see Freud (1900, p. 537).

tional factors. The discussion of ego development in general and of the adaptive and other intrinsic maturational factors involved in it are beyond the scope of this paper, yet I want to conclude this section with the most general formulation of the intrinsic maturational factors to be found in psychoanalytic literature. It is Erikson's:

[In this] sequence . . . the child merely obeys, and on the whole can be trusted to obey inner laws of development, namely those laws which in the prenatal period formed one organ after another, and now (as these organs reach out to reality) create one behavior item after another [1940, p. 717].

[Further:] . . . this evolutionary principle of epigenesis . . . governs the unfolding before birth of the organic basis for all behavior and continues after birth to govern the unfolding of an individual's social potentialities in the successive encounters of impulse systems and cultural realities [1939, pp. 131-132].

I will now briefly survey some observations and some theories other than psychoanalytic which seem to parallel the developmental concepts of psychoanalysis here discussed. The theoretical significance of these similarities is still far from clear. Nor are the observations and theories I will sketch necessarily uncontested. They are presented here partly to show the existence of trends convergent with Freud's conceptions, which stood alone when he advanced them and for a long time thereafter, and partly because some of them seem to have arisen under Freud's influence.

The central implication of the concept of the instinctual drive is that there are certain unlearned appetitive behaviors. The findings obtained by means of the genetic approach show that there exist stages of development determined by intrinsic maturational factors, that these stages are decisive for the effect of experiences encountered during them, and that early experiences are decisive for the whole course of development. The study of the behavior of animals has brought forth many parallel findings. Whether these parallel observations and concepts confirm the basic developmental conceptions of psychoanalysis cannot be unequivocally established at present. Appetitive behaviors in animals have been observed by Whitman (1919), Heinroth (1910, 1938), and Craig (1918). Lashley (1914, 1938) also studied these, called them instincts, and distinguished them from habits as "prefunctional" (that is, independent of experience), and from reflexes as flexible and complex. Whitman's, Heinroth's, and Craig's observations were systematically followed up by Lorenz (1935, 1937a, 1937b, 1937c, 1942-43), who explained these appetitive behaviors in terms of the concepts of "innate releasing mechanisms" and "reaction-specific energies," which are parallel to the psychoanalytic concept of the instinctual drives as intrinsic maturational factors. Lorenz's work was followed up by a group of investigators who call their discipline ethology, and their findings necessitated, among others, the concept of "innate inhibitory mechanisms" (Thorpe, 1956), which seem to parallel the intrinsic restraining factors of psychoanalysis.

Richter's and Young's studies of appetites followed Katz's exploratory studies on hunger and appetite and Davis's studies on self-selection of diet in the human child. Richter (1941), having destroyed the organ or center for the homeostatic regulation of liquid intake, salinity, temperature, etc., observed appetitive behavior which tended to restore the equilibrium previously apparently maintained by the extirpated organ. He concluded from his observations:

> The results . . . establish the fact that, after the physiological means of maintaining a constant internal environment have been removed, the organism itself makes an effort to attain this end. We may conclude either that the behavior factors take over only after the physiological factors have been eliminated or that in the intact organism they both must function more or less at the same time. In all probability the latter conclusion gives the most accurate description of this situation [p. 108].

Richter termed these behavioral factors "drives." Young (1949) in his experiments demonstrated that in the selection of food, three factors, physiological need, a behavioral factor which he termed *preference* or *hedonic arousal*, and learning usually collaborate and can substitute for each other adaptively, but that any one of them may also conflict with the others and can be experimentally manipulated so that either the preference or the learning will result in unadaptive behavior, i.e., behavior contrary to the physiological needs of the organism. It is hardly necessary to say that such relationships between instinctual drives, physiological needs, and experience in man are clinical commonplaces. These observations, in addition to being parallel to psychoanalytic observation and theory, highlight the fact that "drive" and "preference" are not identical with physiological needs, nor is the principle of tension reduction identical with the homeostatic regulations of the organism, though only too many psychoanalysts and psychologists have gratuitously assumed this to be the case.

Stages of maturation whose sequence is independent of experience and which determine the impact and subsequent effects of the experiences taking place in them have been demonstrated in animals by Scott and Marston (1950), Scott, Fredericson, and Fuller (1951), and others. They designate these stages as "sensitive periods," a term which was introduced by Lorenz (1935) to describe the early and brief period when, in certain species of birds, the objects encountered determine the subsequent social relationships of the individual.[7] The process itself he named "imprinting." Imprinting was observed by Craig (1913, 1914), and others before him, and has since been confirmed for various species of birds and for a few species of mammals (see Beach and Jaynes, 1954). Of these studies the outstanding ones are those of Jaynes (1956, 1957) and Hess (1959).

Freud's proposition that early experiences are of particular significance for later development has other parallels besides

---

[7] For Lorenz's further observations, see (1957).

the studies of imprinting. Notwithstanding Orlansky's (1949) conclusion that the evidence for Freud's thesis is meager, and the negative results of the replications of Hunt's (1939, 1941) "hoarding" studies (e.g., McKelvey and Marx, 1951), parallel propositions derived from animal experiments have been accumulating in the literature (see Beach and Jaynes, 1954). An early observation by Lashley (1914) is of historical interest, and Levy's pioneering studies (1934, 1935, 1938) should also be mentioned. More recent studies are those of Fredericson (1951), Kahn (1951), Hall and Whiteman (1951), Christie (1952), Kagan and Beach (1953), Thompson and Woodburn (1954), Thompson and Heron (1954); Bernstein (1952), Scott (1955), Weininger (1956), Levine (1956) (experiments on early handling); Nissen et al. (1951), Riesen (1951) (early sensory and motor deprivation); and Harlow and Zimmermann (1959) ("mothering").

In addition to these observations and concepts, three major theories, those of Piaget, Werner, and Hebb, also show some parallels to Freud's theory. Piaget's concepts are in general radically different from those of psychoanalysis (Piaget, 1956). Nevertheless, both are developmental psychologies, and for this reason a number of parallels exist between them.[8] Two of these are relevant here: first, Piaget (1937a, 1937b) too assumes an intrinsic maturational factor (the circular reflex and its disequilibrium, i.e., the motivation he terms "desirability"); and second, one of his crucial conceptions is that intelligence develops through a series of stages. Werner's (1926, 1949, 1952) theory of development and his physiognomic, sensoritonic theory of perception and cognition also involve intrinsic maturational factors and a conception of stages (levels) of development. Hebb's (1949) neurological theory of behavior emphasizes the pre-experiential and autonomous activity of the brain, the processes which take place between the

---

[8] P. H. Wolff's (1960) comparative study of the theories of psychoanalysis and Piaget develops this point.

stimulus and the response, and the slowness of early learning in contrast to late learning, all of which seem to imply an intrinsic maturational factor and a specific role of early development.[9]

To sum up: The core of psychoanalysis as a developmental psychology is the concepts of instinctual drives and restraining factors and the genetic approach, which are in sharp contrast to the agenetic conceptions of behavioristic learning theories and neo-Freudian psychodynamics. These concepts and the basic observations underlying them have parallels in the concepts, observations, and experimental findings of ethology, in the experimental findings concerning appetites, developmental phases, and the effects of early experiences on mature behavior in animals, in Werner's and Piaget's theories of development, and in the developmental aspect of Hebb's neurological theory.

THE NATURE OF THE INSTINCTUAL DRIVE AND ITS RELATION TO EXPERIENCE

To clarify the relationship between experience and the instinctual drive, a further examination must be made of the concept of instinctual drive, particularly of the subsidiary concepts of cathexis, zone, aim, and object, because it is by means of these that the psychoanalytic theory unites the intrinsic and the experiential components of psychological development. A brief review of Freud's (1905) theory of psychosexual development will provide the background for this discussion.

Freud outlined his theory of the nature and development of the instinctual drive in *Three Essays on the Theory of Sexuality* (1905), primarily in regard to the sexual instinct. He marshaled evidence concerning the developmental levels, variations, and ecology of sexual behavior: he invoked evidence showing that perversions and inversions can occur in people

---

[9] I. H. Paul's study (1959) sheds further light on the parallel characteristics of Freud's and Hebb's theories.

who are not otherwise maladjusted; that some have been accepted practices in high civilizations; that in situations of deprivation they are practiced by people to whom they are alien otherwise; that most of them appear transiently in infancy and childhood; that they are common contents of the fantasies, practices, and symptoms of neurotic and psychotic patients; and that many of them appear as parts of the play preceding sexual intercourse. Most of this evidence is amply supported by statistical studies of human sexual patterns (Kinsey et al., 1948, 1953) and parallel evidence concerning animals is now also available (Ford and Beach, 1951).

What inferences did Freud draw concerning the *development* of the instinctual drive? He concluded that perversions and inversions correspond to early maturational forms of the sexual instinct which in the usual course of development leave a residue that is later integrated with, and functions under the primacy of, the fully developed genital sexual instinct. If this development is impeded, or if the fully developed sexual drive is interfered with, perversions, inversions, or related symbolic substitute behaviors will arise. The implications of Freud's conclusions are paralleled in Werner's conception of the relationship between genetic levels: " . . . all higher organisms manifest a certain range of operations of genetically different levels . . . the more mature individual compared with the less mature has at his disposal a greater number of developmentally different operations" (1957, pp. 20-21).

What inferences did Freud draw as to the *nature* of the instinctual drive? He concluded that the instinctual drive is a force which expends energy in its work, has a source, an aim, and an object (see also Freud, 1915a). The source is the erotogenic zone (e.g., the mouth in the oral phase) which changes from phase to phase. The aim is the tendency to discharge the accumulated energy of the instinctual drive. The object is both the stimulus which releases the energy-discharging action, and the object toward which the action is directed. If internal restraining factors develop prematurely, or if they are excessively strengthened by experience, or if external conditions prevent discharge, the energy of the instinctual drive is diverted (displaced) into collateral channels or is regressively displaced to an earlier maturational (zonal) position, and will be discharged in the form of a perversion, inversion, or symptom.

The phenomenon of displacement was one of Freud's earliest and most original observations. Freud discovered, as early as 1893, by means of the cathartic method, that the abreaction of dammed-up "affects" results in the disappearance of symptoms which are apparently unrelated to the "affect" in question. It was to explain these discoveries that Freud (1894) first introduced a quantitative concept (affect quantity) into his theory:

> . . . among the psychic functions there is something which should be differentiated (an amount of affect, a sum of excitation), something having all the attributes of quantity—although we possess no means of measuring it—a something which is capable of increase, decrease, displacement and discharge, and which extends itself over the memory-traces of an idea like an electric charge over the surface of the body [1894, p. 75].

Later on, Freud conceptualized this quantity as cathexis (energy charge), and this concept plays an important role in his theory of development. For instance, there are at least two ways of accounting for the shifts in the course of maturation from one erogenous zone as the source of instinctual-drive energy to another. These shifts can be explained by assuming that cathexes are displaced from one zone to another, or by assuming that the erogenous zones mature in sequence, each of them, when matured, becoming a source of cathexes of a specific quality.

The concept of cathexis is crucial for psychoanalysis as a developmental psychology not only in connection with displacement, but in another respect as well. Every theory of human behavior must account for the basic observation that there is a difference between those behaviors which are peremptory—that is, over which the individual has no control[10]—and those which the individual can take or leave. Obsessive ideas and compulsive acts are of the former type; everyday behavior is, by and large, of the latter. This difference is significant for developmental psychology because observation shows that peremptory forms of behavior predominate in the early phases of human development, while voluntary ones predominate in later phases. Psychoanalytic theory accounts for the difference between these two types of behavior, and for the shift from the dominance of peremptory behavior, by the proposition that the peremptory behaviors occur when the tendency of cathexes toward displacement and discharge (a tendency common to all energy) is not extensively curtailed by structural limitations (controls). Conversely, in behaviors subject to the control of the individual, the tendency of cathexes toward displacement and discharge is greatly curtailed by controlling structures. The transition from the former to the latter condition is a process of maturation, which involves both instinctual drives and instinctual-drive restraints. Freud (1900) conceptualized this transition as that from the dominance of the primary to that of the secondary process. Present-day psychoanalytic theory (Hartmann, 1950, 1952, 1955; Kris, 1950, 1955; Rapaport, 1959) accounts for this transition by the concept of "neutralization of cathexes" in so far as it refers to the displaceable quantity itself, and "structure formation" (Rapaport, 1951) in so far as it refers to the conditions limiting the displacement and discharge of these quantities. Since neutralization of cathexes is one aspect of the development of instinctual drives, and since structure formation—one of the implications of this development—seems to be codetermined by experience (see

---

[10] This does not include those behaviors whose initiation the individual does control, but whose manner of execution is automatized and thus beyond his conscious control (see Hartmann, 1939).

Rapaport, 1958, on stimulus nutriment), here we encounter one of the ways in which an intrinsic maturational factor interacts with and is modified by experience.

We must now turn to the concepts of zone and aim. According to Freud,

> ... in itself an instinct is without quality ... [it is] a measure of the demand made [by the organism] upon the mind for work. What distinguishes the instincts from one another and endows them with specific qualities is their relation to their somatic sources and their aims. The source of an instinct is a process of excitation occurring in an organ and the immediate aim of the instinct lies in the removal of this organic stimulus [1905, p. 168].

But if the aim is the universal tendency of all drives toward discharge,[11] how can this aim lend distinctive qualities to different instinctual drives? The answer is that Freud used the term "aim" in two different senses.[12] One of these is the tendency toward discharge; the other becomes clear in, for instance, his discussion of the sexual aim in inversion. He wrote:

> Among men, intercourse *per anum* by no means coincides with inversion; masturbation is quite as frequently their exclusive aim, and it is even true that restrictions of sexual aim—to the point of its being limited to simple outpourings of emotion—are common ... [1905, pp. 145-146].

Clearly, in this second sense of the term, the aim can be restricted, displaced, and substituted for. This aim is not the universal discharge tendency itself, but something more specific. What is it? Freud's various attempts to answer this question contain unresolved contradictions.[13] The answer to the question of what endows the instinctual drive with quality,

---

[11] See p. 222 above.

[12] This is particularly striking in "Instincts and Their Vicissitudes" (1915a).

[13] I have attempted to demonstrate this in some detail in my study of activity and passivity (1953b).

that is to say, what the aim in this second sense is, is, I believe, given by Erikson's concept of instinctual modes (1937, 1950b). Erikson points out that all zones—and, indeed, all functioning organs—have modes, determined by the mechanics of their functioning (e.g., the anus expels and retains), and these modes in turn characterize the discharge action proper to the zone. This amounts to the assumption that the various instinctual drives obtain their distinctive quality from these modes, that is, from the functional patterns of the zones, rather than from energies specific to each zone. The maturational shifts from zone to zone would thus be explained by displacement of cathexes rather than by zonal production of specific cathexes. This explanation would lead to the conception of a central rather than zonal origin of instinctual-drive energy. This conception in turn implies that the instinctual drive differentiates and gains a particular quality when it cathects each zone at the appropriate phase of maturation. The added advantage of this explanation, if it should prove to be empirically tenable and consistent with the rest of the theory, is that it would resolve the unsettled issue of the pluralistic vs. the monistic theory of instinctual drives in favor of the monistic. Ultimately, however, this is an empirical question, and we must be prepared for the possibility that the empirical evidence will require the postulation of a dual (both zonal and central) origin of instinctual-drive energy.

The assumption that the modes are the crucial characteristics of the zones has still other important consequences for psychoanalysis as a developmental psychology. Erikson has demonstrated that these modes and their sequence of ascendancy are not determined by experience. Thus they too are intrinsic maturational factors. However, their fate is co-determined by experience. Any given mode, when it reaches its specific phase of ascendancy, as experience accumulates generalizes to and becomes characteristic of other zones, organs, and behaviors also (e.g., the retentive mode of the anal phase will spread to prehensile behaviors, giving them a grabbing and possessive character). Indeed, this "estrangement" of modes (Erikson, 1937) from their zone progressively changes them from modes of instinctual-drive action into modes available for use in adaptive behavior, and ultimately transforms them into basic thought patterns. Both adaptive behavior and thought patterns are molded by experience and imply that this "estrangement" is codetermined by experience. Moreover, Erikson has also demonstrated that the encounter of these modes with the institutions of a given society shapes and selects those behavior modalities in the individual which are viable in that society (1950b), relegating the others to subordinate roles or suppressing them altogether. Here again we encounter an interaction between an intrinsic maturational factor and experience.

We turn now to the object of the instinctual drive (Freud, 1905, 1915a). On scrutiny, the concept of object proves to be one of Freud's most important conceptual inventions. It is the core of his solution of the problem of the purposiveness of human behavior. The instinctual drive is a force concept, that is, a causal concept, which cannot per se explain the purposiveness of behavior. The proposition that the object is one of the defining characteristics of the instinctual drive implies, however, that this force exerts an effect only when it encounters its object. Thus the instinctual drive is conceived of not as a blind but as a purposively acting force. The coordination of instinctual drive and object is assumed to be innate, i.e., given by evolution. While this coordination is rigid in lower-order animals, it is relatively flexible in man (see Hartmann, 1948), so that experience can modify the gratification of the instinctual drive by the substitution of objects. Thus in the variability of the object of the instinctual drive we again encounter the interaction of an intrinsic maturational factor with experience.

We may conclude that while in the psychoanalytic theory of development the defining characteristics of the instinctual

drive, its cathexis, mode, and object, are intrinsic maturational factors, their vicissitudes are codetermined by experience. Thus the psychoanalytic theory of development unites
maturational and experiential factors.

I will now review some nonpsychoanalytic parallels to the
observations, concepts, and theories discussed in this section.
Some of them have already been mentioned, and since parallels to the concepts of mode and object would carry us deep
into the literature on learning and into the work of Piaget,
I will concentrate on the parallels to the cathectic theory,
which are mostly in the literature of ethology.[14] In reviewing
these, however, we will also encounter parallels to the concepts of zone, mode, and object.

Lorenz (1937a, 1937b), as we have already seen, introduced
two concepts in his study of appetitive behavior: "innate releasing mechanisms" and "reaction-specific energy." It is the
latter of these that is of importance here. Lorenz defined it as
"energy, specific to one definite activity, [which] is stored up
while this activity remains quiescent and [which] is consumed
in its discharge" (1950, p. 249). This conception appears to be
parallel to the psychoanalytic conception of the zones as the
sources of instinctual drive energy. Lorenz's conception of
instinct also involves an object, the "releaser" which activates
the "innate releasing mechanism." Analyzing experimentally
the characteristics of such objects, he and others (Lorenz,
1950; Tinbergen, 1951) discovered that these objects are aggregates of stimuli, only some of which are indispensable for
effecting release, and various combinations of which can
effect adequate release. The concept of releaser, like Freud's
instinctual-drive object, implies some flexibility of the relation between the innate releasing mechanism and the releaser.

More recent ethological work, however, has led to a broader
conception of the instinct and its relation to the object. Ob-

---

[14] Schur has explored some of these parallels in his recent papers (1958, 1959).

servation and study of the so-called "displacement activities" led at least some ethologists (see Thorpe, 1956) to the assumption of a "drive-specific energy" pertaining to certain groups of innate releasing mechanisms rather than a "reaction-specific energy" pertaining to a single such mechanism. This concept of general drive appears to parallel the conception of the central origin of instinctual-drive energy discussed above.

The displacement activities, named by Armstrong (1947, 1950), were first studied systematically by Tinbergen (1952), who defined them as follows:

> The irrelevancy is found in the fact that although an animal is clearly in fighting motivation, or, in other cases, in mating motivation—in general, when instinct "a" is activated—and although we know by experience that we must expect movements belonging to the executive pattern of this instinct "a," we observe movements belonging to the executive pattern of another instinct, "b." The activity seems to be displaced from instinct "b," to which it belongs, to instinct "a" which uses it as if it were a part of its executive pattern [p. 6].

According to Tinbergen, such displacements occur (a) when there is a conflict between two antagonistic drives (e.g., birds in a conflict between flight and fight may display, instead of either of these behaviors, a fragment of nesting behavior); (b) when an instinct is aroused but cannot be discharged (e.g., when the sex partner is dilatory, foreplay consisting of fragmentary fighting behavior may occur); (c) when excessive arousal has taken place (e.g., after a bird is flushed but encounters no danger, copulation may occur); (d) when stimulation suddenly ceases (e.g., when the opponent suddenly flees, nesting behavior or copulation may ensue); and (e) as an "afterdischarge" when the drive dies down gradually (e.g., after coition, fighting or nesting behavior may occur).

Tinbergen concluded that (a) displacement activities serve as outlets for residual drive-energy; (b) the behavior patterns used as outlets are those which, for some reason, offer least resistance; (c) displacement activities are usually incomplete forms of the drive activity from which the displacement occurred; and finally (d), on Liddell's evidence, " . . . the fact that displacement activities appear before a neurotic stage is reached . . . indicates that outlet through displacement behavior is a form of defense against neurotic disorder of the central nervous system, enabling it to 'get rid' of the surplus of impulses which would otherwise damage it" (1952, p. 22).

The parallel between the psychoanalytic and ethological concepts of displacement needs no further comment.

But what of the relation between drive and object? I have already discussed the object as a releaser. Another relevant finding of the ethologists (see Lorenz, 1950; Tinbergen, 1952) is that the more the object fits the innate releasing mechanism, the lower the drive tension which it will release, and the higher the tension the less fitting the object need be to effect its release. But [15] ethology has made still other discoveries about the object. I have in mind the already-mentioned process of "imprinting," discovered by Craig (1914). Lorenz (1935, 1937c), who explored and named the phenomenon, concluded that (a) in certain species the objects of the social following instinct and of the sexual instinct are not entirely determined as innate receptory patterns, but must be completed by experience; (b) the limits on what objects can be imprinted are, however, innate, though they vary from species to species; (c) once imprinting has occurred, it is practically unalterable; (d) though imprinting occurs in relation to the social following instinct, it determines the object of the sexual instinct; (e) imprinting occurs only in a well-defined, early sensitive period of the animal's life. Most of these conclusions have been confirmed in rigorously controlled experiments by

---

[15] Note the analogy to Freud's formulation that "Where the [drive] constitution is a marked one it will perhaps not require the support of actual experiences; while a great shock in real life will perhaps bring about a neurosis even in an average constitution . . . this view of the relative aetiological importance of what is innate and what is accidentally experienced applies equally in other fields" (1905, p. 171).

Jaynes (1956, 1957), Hess (1959), and others (see Beach and Jaynes, 1954).

Imprinting is a remarkable parallel not only to fixation and to the critical, sensitive periods familiar from the study of both libido and ego development (see Erikson, 1950a, 1950b), but also to Freud's (1905, 1914) propositions that (a) libidinal object choice is not specifically determined by the sexual drive in man, and (b) the first objects of the sexual drive are the objects of the self-preservative drive, that is to say, the people who take care of the infant. Thus in both psychoanalytic and ethological theory, experience plays a role in determining the choice of object, though psychoanalysis finds the role of experience broader than ethology does. This difference is—as Hartmann (1939, 1948) has suggested— probably due to the difference between the role instincts play in the animal's adaptation to reality and the role instinctual drives play in man's.

Object attachment and fixation in psychoanalysis and imprinting in ethology refer to processes which create enduring relations between drives and objects. Since the processes which create enduring relationships of any sort are what we have in mind when we speak of learning, the study of imprinting and fixation might well serve as a point of departure for a learning theory relevant to developmental psychology.

To sum up: The crucial factors in the interaction between the instinctual drive and experience are the cathexes (since their displacements can be and are modulated by experience), the modes (since their capacity to become estranged from their zone, to be displaced to other zones, and to be selectively turned into dominant modalities of behavior can be and is regulated by experience), and the object (because it is subject to substitutions in the course of experience). The literature of ethology provides observations and conceptions which parallel the psychoanalytic observations and conceptions pertaining to the interaction of instinctual drives and experience.

THE DEVELOPMENT OF THINKING

In this attempt to clarify what the basic concepts of psychoanalysis as a developmental psychology are, I have chosen the development of thinking for the third area of discussion partly because the relationship of the primary to the secondary process which plays a central role in it is also crucial for the theory of development in general, and partly because in it we encounter both of the relationships discussed so far (instinctual drives vs. drive-restraining factors, intrinsic maturational vs. experiential factors of development). My purpose in what follows here is to explore the connection between these two relationships in the realm of thinking, and therefore my discussion of the development of thinking will of necessity be a limited one. Even though the development of thinking has many other aspects, I will concentrate only on the relation between the primary and the secondary thought processes. Moreover, though the development of thinking is an integral part of ego development and best discussed in that context, I will avoid a general discussion of its place and role in ego development.

The problem of the relation between instinctual drive and experience arose in Freud's studies not only in the form in which I have presented it above, but also in the form of the relation between drive-representing, wish-fulfilling thought and reality-representing adaptive thought. Freud did much to clarify the relationship between these two types of thought process, particularly in regard to the usual dominance of the latter over the former (see especially *The Interpretation of Dreams*, 1900), but many aspects of their relationship, and in particular their maturational and developmental relationship, remained ambiguous. Freud's discussion of this relationship left the general impression that the secondary process arises from the primary under the impact of experience. Yet, as we shall see, this may not be quite what Freud intended.

In *The Interpretation of Dreams* and *The Psychopathology of Everyday Life* (1901), Freud demonstrated the common characteristics of thinking in dreams, pathological states, and childhood. He termed the process responsible for these characteristics the primary process, in contrast to the process responsible for the ordered forms of adult thought which he termed the secondary process. The proposition that the forms of thought characteristic of dreams, pathological states, and childhood show striking common characteristics and thus belong to closely related developmental levels is paralleled by Werner (1926). But Freud's (1900, 1911) assertion that the primary process is the matrix out of which the secondary process arises involves him in contradictions. He wrote (1900):

> The bitter experience of life must have changed this primitive thought-activity into a more expedient secondary one [p. 566].[16]
> [And:] . . . [the] primitive psychical apparatus . . . [is] regulated by an effort to avoid an accumulation of excitation . . . [and avoids it by] repeating the experience of satisfaction, which involved a diminution of excitation . . . A current of this kind . . . we have termed a 'wish'. . . . The first wishing seems to have been a hallucinatory cathecting of the memory of satisfaction. Such hallucinations, however, . . . proved to be inadequate to bring about . . . satisfaction. A second activity—or, as we put it, the activity of a second system—became necessary, which . . . diverted the excitation arising from the need along a roundabout path which ultimately, by means of voluntary movement, altered the external world in such a way that it became possible to arrive at a real perception of the object of satisfaction [pp. 598-599].
> [Further:] Thought is after all nothing but a substitute for a hallucinatory wish . . . nothing but a wish can set our mental apparatus at work [p. 567].

Finally, he links the secondary process to the restraining factors:

> . . . the *first* . . . system is directed towards securing the *free discharge* of the quantities of excitation, while the *second* system . . . succeeds in *inhibiting* this discharge and in transforming the cathexis into a quiescent one . . . [p. 599].

---

[16] See also Freud (1911, p. 219).

Clearly, here Freud assumed that the secondary process arises from the primary process owing to "the bitter experience of life," and is motivated by the same wishes as the primary process; so that secondary-process thinking is merely a detour toward the memory of gratification; and although it has a controlling function over the primary process (in suppressing, delaying, and detouring it), it does not contribute anything to the thought process other than what is required by the demands of reality. We may paraphrase this conception as follows: the secondary process is a learned modification of the primary one and no intrinsic maturational factor contributes to its development. But Freud did not consistently carry out the conception just summarized in that he treated the idea of a primordial mental apparatus possessing only a primary process as a theoretical model, rather than as an actuality:

> It is true that, so far as we know, no psychical apparatus exists which possesses a primary process only and that such an apparatus is to that extent a theoretical fiction. But this much is a fact: the primary processes are present in the mental apparatus from the first, while it is only during the course of life that the secondary processes unfold, and come to inhibit and overlay the primary ones; it may even be that their complete domination is not attained until the prime of life [1900, p. 603].

Here we are faced with a difficulty. If a purely primary-process mental apparatus is a theoretical fiction, then it must be assumed that the secondary process exists from the beginning. But Freud asserts that the secondary process develops "only during the course of life." If he means that it is not there in the beginning and arises only from the impact of "the bitter experience of life," then his theory at this point is a purely environmentalistic one, and contradicts not only his assertion that no pure primary-process psychical apparatus can exist, but his conception of intrinsic maturational restraining factors as well. One obvious way out of this difficulty is to interpret Freud's proposition as follows: rudiments of the secondary process are present from the beginning but their maturation is slow and dependent on "the bitter experience of life." This assumption would be consistent with a developmental theory of thinking.[17] *The Interpretation of Dreams* provides no grounds for the assumption that this is what he meant, and we can only conclude that Freud at that time did not perceive the difficulty, and therefore could not resolve it. It seems that when Freud introduced the concept of the instinctual drive he only partially overcame his early environmentalism,[18] and it is still very much in evidence in his conception of the secondary process.

A reconsideration of *Totem and Taboo* (1913) will shed further light on Freud's conception of the secondary process. His discussion of animism as a theoretical system and of the synthetic function inherent in it came close to an explicit recognition of an intrinsic maturational factor in the development of the secondary process. Yet Freud did not disentangle the intrinsic factor but, rather, gave an experiential explanation of the origins of taboos.

In *Totem and Taboo* Freud amassed evidence of the striking correspondence between the magic and animistic conceptions and practices of primitives and compulsion-neurotics (pp. 28-29), and set out to explain these correspondences. He concluded that the conceptions and practices of primitives and compulsion-neurotics reflect and restrain the same sexual and hostile impulses. Once he had reached this conclusion, he was faced with the question, Whence the tendency toward this restraint?

In other writings of the same period he explained the restraint in neurotics by the "antithesis between ego-instincts and sexual instincts" (1914, p. 79). From our present vantage point these ego instincts, like other instinctual drives, would represent an intrinsic maturational factor. In *Totem and Taboo*,

[17] With Piaget's in particular; see Wolff (1960).
[18] See p. 212 above.

however, Freud rejected the possibility that the restraint is
exerted by instincts with the argument that if this were the
case, no external restraining laws like taboos would be necessary. Freud quotes Frazer in support of his argument:

> 'It is not easy to see why any deep human instinct should need
> to be reinforced by law. There is no law commanding men to eat
> and drink or forbidding them to put their hands in the fire. . . .
> The law only forbids men to do what their instincts incline them
> to do; what nature itself prohibits and punishes, it would be super-
> fluous for the law to prohibit and punish' [1913, p. 123].

With Wundt, he regarded taboo as "the oldest human unwritten code of laws" (1913, p. 18). Searching for the origin
of this law, he arrived, by his method of reconstruction, at the
conclusion that these taboos have a historical, experiential
origin in the murder of the primal father by his sons, followed by the sons' establishment of rules to prevent the recur-
rence of such deeds:

> Taboos we must suppose are prohibitions of primaeval antiquity
> which were at some time externally imposed upon a generation of
> primitive men; they must . . . no doubt have been impressed on
> them violently by the previous generation [p. 31].

Thus his explanation of the origins of taboo, like his explanation of the secondary process, was environmental, experiential, and not one in terms of an intrinsic maturational
factor. But since he assumed that "Unless psychical processes
were continued from one generation to another, if each
generation were obliged to acquire its attitude to life anew,
there would be no progress" (1913, p. 158), he had to explain
how these environmentally imposed restrictions were transmitted, and his explanation was Lamarckian:

> A part of the problem seems to be met by the inheritance of psychi-
> cal dispositions which, however, need to be given some sort of
> impetus in the life of the individual before they can be roused into
> actual operation [1913, p. 158].

The difficulties involved in adopting Lamarck's "inheritance of acquired characteristics" are obvious. But this explanation had still other difficulties. Freud himself wondered whether he was making the same mistake which led him, before 1897, to assume the reality of seduction in infancy. He wrote:

> If . . . we inquire among these neurotics to discover what were the deeds which provoked these reactions, we shall be disappointed. We find no deeds, but only impulses and emotions, set upon evil ends but held back from their achievement. What lie behind the sense of guilt of neurotics are always *psychical* realities and never *factual* ones. . . . May not the same have been true of primitive men? [1913, p. 159].

A positive answer to this question—a rejection of the assumption of the murder of the primal father as a historical fact—would have opened the way to a generalized conception of the secondary process and of drive restraint in terms of an intrinsic maturational factor, just as the rejection of the historical reality of seduction in infancy led to the conceptualization of the instinctual drive as an intrinsic maturational factor. However, Freud rejected this solution, even though, as we have seen (p. 215ff.), he did have a partial conception of an intrinsic developmental restraining factor.

> Nor must we let ourselves be influenced too far in our judgment of primitive men by the analogy of neurotics. There are distinctions, too, which must be borne in mind . . . neurotics are above all *inhibited* in their actions: with them the thought is a complete substitute for the deed. Primitive men, on the other hand, are *uninhibited* . . . the deed . . . is a substitute for the thought. And that is why, without laying claim to any finality of judgment, I think that in the case before us it may safely be assumed that 'in the beginning was the Deed' [1913, p. 161].

Thus we see that here Freud made a decision analogous to the one which he had to revoke in 1897.

But if we shift our attention from Freud's conception of the origins of taboos to his discussion of their nature, we obtain a very different picture of his conception of the origins and nature of the secondary process. Throughout *Totem and Taboo* Freud stressed that taboos are not isolated phenomena but part of a broad system of thought:

> The human race . . . [has] in the course of ages developed three such systems of thought—three great pictures of the universe: animistic (or mythological), religious and scientific. Of these, animism . . . is perhaps the one which is most consistent and exhaustive and which gives a truly complete explanation of the nature of the universe [p. 77].
> . . . man's first theoretical achievement—the creation of spirits—seems to have arisen from the same source as the first moral restrictions to which he was subjected—the observances of taboo [p. 93].

Thus Freud viewed totem and taboo as integral parts of the animistic theory of the world. The question which now presents itself to us is: how can such an all-embracing system of thought arise from specific prohibitions imposed in ancient times and transmitted by the "inheritance of acquired characteristics?" Freud was aware of this problem:

> . . . we shall have to investigate that system's psychological characteristics . . . . For the moment I will only say that the prototype of all such systems is what we have termed the 'secondary revision' of the content of dreams. And we must not forget that, at and after the stage at which systems are constructed, two sets of reasons can be assigned for every psychical event . . . one set belonging to the system and the other set real but unconscious [p. 65].

Thus here Freud places "systems" on the same level as unconscious impulses, refers to them as "reasons" (that is, causal factors), and, as we shall see, attributes to them a function independent from both external environmental pressure and id forces.

> The secondary revision of the product of the dream-work is an admirable example of the nature and pretensions of a system. There is an intellectual function in us which demands unity, connection and intelligibility from any material, whether of perception or

thought, that comes within its grasp; and if, as a result of special circumstances, it is unable to establish a true connection, it does not hesitate to fabricate a false one. Systems constructed in this way are known to us not only from dreams, but also from phobias, from obsessive thinking and from delusions. The construction of systems is seen most strikingly in delusional disorders (in paranoia) . . . [p. 95].

Later on—when he had already laid down the foundations of his ego psychology in which thinking was conceived of as a function of the ego and the apparatuses used in thinking as ego apparatuses—Freud (1926) conceptualized these unifying, connecting, rationalizing processes as the synthetic functions of the ego. His reference here to these synthetic functions throws new light on his conception of the secondary process. In *The Interpretation of Dreams* (1900) the main attributes of the secondary process were the instinctual drive-restraining function and reality orientation. In "Formulations on the Two Principles of Mental Functioning" (1911), this reality orientation was elaborated into the reality principle, whose relation to the secondary process was conceived to be analogous to the relation of the pleasure principle to the primary process. The conception of the secondary process changes radically, however, when in *Totem and Taboo* Freud attributes a unifying, connecting, and rationalizing synthetic function to it.[19] Since the synthetic function emerges here as a new function unique to the secondary process, independent of the demands of instinctual drives as well as of those of reality, it is no longer a mere superimposition upon the primary processes by the dire necessities of reality. In the terminology of present-day psychoanalytic ego psychology, we formulate this state of affairs as follows: the secondary process and its synthetic function are autonomous ego functions in relation to both instinctual drives and external stimulation (Rapa-

---

[19] In *The Interpretation of Dreams* there were already traces of such a conception, but they were not made explicit.

port, 1958). Furthermore, Freud's formulation implies that there are various such synthetic functions which differ from one another: we observe these in, for instance, paranoia, dream, phobias, animism, religion, and science. In my study of states of consciousness (Rapaport, 1957) I offered independent evidence in support of this proposition.

We may conclude that Freud's study of animism as a theoretical system brought him to the threshold of the discovery of an autonomous synthetic function of the secondary process in addition to the restraining function he had already attributed to it (1900, p. 599). As already mentioned, he finally crossed this threshold in *The Problem of Anxiety* (1926). In "Analysis Terminable and Interminable" (1937) he went further and spoke of innate ego factors in general, not limiting them to the restraining and integrating factors. These beginnings led Hartmann (1939) and Hartmann, Kris, and, Loewenstein (1946) to the conclusion that the id and the ego both arise from a common undifferentiated matrix, and that the ego apparatuses of primary autonomy—the psychological apparatuses of motility, perception, and memory—already exist in the undifferentiated phase. I have argued elsewhere (1951) that the discharge thresholds of the instinctual drive too are primarily autonomous apparatuses, and are, in fact, the prototypes of all restraining structures. Hartmann, Kris, and Loewenstein's, as well as my own propositions imply that the primary and secondary processes also arise by differentiation from a common matrix and that therefore the rudiments of the secondary process too exist from the beginning—a hypothesis which clarifies Freud's proposition that an organism which operates by primary processes alone does not exist.

We have already discussed some of the relationships[20] which suggest the assumption of an intrinsic maturational restraining factor. We have now encountered a set of considerations which seems to make such an assumption inevitable: (1) the

---

[20] See p. 215ff. and p. 233ff. above.

close relation between restraining factors and secondary process; (2) the autonomous character of the secondary process and of the synthetic function, eliminating the possibility that their origins are environmental; (3) the primary autonomous ego apparatuses involved in secondary-process thinking.

My review of *Totem and Taboo* and particularly of the concept of animism has led to two conclusions: First, the secondary process does not simply arise from the primary process under the pressure of environmental necessity, but, like the primary process, arises from an undifferentiated matrix in which its intrinsic maturational restraining and integrating factors are already present.[21] Second, animism, which is so striking a form of the primary process in pathological states, preliterates, children, etc., is a "theoretical" system and as such is organized in terms of a synthetic function alien to the primary processes,[22] demonstrating that animistic thought and practices involve secondary processes as well as primary. But if secondary processes are involved in the thinking of primitives just as much as in our everyday, ordered, logical, and scientific thinking, how does our thinking differ from that of primitives? To answer this question we must again go somewhat beyond what Freud had to say. The first answer restates the obvious: the primitive is in his own way no less realistic, logical, and adroit in using his thinking in the service of adaptation than we are.[23] The second answer we have already anticipated: all thought forms involve both primary and secondary processes, but differ from each other in the kind of synthetic function they involve; that is to say, they differ in the degree of dominance the secondary process achieves over the primary. Not even our ordered thinking is free of primary processes. As Freud wrote:

---

[21] See Bergman and Escalona's (1949) observations showing that this process of differentiation misfires in autistic children.

[22] See Freud (1915b, p. 119).

[23] Hartmann (1939, 1956) has demonstrated that adaptation to reality is subserved by both rational and irrational processes.

... thinking must aim at freeing itself more and more from exclusive regulation by the unpleasure principle and at restricting the development of affect in thought-activity to the minimum required for acting as a signal. ... As we well know, however, that aim is seldom attained completely, even in normal mental life, and our thinking always remains exposed to falsification by interference from the unpleasure principle [1900, pp. 602-603].

In arguing that in both the primitive's and our everyday thinking, primary-process forms of thought are integrated by the synthetic function of the secondary process, I have, by implication, equated our wishful thinking and the primary-process forms in the everyday thinking of primitives. But this equation is fallacious. Wishful distortions (e.g., parapraxes) are *intrusions* of primary processes into our secondary-process thinking. The primitive's everyday thinking is not an intrusion into anything: it is subject to a synthetic function and has a secondary-process organization, though this synthesis and organization are by no means as stringent as those of our everyday thinking. The primitive's thinking should be compared only to our own socially sanctioned superstitions, biases and values which, although their form often reveals their primary-process origin, are integrated into our secondary-process thinking. The primitive's socially sanctioned animistic thinking, which has its own secondary-process organization, cannot be compared with our "personal" primary processes (e.g., in dreams, hallucinations, etc.): the primitive too has "personal" primary processes and these are just as much restrained by his secondary processes as are ours by our secondary processes. The secondary processes (of whatever kind) integrate and use primary-process mechanisms, which were originally means of wish fulfillment, as means of adaptation (see Hartmann, 1939; Kris, 1950). It is the primary processes *not* so integrated over which the system of secondary processes exerts its controlling function. Paradoxical as it may sound, one might speak here of a difference between structuralized and nonstructuralized primary-process mechanisms. [24] The essence of this difference seems to be that structuralized primary-process mechanisms integrated by secondary processes are energized by cathexes of greater neutralization than are nonstructuralized primary-process mechanisms.

We may conclude, then, that both the primary processes and the secondary processes involve intrinsic maturational factors. The intrinsic maturational factors involved in the primary processes are related to the instinctual drives, and those involved in the secondary processes are related to instinctual-drive restraints and synthetic functions. We must add, however, that the ontogenetic course of these restraining factors, and their interaction with experience (see Rapaport, 1958), have been given very little attention so far. It is probable that the study of these relations of restraining factors will center on the problem of structure development and will lead to a learning theory compatible with developmental psychology.

Now, for some parallels to the psychoanalytic conception of the relation between the primary and secondary processes. The first of these is a historical example of the transition from one form of the synthetic function to another, higher one. The second is an example of the various forms the synthetic function takes in the young child. The third is an observational and theoretical parallel to the proposition that the secondary process involves intrinsic maturational factors and its course of development consists of a succession of predetermined stages.

F. M. Cornford, the philosopher, re-examined the thesis that the Greek philosophers of Miletus were the first empirical

---

[24] The primary-process mechanisms (displacement, condensation, substitution) are basically means of immediate drive discharge. In this role they have a structural characteristic, since the discharge attained through them is slower than a discharge which can take place without them. Nevertheless, they are at best *ad hoc*, short-lived structures. When they appear in a form which is integrated into the secondary process, their lifetime is increased: they have become further structuralized.

scientists of the Western world. In *Unwritten Philosophy* (1950) and *Timor Dei Principium Sapientiae* (1952) he demonstrated that these Greek "scientists" were not empiricists, but dogmatists who took the world explanation contained in the Orphic myths, gave it rational form, and arrived at what appeared to be a theory based on empirical observations. He concluded:

> ... Anaximander's cosmogony ... [is] a rationalization of an ancient Creation Myth. ... He inherited from mythical thought a scheme of cosmogony in which the operating factors had originally been conceived as personal God. Expurgating the factors he could recognize as mythical, he substituted for the Gods the operation of powers, such as "the hot" and "the cold" which he took to be unquestionably natural. But he kept the fundamental framework of the myth [1950, pp. 121-122].
>
> What we claim to have established ... is that the pattern of Ionian cosmogony, for all its appearance of complete rationalism, is not a free construction of the intellect, reasoning from direct observation of the existing world [1952, p. 201].

The Orphic myths and practices, just like the animistic conceptions and practices of primitives, were on the one hand dominated by primary-process mechanisms, and on the other hand were welded into a system by a synthetic function. The rationalized form the Milesian philosophers gave to the mythological world view, which made their assertions appear to be the results of observation, was but a new system, a new synthesis, a shift to a new level of the secondary process,[25] which initiated a new integration of the primary processes by the secondary, an achievement which affected not only Greek civilization but ultimately all Western civilization.

Piaget showed that the dominance of primary-process forms of thought in children—which Freud inferred, by the genetic approach, from the reports of his adult patients—can be demonstrated by direct interviews. He showed (1928, 1929, 1930, 1931) that children's thinking develops from what he calls a naïve realism through animism to artificialism. These

---

[25] See Freud (1915a, pp. 124-125).

forms of thought characterize children's explanations of both familiar and unfamiliar phenomena, and are not limited to thought pertaining to instinctual-drive objects. Thus here too we encounter structured primary-process mechanisms, to use the terminology we suggested. The child's primary-processlike thinking orients his actions to his limited world and to his limited objectives more or less as adequately as the primitive's orients him to his.

In his studies of the first years of life Piaget (1937a, 1937b) demonstrated that "abstract" intelligence develops from sensorimotor intelligence. According to him, circular reflexes, i.e., reflexlike, but self-stimulating, behaviors (e.g., grasping which engenders further grasping) are the innate sensorimotor foundations of the development of intelligence. These behaviors are activated by appropriate objects (e.g., objects which are suckable, graspable, visible, etc.) to which they are "preadapted." When different—but not too different—objects activate these circular reflex behaviors, the behaviors (more precisely, the schemata underlying them) begin to accommodate to these objects and, in doing so, differentiate. When an object becomes the object of several of these circular reflexes (e.g., vision and prehension), the reflex behaviors begin to coordinate and a different kind of self-stimulating (circular) behavior (one which is capable of a primitive degree of anticipation), termed a "primary circular reaction," takes shape. The primary circular reactions lead progressively to secondary ones, which in turn initiate tertiary ones, which in turn yield to abstract, though primitive, thinking which can discover, anticipate, and intend without overt sensorimotor action. At each of these stages, behavior has its own form of integration, primitive though it may be, and is realistic and adaptive in its own way, that is to say, is not exclusively guided by somatic need or instinctual-drive satisfaction. Yet behavior at all of these stages is pervaded by phenomena similar to condensation, displacement, and substitution, which are characteristic of the primary process.

CONCLUSION

The most general propositions of psychoanalytic developmental psychology may be tentatively formulated as follows:

1. Behavior is determined by both intrinsic maturational factors and experience.

2. The central intrinsic maturational factors are instinctual drives and the structures restraining them.

3. The process of development is not a continuous quantitative growth but a sequence of discontinuous, qualitatively distinct phases.

4. The interaction of the instinctual drive with experience can be traced by the vicissitudes of its defining characteristics: the cathexes, modes, and objects.

5. The development of thought is a progression from the dominance of primary-process forms to the dominance of secondary-process forms. Both of these forms involve intrinsic maturational factors, which can be modified by experience. The particular kind of integration of primary-process forms into the secondary process produces the thought form characteristic of a given culture or state of consciousness. The restraint of the primary process by the secondary process creates the balance between reality adaptation and instinctual-drive satisfaction in the individual.

While the interaction of the intrinsic motivational factors with experience has been demonstrated by psychoanalysis, and while many of the general effects of these interactions are known and understood, the specific mechanisms involved in these interactions—which may be termed learning—are yet to be explored.

BIBLIOGRAPHY

Armstrong, E. A. (1947), *Bird Display and Behaviour*. Oxford: Oxford University Press.
———— (1950), The Nature and Function of Displacement Activities. In *Physiological Mechanisms in Animal Behavior*, Symposia

of the Society for Experimental Biology. New York: Academic Press, pp. 361-382.

Beach, F. A. and Jaynes, J. (1954), Effects of Early Experience upon the Behavior of Animals. *Psychological Bulletin, 51*:239-263.

Benjamin, J. (1959), Prediction and Psychopathological Theory. In *Dynamic Psychopathology in Childhood*, ed. L. Jessner and E. Pavenstedt. New York: Grune & Stratton.

Bergman, P. and Escalona, S. (1949), Unusual Sensitivities in Very Young Children. *The Psychoanalytic Study of the Child, 3/4*:333-352. New York: International Universities Press.

Bernstein, L. (1952), A Note on Christie's "Experimental Naiveté and Experiential Naiveté." *Psychological Bulletin, 49*:38-40.

Breuer, J. and Freud, S. (1895), Studies on Hysteria. *Standard Edition, 2*. London: Hogarth Press, 1955.

Christie, R. (1952), The Effect of Some Early Experiences on the Latent Learning of Adult Rats. *Journal of Experimental Psychology, 43*:281-288.

Coleman, R. W.; Kris, E.; and Provence, S. (1953), The Study of Variations of Early Parental Attitudes. *The Psychoanalytic Study of the Child, 8*:20-47. New York: International Universities Press.

Cornford, F. M. (1950), *Unwritten Philosophy*. Cambridge: Cambridge University Press.

―――― (1952), *Timor Dei Principium Sapientiae*. Cambridge: Cambridge University Press.

Craig, W. (1913), The Stimulation and the Inhibition of Ovulation in Birds and Mammals. *Journal of Animal Behavior, 3*:215-221.

―――― (1914), Male Doves Reared in Isolation. *Journal of Animal Behavior, 4*:121-133.

―――― (1918), Appetites and Aversions as Constituents of Instincts. *Biological Bulletin, 34*:91-107.

Escalona, S., et al. (1952), Early Phases of Personality Development: a Non-normative Study of Infant Behavior. *Monograph of the Society for Research in Child Development, 17*(1); Ser. No. 54.

Erikson, E. H. (1937), Configurations in Play: Clinical Notes. *Psychoanalytic Quarterly, 6*:139-214.

―――― (1939), Observations on Sioux Education. *Journal of Psychology, 7*:101-156.

————— (1940), Problems of Infancy and Early Childhood. In *Cyclopedia of Medicine.* Philadelphia: Davis, pp. 714-730. Also in *Outline of Abnormal Psychology,* ed. G. Murphy and A. Bachrach. New York: Modern Library, 1954, pp. 3-36.

————— (1950a), Growth and Crises of the Healthy Personality. In *Symposium on the Healthy Personality.* Supplement II; Problems of Infancy and Childhood, Transactions of Fourth Conference, March, 1950, ed. M. J. E. Senn. New York: Josiah Macy, Jr. Foundation. Also in *Personality in Nature, Society and Culture,* 2nd ed., ed. C. Kluckhohn and H. Murray. New York: Knopf, 1953, pp. 185-225. Also in Identity and the Life Cycle. *Psychological Issues, 1*:50-100. New York: International Universities Press, 1959.

————— (1950b), *Childhood and Society.* New York: Norton.

Ford, C. S. and Beach, F. A. (1951), *Patterns of Sexual Behavior.* New York: Harper.

Fredericson, E. (1951), Competition: The Effects of Infantile Experience upon Adult Behavior. *Journal of Abnormal and Social Psychology, 46*:406-409.

Freud, A. (1936), *The Ego and the Mechanisms of Defence.* New York: International Universities Press, 1946.

————— and Burlingham, D. T. (1943), *War and Children.* New York: International Universities Press.

————— ————— (1944), *Infants Without Families.* New York: International Universities Press.

————— and Dann, S. (1951), An Experiment in Group Upbringing. *The Psychoanalytic Study of the Child, 6*:127-168. New York: International Universities Press.

Freud, S. (1887-1902), *The Origins of Psychoanalysis: Letters to Wilhelm Fliess, Drafts and Notes: 1887-1902.* New York: Basic Books, 1954.

————— (1893-1896), *Collected Papers, 1*:9-219. London: Hogarth Press, 1948.

————— (1894), The Defence Neuro-Psychoses. *Collected Papers, 1*:59-75. London: Hogarth Press, 1948.

————— (1900), The Interpretation of Dreams. *Standard Edition,* Vols. *4* & *5.* London: Hogarth Press, 1953.

————— (1901), The Psychopathology of Everyday Life. In *The Basic Writings of Sigmund Freud.* New York: Random House, 1945.

—— (1905), Three Essays on the Theory of Sexuality. *Standard Edition*, 7:123-245. London: Hogarth Press, 1953.

—— (1911), Formulations on the Two Principles of Mental Functioning. *Standard Edition*, 12:218-226. London: Hogarth Press, 1958.

—— (1913), Totem and Taboo. *Standard Edition*, 13:1-161. London: Hogarth Press, 1955.

—— (1914), On Narcissism: An Introduction. *Standard Edition*, 14:73-102. London: Hogarth Press, 1957.

—— (1915a), Instincts and Their Vicissitudes. *Standard Edition*, 14:117-140. London: Hogarth Press, 1957.

—— (1915b), The Unconscious. *Standard Edition*, 14:166-215. London: Hogarth Press, 1957.

—— (1923), *The Ego and the Id*. London: Hogarth Press, 1927.

—— (1926), *The Problem of Anxiety*. New York: Norton, 1936.

—— (1932), *New Introductory Lectures on Psychoanalysis*. New York: Norton, 1933.

—— (1937), Analysis Terminable and Interminable. *Collected Papers*, 5:316-357. London: Hogarth Press, 1950.

Hall, C. S. and Whiteman, P. H. (1951), The Effects of Infantile Stimulation upon Later Emotional Stability in the Mouse. *Journal of Comparative and Physiological Psychology*, 44:61-66.

Harlow, H. and Zimmermann, R. (1959), Affectional Responses in the Infant Monkey. *Science*, 130:421-432.

Hartmann, H. (1939), *Ego Psychology and the Problem of Adaptation*. New York: International Universities Press, 1958. See also abbreviated, annotated version in *Organization and Pathology of Thought*, ed. D. Rapaport. New York: Columbia University Press, 1951, pp. 362-396.

—— (1948), Comments on the Psychoanalytic Theory of Instinctual Drives. *Psychoanalytic Quarterly*, 17:368-388.

—— (1950), Comments on the Psychoanalytic Theory of the Ego. *The Psychoanalytic Study of the Child*, 5:74-96. New York: International Universities Press.

—— (1952), The Mutual Influences in the Development of the Ego and Id. *The Psychoanalytic Study of the Child*, 7:9-30. New York: International Universities Press.

—— (1955), Notes on the Theory of Sublimation. *The Psycho-*

analytic Study of the Child, *10*:9-29. New York: International Universities Press.

———— (1956), Notes on the Reality Principle. *The Psychoanalytic Study of the Child*, *11*:31-53. New York: International Universities Press.

———— and Kris, E. (1945), The Genetic Approach in Psychoanalysis. *The Psychoanalytic Study of the Child*, *1*:11-30. New York: International Universities Press.

———— ———— and Loewenstein, R. M. (1946), Comments on the Formation of Psychic Structure. *The Psychoanalytic Study of the Child*, *2*:11-38. New York: International Universities Press.

Hebb, D. O. (1949), *The Organization of Behavior*. New York: Wiley.

Heinroth, O. (1910), Beiträge zur Biologie, namentlich Ethologie und Physiologie der Anatiden. *Verhandlungen des 5. Internationalen Ornithologischen Kongresses*, Berlin, pp. 589-702.

————(1938), *Aus dem Leben der Vögel*. Leipzig.

Hess, E. H. (1959), Imprinting: An Effect of Early Experience, Imprinting Determines Later Social Behavior in Animals. *Science*, *130*:133-141.

Hunt, J. McV. (1941), The Effects of Infant Feeding-Frustration upon Adult Hoarding in the Albino Rat. *Journal of Abnormal and Social Psychology*, *36*:338-360.

———— and Willoughby, R. R. (1939), The Effect of Frustration on Hoarding in Rats. *Psychosomatic Medicine*, *1*:309-310.

Jaynes, J. (1956), Imprinting: The Interaction of Learned and Innate Behavior: I. Development and Generalization. *Journal of Comparative and Physiological Psychology*, *49*:201-206.

———— (1957), Imprinting: The Interaction of Learned and Innate Behavior: II. The Critical Period. *Journal of Comparative and Physiological Psychology*, *50*:6-10.

Kagan, J. and Beach, F. A. (1953), Effects of Early Experience on Mating Behavior in Male Rats. *Journal of Comparative and Physiological Psychology*, *46*:204-208.

Kahn, M. W. (1951), The Effect of Severe Defeat at Various Age Levels on the Aggressive Behavior of Mice. *Journal of Genetic Psychology*, *79*:117-130.

Kardiner, A. (1939), *The Individual and His Society: the Psychodynamics of Primitive Social Organization*. New York: Columbia University Press.

———(1945), *The Psychological Frontiers of Society*. New York: Columbia University Press.

Kinsey, A. C., et al. (1948), *Sexual Behavior in the Human Male*. Philadelphia: Saunders.

——— (1953), *Sexual Behavior in the Human Female*. Philadelphia: Saunders.

Kris, E. (1950), On Preconscious Mental Processes. *Psychoanalytic Quarterly*, *19*:540-560. Also in *Organization and Pathology of Thought*, ed. D. Rapaport. New York: Columbia University Press, 1951, pp. 474-493.

——— (1951), Some Comments and Observations on Early Autoerotic Activities. *The Psychoanalytic Study of the Child*, *6*:95-116. New York: International Universities Press.

——— (1955), Neutralization and Sublimation: Observations on Young Children. *The Psychoanalytic Study of the Child*, *10*:30-46. New York: International Universities Press.

Lashley, K. S. (1914), A Note on the Persistence of an Instinct. *Journal of Animal Behavior*, *4*:293-294.

——— (1938), Experimental Analysis of Instinctive Behavior. *Psychological Review*, *45*:445-471.

Leitch, M. (1948), A Commentary on the Oral Phase of Psychosexual Development. *Bulletin of the Menninger Clinic*, *12*:117-125.

——— and Escalona, S. (1949), The Reaction of Infants to Stress. *The Psychoanalytic Study of the Child*, *3/4*:121-140. New York: International Universities Press.

Levine, S. (1956), A Further Study of Infantile Handling and Adult Avoidance Learning. *Journal of Personality*, *25*:70-80.

Levy, D. M. (1934), Experiments on the Sucking Reflex and Social Behavior of Dogs. *American Journal of Orthopsychiatry*, *4*:203-224.

——— (1935), A Note on Pecking in Chickens. *Psychoanalytic Quarterly*, *4*:612-613.

——— (1938), On Instinct-Satiation: An Experiment on the Pecking Behavior of Chickens. *Journal of General Psychology*, *18*:327-348.

Lorenz, K. (1935), Der Kumpan in der Umwelt des Vogels. *Journal of Ornithology*, *83*:137-214, 289-413. Also in *Instinctive Behavior*, ed. and tr. C. Schiller. New York: International Universities Press, 1957.

—— (1937a), Über den Begriff der Instinkthandlung. *Folia Diotheoretica*, 2:17-50.

—— (1937b), Über die Bildung des Instinktbegriffs. *Die Naturwissenschaften*, 25:289-300, 307-318, 324-331. Also in *Instinctive Behavior*, ed. and tr. C. Schiller. New York: International Universities Press, 1957.

—— (1937c), The Companion in the Bird's World. *The Auk*, 54:245-273.

—— (1942-43), Die angeborenen Formen möglicher Erfahrung. *Zeitschrift für Tierpsychologie*, 5:235-409.

—— (1950), The Comparative Method in Studying Innate Behaviour Patterns. In *Physiological Mechanisms in Animal Behavior*, Symposia of the Society for Experimental Biology. New York: Academic Press, pp. 221-268.

—— (1957), The Role of Aggression in Group Formation. In *Group Processes*, Transactions of the Fourth Conference, October 13-16, 1957. New York: Josiah Macy, Jr. Foundation, 1959, pp. 181-252.

McKelvey, R. K. and Marx, M. H. (1951), Effects of Infantile Food and Water Deprivation on Adult Hoarding in the Rat. *Journal of Comparative and Physiological Psychology*, 44:423-430.

Nissen, H. W.; Chow, K. L.; and Semmes, J. (1951), Effects of Restricted Opportunity for Tactual, Kinesthetic and Manipulative Experience on the Behavior of a Chimpanzee. *American Journal of Psychology*, 64:485-507.

Orlansky, H. (1949), Infant Care and Personality. *Psychological Bulletin*, 46:1-48.

Paul, I. H. (1959), Studies in Remembering: The Reproduction of Connected and Extended Verbal Material. *Psychological Issues*, 1 (2). New York: International Universities Press.

Piaget, J. (1928), *Judgment and Reasoning in the Child*. New York: Harcourt, Brace.

—— (1929), *The Child's Conception of the World*. New York: Harcourt, Brace.

—— (1930), *The Child's Conception of Physical Causality*. New York: Harcourt, Brace.

—— (1931), Children's Philosophies. In *A Handbook of Child Psychology*. Worcester, Mass.: Clark University Press.

—— (1937a), *The Origins of Intelligence in Children*. New York: International Universities Press, 1952.

—— (1937b), *The Construction of Reality in the Child*. New York: Basic Books, 1954.

—— (1956), Essay on the General Problem of the Psychobiological Development of the Child. Unpublished manuscript.

Rapaport, D., ed. (1951) *Organization and Pathology of Thought*. New York: Columbia University Press.

—— (1952), Book review: *Learning Theory and Personality Dynamics*, by O. Hobart Mowrer. New York: Ronald Press, 1950. *Journal of Abnormal and Social Psychology*, *47*:137-142.

—— (1953a), Book review. *Personality and Psychotherapy: an Analysis in Terms of Learning, Thinking and Culture*, by John Dollard and Neal E. Miller. New York: McGraw-Hill, 1950. *American Journal of Orthopsychiatry*, *23*:204-208.

—— (1953b), Some Metapsychological Considerations Concerning Activity and Passivity. Unpublished manuscript.

—— (1957), Cognitive Structures. In *Contemporary Approaches to Cognition*. Cambridge: Harvard University Press, pp. 157-200.

—— (1958), The Theory of Ego Autonomy: A Generalization. *Bulletin of the Menninger Clinic*, *22*:13-35.

—— (1959), The Structure of Psychoanalytic Theory: A Systematizing Attempt. In *Psychology: A Study of a Science*, Vol. *3*, ed. S. Koch. New York: McGraw-Hill, pp. 55-183. Also in *Psychological Issues*, Vol. *2*. New York: International Universities Press, 1960.

Richter, C. P. (1941), Biology of Drives. *Psychosomatic Medicine*, *3*:105-110.

Riesen, A. H. (1951), Post-partum Development of Behavior. *Chicago Medical School Quarterly*, *13*:17-24.

Schur, M. (1958), The Ego and the Id in Anxiety. *The Psychoanalytic Study of the Child*, *13*:190-220. New York: International Universities Press.

—— (1959), Ontogenesis and Phylogenesis of Affect- and Structure-Formation and the Concept of Repetition Compulsion. Paper read at the International Congress of Psychoanalysis, Copenhagen. *International Journal of Psycho-analysis* (in press).

Scott, J. H. (1955), Some Effects at Maturity of Gentling, Ignoring, or Shocking Rats During Infancy. *Journal of Abnormal and Social Psychology*, *51*:412-414.

Scott, J. P.; Fredericson, E.; and Fuller, J. L. (1951), Experimental Exploration of the Critical Period Hypothesis. *Personality*, *1*:162-183.

————— and Marston, M. V. (1950), Critical Periods Affecting the Development of Normal and Mal-adjustive Social Behavior of Puppies. *Journal of Genetic Psychology*, *77*:25-60.

Spitz, R. A. (1946a), Anaclitic Depression. *The Psychoanalytic Study of the Child*, *2*:313-342. New York: International Universities Press.

————— (1946b), The Smiling Response: A Contribution to the Ontogenesis of Social Relations. *Genetic Psychology Monographs*, *34*:57-125.

————— (1949), Autoerotism. *The Psychoanalytic Study of the Child* *3/4*:85-120. New York: International Universities Press.

Sullivan, H. S. (1953), *The Interpersonal Theory of Psychiatry*. New York: Norton.

Thompson, W. R. and Heron, W. (1954), The Effect of Early Restriction on Activity in Dogs. *Journal of Comparative and Physiological Psychology*, *47*:77-82.

————— and Woodburn, W. (1954), The Effects of Restricting Early Experience on the Problem Solving Capacity of Dogs. *Canadian Journal of Psychology*, *8*:17-32.

Thorpe, W. H. (1956), *Learning and Instinct in Animals*. Cambridge: Harvard University Press.

Tinbergen, N. (1951), *The Study of Instinct*. Oxford: Clarendon Press.

————— (1952), "Derived" Activities; Their Causation, Biological Significance, Origin and Emancipation During Evolution. *Quarterly Review of Biology*, *27*:1-32.

Weininger, O. (1956), The Effects of Early Experience on Behavior and Growth Characteristics. *Journal of Comparative and Physiological Psychology*, *49*:1-9.

Weiss, P. (1939), *Principles of Development*. New York: Holt.

Werner, H. (1926), *Comparative Psychology of Mental Development*. Rev. ed., 2nd printing. New York: International Universities Press, 1957.

————— (1957), The Concept of Development from a Comparative and Organismic Point of View. In *The Concept of Development*,

ed. D. B. Harris. Minneapolis: University of Minnesota Press.
—— and Wapner, S. (1949), Sensory-Tonic Field Theory of Perception. *Journal of Personality*, *18*:88-107.
—— —— (1952), Toward a General Theory of Perception. *Psychological Review*, *59*:324-338.
Whitman, C. O. (1919), The Behaviour of Pigeons. *Posthumous Works of C. O. Whitman*, *3*:1-161.
Wolff, P. H. (1959), Observations of Newborn Infants. *Psychosomatic Medicine*, *21*:110-118.
—— (1960), The Developmental Psychologies of Jean Piaget and Psychoanalysis. *Psychological Issues*, *2* (in press). New York: International Universities Press.
Young, P. T. (1949), Food-Seeking Drive, Affective Process, and Learning. *Psychological Review*, *56*:98-121.

Cognitive Embeddedness
in Problem Solving:
A Theoretical and Experimental Analysis

MARTIN SCHEERER

MAURICE D. HULING

University of Kansas

THE PROBLEM OF COGNITIVE EMBEDDEDNESS

It is a common experience to discover, often to our chagrin, that we could have easily solved a problem by using something that has been "under our nose" all along and that we have "overlooked." In one of Poe's stories the police inspectors make an exhaustive and microscopic search for a valuable letter they know to be in a certain room. The letter was in plain sight all the time, but defaced and soiled, sticking out of an open calling-card rack on the mantle piece. By leaving the letter openly exposed and giving it the appearance of

The writers gratefully acknowledge support received from the General and Graduate Research Funds of the University of Kansas for use in connection with this study.

being worthless, the thief cleverly "hid" it. Closer to experimental psychology is an observation by Köhler on his chimpanzees. They were familiar with using boxes to stand on for reaching a stick on the roof with which to rake in fruit lying outside the cage. In this instance Chica needed to move a box across the cage so that she could climb on it to reach the stick. She did not use the box in the habitual way, even though she had squatted on it repeatedly to catch her breath. Instead, she was leaping in vain from the floor for the stick.

But presently the reason became evident; as soon as Tercera, who had been reposing on the box all this time, descended for some purpose, Chica seized it and pulled it forward, mounted it and seized the stick. . . . One can hardly assume that Chica had already seen the box as an implement, while Tercera was still lying on it. To judge by the conduct of the animals at other times, she would in that case have tried to remove her friend by pleading and complaining and by pulling at her hands and feet, or would at least have made an attempt to move the box in spite of its weight. . . . It is only when the box is freed of Tercera that it is recognized as an implement. It is not thus recognized while being occupied as a seat [Köhler, 1917, p. 141; 1931, p. 178ff.].

The foregoing instances illustrate a general phenomenon which has been called "fixedness of thought material" (Duncker, 1945). We propose that they point to a hitherto unexplored subtype of such fixedness, namely, cognitive embeddedness. Previous research in visual perception has demonstrated the phenomenon of perceptual embeddedness. The latter is usually subsumed under the laws of perceptual unit formation. Familiar examples are planned or natural camouflage, hidden face puzzles, or the Gottschaldt figure experiment (1926), in which a previously inspected figure is not readily seen after its contours have become parts within another figure, i.e., absorbed by the unit-forming properties of a more *complex* design.

In 1941 an experimental situation was conceived by Zelda Klapper, H. Witkin, and M. Scheerer, for the purpose of exploring perceptual embeddedness in problem solving. This was a modification of Köhler's well-known two-stick situation.

The subject has to find a way to place two rings over an upright peg, while standing behind a chalk line about six feet from the peg. Since the peg and rings are patently out of his reach, he needs a tool to extend his arm. Except when placing the rings, he is allowed to move freely about the room, even across the chalk line, and to utilize any object in the room. There are two dowel sticks of equal length in the room. Neither stick alone is long enough to bridge the gap. Only if the two sticks are joined together, to make a longer tool, can the subject place the rings on the peg from behind the chalk line. On the wall, directly above the rings and peg, and clearly in view, a "No Smoking" sign hangs by a string. The string is crucial for the solution because it is the only object in the room which can be used to fasten the sticks together.

This problem proved surprisingly difficult.[1]

Originally the difficulty seemed explainable by the perceptual unit formation between sign and string which hindered visual isolation of the string. Subsequent experiments have cast doubt on perceptual embeddedness as the primary cause of the problem's difficulty.[2] A closer analysis of the experimental situation led the present authors to hypothesize that cognitive factors were the principal determinants of the string's psychological inaccessibility. We propose that the locus of the difficulty does not lie in perceptual unit formation alone, but that the string's inaccessibility is related to the meaning which the crucial object has assumed; and that this meaning chiefly derives from the context in which the object functions for the observer.

---

[1] For this reason it has since become a frequent experiment in laboratory courses at Brooklyn and City Colleges as well as the New School for Social Research.

[2] Some of these experiments have been reported by M. D. Huling (unpublished Ph.D. thesis, University of Kansas, 1956, under the sponsorship of M. Scheerer); and by Huling and Scheerer in a paper read at the Meetings of the American Psychological Association, 1959; and also by J. Lyons (unpublished Ph.D. thesis, University of Kansas, 1952).

In the previously mentioned examples of the "sat-on" box and the "hidden" letter, the crucial object is visually available. Why is it psychologically unavailable? Here, in contrast to ordinary perceptual embeddedness, the contours of box and letter do not have boundaries in common with other surrounding figures, making for "unit formation." Nor does this law obtain here in the sense that the adjacent configuration is a "good continuation" of the respective outlines of the objects; viz., the contours of chimp and box are partially in contact but their respective identities as visual units remain preserved, leaving little doubt where box ends and chimp begins. True, the defacing of the letter, its protruding from the card rack, and the partial figural contact of chimp and box may be considered as certain alterations of the crucial object's perceptual qualities. But these minor changes do not fulfill the conditions of genuine perceptual embeddedness. Rather the embeddedness of the critical object derives from the meaning it has for the perceiver in the context of its particular setting. The slightly changed appearance fits as a supporting cue consonant with the meaning which the particular context presents to the observer, thereby embedding the critical object.

We may apply an analogous line of reasoning to the experiment with the "No Smoking" sign. The type of perceptual unity which string and sign form does not constitute perceptual embeddedness. There is no double function of contours, no "good continuation" between string and sign (e.g., direction), and no loss of identity of each respective visual unit. One sees where string ends and sign begins; each is optically available. The "inaccessibility" of the string must stem from factors that transcend sensory organization proper: namely, from the meaning it has for the subject in the given context.

For the purpose of this paper we are using "meaning" as follows:

1. An object has meaning in terms of its known as well as its discoverable functions. Both the known and potential

functions of an object are intrinsically related to its structural characteristics.[3] These are experienced by the person via "physiognomic" aspects (Werner, 1940), and via commerce with the object when "phenomenal causality" comes into play (Duncker, 1945). The object's functions that are thus "known" derive from experienced usage, and the physiognomic aspects connected with this usage become "figure." Other functional and physiognomic aspects of the object are "ground" and constitute its potentialities which are discoverable.

2. A meaning unit between two (or more) objects may be formed when they make perceptual contact, which suggests their functional union, but does not obliterate their respective perceivable identities (e.g., a horse and rider, pen and ink, lamp and lampshade, garbage can and cover). This perceptual contact is a necessary but not sufficient condition.[4] To fulfill the sufficient condition for a meaning unit, the functions of the two objects must be linked so as to interact in mutual support or interdependency. For instance, the string suspends a painting which in turn requires support to fulfill its function. By contrast, when a string lies on a table, the two do not form a meaning unit, although they make perceptual contact.

3. The above definition of a meaning unit is incomplete without including the broader framework in which it has come to operate. This is the psychological context or behavior setting which constitutes a "sphere of meaning" (Scheerer, 1959), and which functionally contains the unit. For instance, the same "No Smoking" sign with string, when hanging on a pinnacle of rock in a barren desert, would not repre-

---

[3] What we call known or potential functions of an object may be related to Carnap's term, "dispositional" (1937).

[4] Meaning units may also form without actual perceptual contact. These exceptions may occur via functional proximity, as in cases of "pairing," for example, knife and fork, the red and green of a traffic signal. Here even perceptual similarity is wanting. In other cases of pairing, meaning units may be supported by perceptual similarity, as in pen and pencil, or salt and pepper shakers.

sent the same meaning unit as when hanging on a wall in a hospital room, though the identical perceptual contact and relation between sign and string are present in both cases. Hence, in fully defining the characteristics of a meaning unit, the relationship to its context, i.e., its pertinence and appropriateness, has to be specified. Obviously, meaning, as treated under points 1 to 3, results from past experience and commerce with the objects whose functions have become relatively stable and appropriate.

4. It is characteristic of the described meaning unit that the objects contained in it become "subparts." In becoming a subordinate part in such a whole, an object may change its independent meaning to one which is more consonant with the total unit. The unit may influence the object's meaning so strongly that the latter loses its independence and becomes embedded or "camouflaged." Thereby it may become psychologically inaccessible for other functions although it is perceptually identifiable. A person on a hike may urgently need a piece of string for tying something, but not immediately think of using his shoelace, and will consequently "walk a mile" for a bit of string. In such cases we speak of cognitive embeddedness.

Which of the member objects that form a meaning unit will be more strongly cognitively embedded than the others depends on a variety of factors which have not yet been fully explored. Here we can only touch upon them. To illustrate, in the case of the shoe and shoelace, these two objects are not embedded to an equivalent extent; one is more dominant in the meaning unit. The same person may more readily think of removing his shoe to swat an insect than of using his shoelace for tying something. The string and shoe form a meaning unit in which the string is cognitively embedded. Person-shoe-lace also form a meaning unit, but the shoe is less cognitively embedded in this unit than the string. An explanation of these differences would require an analysis of the stability and plasticity of the functional properties of objects (see

p. 263). One would also have to determine how the *behavior setting* interacts with the meaning unit. Thus, in the wearing and owning of shoes, shoe and shoelace form a unit in which the laces are functionally "contained" by the shoe in a relatively permanent way, whether it is off or on the person. In the unit person-shoe-lace, the shoe is not as permanently contained in the behavior of the person, and may therefore be more easily available. By contrast, in putting on shoes, breaking a lace, or in polishing shoes, the laces become more easily available.

Let us examine the "No Smoking" sign experiments from this position. The meaning of objects that usually hang on the walls of a room depends on their having acquired functional fittingness and permanent purpose there. We propose to call this "functional stay-putness character." A painting, a mirror, a calendar, a wall clock, an eye chart, etc., all have this functional belongingness. We have come to "know" that these things belong on the walls of rooms when serving their respective purposes and would be surprised to find them elsewhere, e.g., outdoors. The subject brings to the experimental situation previously established cognitive habits or sets; he structures the "No Smoking" sign as having the "functional stay-putness character" formerly encountered in equivalent behavior settings. The sign suspended by the string on the wall forms a meaning unit in which the string is embedded. This is so because the sign plays the dominant role in this meaning unit, i.e., giving a message. (Also, the sign could form the identical meaning unit with suspending agents other than string, e.g., a nail, tape, etc.) The fact that the subject's cognitive set structures the "No Smoking" sign as a permanent fixture customarily belonging on the wall hinders him from isolating the string for use. Putting it concretely, and perhaps oversimplifying, when the subject sees this sign upon entering the room, he takes it for granted that it fits there, was there before, and is there to stay. If he knew that the experimenter purposely hung it there, the subject would succeed with ease. But the sign is cognitively placed by the subject into a "meaning sphere" which is only tangentially related to the experimental situation, i.e., the subject sees the sign, but does not view it as relevant. The required restructuring demands that the subject actually overcome or suspend the functional stay-putness character of the sign. Once this is accomplished, the meaning unit of sign and string becomes less cohesive, and the embedded string can be isolated for use.

If the foregoing psychological analysis is correct, the following hypotheses are suggested: (1) Objects which have stable functional stay-putness character in the subject's experience will be cognitively structured as belonging to a definite sphere of meaning (this has the permanent purpose of such and such). Such objects will not be readily considered as containing any properties that can be used in another sphere of meaning. (2) Such objects can have an embedding ("hiding") influence on others with which they form a meaning unit, so that the embedded object will not be readily isolated. (3) The stronger the functional stay-putness character, the stronger will be the embedding influence.

Hypothesis 1 belongs to the general category of fixedness of thought material described by Duncker; especially, it may seem related to his subtype, functional fixedness. Our functional stay-putness character could be called, in Duncker's terms, the result of a "static preutilization"[4a] through which the sign, mirror etc., have become fixed in their own respective functions (F 1). This F 1 is not derived from concrete action (as other F 1's) but through preceding experience. However, a certain difference should be noted here: we have introduced the concept of meaning unit defined as the functional union of one or more objects. To this we have added a temporal dimension (forward and backward) as well as the belongingness of the unit to cognitive structures called spheres of

---

[4a] Because of editorial policy, the term *pre-utilization* will not be hyphenated in this paper.

meaning. Functional fixedness of the unit was then derived from this meaning sphere.

Hypotheses 2 and 3 fall outside of Duncker's framework and represent a hitherto unexplored aspect of fixedness of thought material. This aspect concerns the embedding influence of one object on another, not the fixation of the object's own function. We are asking whether and how a meaning unit embeds one of its substructures (cognitive embeddedness). If one were to use Duncker's terminology, one could say we are studying the potentialities of an F 1 to embed *another* object as contrasted with Duncker's F 1 object, which fixes *itself*.

Stated in this theoretical form, the above hypotheses cover a wide range of everyday behavior, much of which eludes scientific scrutiny because of the difficulty in controlling the postulated variables. A problem-solving situation allows experimental manipulation of such variables. In our experimental design, cognitive embeddedness was systematically varied by changing the stay-putness meaning. Cognitive embeddedness of the crucial object assumed the role of an independent variable. Thus we could formulate specific predictions in which the degree of difficulty in problem solution would be the dependent variable. A series of experiments was conducted with 240 subjects to implement this design: they will be presented in five parts.[5]

EXPERIMENTAL ANALYSIS OF COGNITIVE EMBEDDEDNESS

PART I

Experimental Design

The experimental task was always the Köhler two-stick problem. The subject has to discover that the two sticks must be joined together in order to extend his reach beyond the chalk line so that he can lift the rings onto the peg. The crucial and only suitable object in the room for tying the sticks together

---

[5] The contributions of J. Elliot, G. Goldstein, and R. Mecham, University of Kansas, as experimental assistants, are gratefully acknowledged.

is the string on the wall. It was predicted that the subjects would have no difficulty when the string was neither embedded in a meaning unit nor had functional stay-putness, so that it was maximally available. The first step was to establish this, by presenting the problem with the string hanging in plain sight on the wall, supporting nothing, and looped over a nail. Since a pilot experiment showed that all subjects solved this rapidly, it was concluded that (1) the problem itself was not inherently difficult for normal adult subjects; and (2) this condition could serve as a control, i.e. a baseline, against which to compare others where the string is embedded in varying degrees. The different objects were presented, hanging on the wall suspended by the identical string. Two degrees of embeddedness were used:

1. Strong embeddedness: (a) "No Smoking" sign; (b) intact mirror; (c) a current calendar. Items (a), (b), and (c) are meaning units having potent functional stay-putness character where the string is strongly embedded (strong embeddedness conditions will henceforth be referred to as E+ conditions).

2. Weak embeddedness: (a) a blank white cardboard. This was hypothesized to have little embedding influence on the string because the blank cardboard connotes a minimal functional stay-putness or specific meaning. Lacking these, string and cardboard form a very weak meaning unit. (b) An obsolete calendar (from the last year). This object was also predicted to embed the string weakly because the calendar was obsolete. Its *raison d'être* on the wall was not actual, and therefore the functional meaning of temporal permanence usually associated with wall calendars would be diminished. (c) A cloudy mirror. Since its mirroring functioning is partially reduced, the stay-putness value of this object on the wall was hypothesized to be lessened so that the meaning unit of string and cloudy mirror would be less cohesive (weak embeddedness conditions will henceforth be referred to as E− conditions).

Predictions

Specifically it was predicted:

1. In the E+ conditions more subjects would fail than in the E− conditions.

2. Those subjects who would solve the problem in E+ conditions would take a longer time than those subjects solving it in E− conditions.

3. Frequency of failure and solution time would not differ significantly from the control condition in the E− conditions; but in the E+ conditions, frequency of failure would be significantly greater and solution time significantly longer than in the control condition.

Method

The experiments were conducted in a laboratory cubicle about 7 by 9 feet. The room was sparsely furnished with a desk, two chairs, and a waste basket. Care was taken to remove objects such as window shade cords which might have been used to solve the problem. A nail was driven into one wall, slightly above eye level, i.e., at a height which is customary for the hanging of objects. On this nail the identical string always hung in the various conditions, supporting in each case one of the experimental objects. Otherwise the walls were completely bare. The rings and pegs were placed on the floor touching the baseboard and standing directly beneath the hanging object. Six feet back and parallel to the same wall, the white chalk line was drawn on the floor across the room. The experimenter sat at the table on which were papers for recording the protocols of the experiment, instructions for the subjects, pencils, a stop watch, and a piece of chalk, etc.

Both intact and cloudy mirrors were enclosed in a white wooden frame. The "No Smoking" sign was made of white cardboard bearing the printed legend "No Smoking" in bold black lettering. The current and obsolete calendars were both of identical format. The cardboard was simple blank white posterboard. Each object measured 11 by 15 inches. When any of the objects hung from the nail, the same amount of string showed, namely, a total of 11 inches, or 5½ inches on each of the two sides of a triangle formed by the supporting string above the object. The string was common white package cord and was tied with a square knot which rested on the nail. The knot was tied with clearly visible "tails," each measuring 1½ inches, so that it would be unmistakably clear that the string could be untied.

Thus all experimental conditions were identical, except that the objects hanging from the string differed essentially only in meaning.

Instructions and Procedure

All subjects were given the following instructions:

[A] This experiment has been designed to collect some data about the way in which people think while they are solving a problem. I am not interested at all in the success or failure of individuals—I don't care if some people are fast or slow in getting the solution, since this is not a test of individual ability. I am interested only in the process that people in general use in solving problems. So that I can better understand how you solve problems, I'll ask you to think out loud while you are working, that is, tell me what you are doing as you go along. Since I am not interested in individual performances, I will identify your record of this experiment with the first, middle, and last letters of your last name. In this way you remain completely anonymous. I must ask your cooperation in not discussing with *anyone* any part of this experiment until the semester is over. If you don't feel that you can pledge yourself to be discreet, I would rather not have you for a subject. If you are interested in the results of this work, I will be glad to tell you all about it when I am finished testing subjects.

[B] The problem I should like you to solve is to put those two wooden rings over that peg *while standing in back of the white line.* Now from this position you are to try to get the rings, which lie next to the peg, onto the peg. This must be done *without crossing the white line.* If you see *anything* anywhere in the room which you think may be useful to you in solving the problem, feel entirely free to use it. Furthermore, you may walk to any part of the room to obtain any item you want. The only restriction is that at the very time you are placing the rings onto the peg, you must be *standing* in back of the chalk line.

[C] Since this is a study in problem solving, I want to remind you again that it is of utmost importance that you think aloud while working on the problem, so that I know what you are trying to do. Please give expression to *all* your thoughts as they occur to you, whatever they may be. Do not be afraid to tell me of any idea that you may have about the solution, no matter how foolish you may think it will sound.[6] Remember, this is *not* an intelligence test. If there is any doubt, or if there are any questions that come up, don't hesitate to ask. If a solution occurs to you and you reject it, please mention this thought to me.

[D] I also want to assure you that there is a solution to this problem. If you have not understood the instructions completely or if you have any questions concerning anything about the problem, do not hesitate to ask at any time. Have you any questions now?

After answering any questions that arose, the experimenter asked the subject actually to stand behind the chalk line while he recapitulated the instructions as given in Part B. The subject was then told to begin.

As the subject worked, his actions were noted and his verbalizations recorded as nearly as possible verbatim. A running time record was kept along the margin of the protocol sheet so that any verbalization or action could be located in terms of the amount of time elapsed since the beginning of the problem. If the subject was not verbalizing, he was asked every minute, "Tell me what you are thinking, please." If he was performing some action and not explaining it, he was asked to do so. If a subject had questions during the time

---

[6] The instruction "Think aloud," as distinguished from introspection, was adopted from Duncker who claims, "This instruction . . . is not identical with the instruction to introspect which has been common in experiments on thought-processes. While the introspector makes himself as thinking the object of his attention, the subject who is thinking aloud remains immediately directed to the problem, so to speak allowing his activity to become verbal" (1945, p. 2).

he was working on the problem, they were answered according to the conditions originally set up in the instructions. If the subject attempted a solution using some of his own property (his shoestrings or handkerchief or belt to tie the sticks) he was told that he could not use his personal property but must solve the problem with what was in the room. Whenever the subject wanted to give up before the time limit, he was urged to continue and assured that there was a solution to the problem. The subject was considered to have solved the problem when he utilized the string on the wall, either by actually taking it down and tying the sticks together, or by verbalizing this intention clearly. If the subject had done neither of these after working for twenty minutes, he was stopped and considered to have failed. After the subject completed the experiment, he was interviewed with a standard questionnaire.

Subjects

All subjects were university students, which made the intelligence of our sample more homogeneous than that of the general population. All subjects volunteered, and were assigned at random to the various conditions. Intelligence differences within the various groups were thus assumed to cancel each other. The variable of sex was controlled to the extent that no experimental group was predominantly of either sex, since pilot studies revealed no sex differences related to solution efficiency. In Part I, a total of 93 subjects (including controls) were assigned to the various conditions. The number of subjects serving under each condition will be presented with the results.

Analysis of Results

The results were quantitatively analyzed by applying two independent measures of problem difficulty: (1) the frequency of failure; (2) the solution time needed by successful subjects.

The first measure gives us the number of subjects who failed to solve the problem within twenty minutes. This generous time limit gave the subjects ample opportunity for thinking and for exploring the room. All protocols showed that the subjects discovered early (usually during the first two minutes) the problem could be solved by joining the two sticks. Most subjects also verbalized the need for something—wire, string, tape, etc.—to bind the two sticks together. The attainment of this stage was considered a "conceptual solution" as opposed to the actual solution, using the string. Hence the approximately eighteen remaining minutes were available for searching the room for a suitable fastener. At this point we remind the reader that the article with string was the only thing on the walls of this small barren room, and that it faced the subject directly in his line of vision as he manipulated the sticks. Under these circumstances, a fruitless twenty-minute effort seems quite remarkable, and is a convincing demonstration of cognitive embeddedness as affecting problem difficulty.

It was, of course, possible to succeed at any time during the twenty-minute period, but whether a solution occurred after three minutes or after seventeen, it was recorded as a success. Such time differences as the above are obscured by mere success-failure count, and they would offer an additional measure of the effects of embeddedness, since solution time should vary directly with problem difficulty. The data of the failure and solution time analyses will be presented and discussed separately.

Table I summarizes frequency of failure for the control and all experimental conditions.

TABLE I

Frequency of Failure; All Conditions

Conditions	N	Number Failing	% of Failing	Significance of Differences from Control Condition*
Control (string alone)	16	0	0	——
Weakly embedded				
Cardboard	10	1	10	not sig.
Obsolete calendar	10	1	10	not sig.
Cloudy mirror	10	0	0	not sig.
Strongly embedded				
Current calendar	16	9	56.25	$p < .003$
Intact mirror	16	11	68.75	$p < .003$
"No Smoking" sign	15	8	53.33	$p < .002$

*Tested with Fisher's Exact Method for the Probability of a 2 x 2 Contingency Table using Finney's (1948) and Latscha's (1953) tables.

It is evident that the problem was easier with the cardboard, obsolete calendar, and cloudy mirror where the embedding influence was predicted to be weaker. Of the 30 subjects in these three conditions, only 2 failed. By contrast, 28 of the 47 subjects in the cases of the current calendar, intact mirror, and "No Smoking" sign failed. Here, as predicted, the problem difficulty was much greater and embeddedness stronger. It should be re-emphasized that throughout only object *meaning* was varied, object size and form being held constant, with the same string suspending all objects.

As hypothesized none of the E − conditions differs significantly from the control; and each of the E + conditions has a significantly greater frequency of failure. Moreover, comparing the E + conditions among themselves, no significant differences were found.

Table II gives the mean solution times for the successful subjects in the control and all experimental conditions.

TABLE II

Comparison of Solution Times under Experimental and Control
Conditions

Conditions	N	Mean Solution Time	Significance of Difference from Control Condition*
Control	16	2'8"	——
Weakly embedded			
Cardboard	9	3'40"	not sig.
Obsolete calendar	9	2'54"	not sig.
Cloudy mirror	10	2'37"	not sig.
Strongly embedded			
Current calendar	7	6'05"	not sig. (p = .08)
Intact mirror	5	2'12"	not sig.
"No Smoking" sign	7	13'03"	p < .001

*Significance tested with White's extension (1952) of the Mann-Whitney and Wilcoxen tests.

Inspection shows the mean solution times of the E — conditions to be much closer to the control time than those of the E + ones—with one exception. This was the intact mirror, and was quite unexpected, because this same condition produced the greatest number of failures in the entire experiment. Because of the small numbers of successful subjects in each E + condition and the skewed distribution of the time scores, it was considered inappropriate to use a parametric test of significance. Therefore, the significance figures of Table II were calculated using the rank order test developed by White (1952). As predicted, none of the E — conditions had a significantly different solution time from the control. Of the E + conditions, only with the "No Smoking" sign was the expected significance achieved. The solution times for the current calendar fell short of the 5 per cent level of confidence but approached this criterion with a probability of .08, indicating a trend in the expected direction. Of 16 subjects, only 5 solved the intact mirror problem, but did so with solution times not significantly exceeding those of the control. We have no ready explanation for this finding.

Summarizing the results on both measures, all six predictions for failure frequency, and four of the six for solution times were upheld. Thus, ten of twelve specific hypotheses were confirmed. In principle the above results support our expectations, although the solution time data are not as confirmatory as the failure data.

Another analysis of the results which focuses on the persistence of embeddedness through time may be made by determining the proportion of failure at elapsed time intervals for all experimental groups as compared to the controls. This method would show whether solutions in the various groups tended to distribute themselves early or late during the twenty-minute experimental period.

Figure 1 presents such an analysis based on four time samples, the first covering the first three minutes, the subsequent ones drawn after six, twelve, and eighteen minutes.

Even after the first three-minute period, a fairly clear differentiation is apparent between per cent of failures in the E + and in the E − conditions. This differentiation becomes unequivocal after six minutes and persists through the last sample. Comparing each condition with the control, the current calendar, intact mirror, and "No Smoking" sign show significantly more failure after three minutes and continue to do so. Turning to the E − conditions, the per cents of failure in the cardboard and cloudy mirror do not differ significantly from the control at the end of the first three-minutes, but the obsolete calendar does, having 80 per cent failures. This, however, drops to nonsignificance at the six-, twelve-, and eighteen-minute points, becoming consistent with the E − conditions. Cognitive embeddedness appears to persist through time in the cases where its potency was predicted. The converse is true for this persistence in the E − conditions.

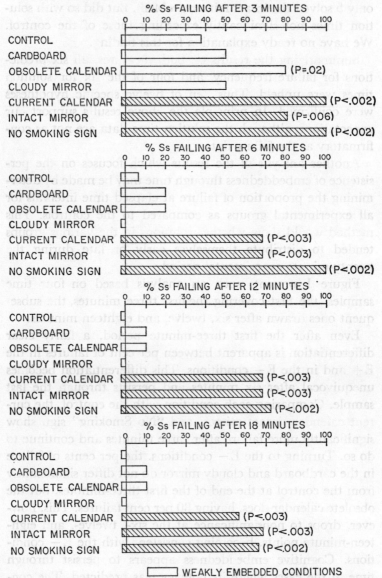

PERSISTENCE OF EMBEDDEDNESS THROUGH TIME

% Ss FAILING AFTER 3 MINUTES

CONTROL
CARDBOARD
OBSOLETE CALENDAR (P=.02)
CLOUDY MIRROR
CURRENT CALENDAR (P<.002)
INTACT MIRROR (P=.006)
NO SMOKING SIGN (P<.002)

% Ss FAILING AFTER 6 MINUTES

CONTROL
CARDBOARD
OBSOLETE CALENDAR
CLOUDY MIRROR
CURRENT CALENDAR (P<.003)
INTACT MIRROR (P<.003)
NO SMOKING SIGN (P<.002)

% Ss FAILING AFTER 12 MINUTES

CONTROL
CARDBOARD
OBSOLETE CALENDAR
CLOUDY MIRROR
CURRENT CALENDAR (P<.003)
INTACT MIRROR (P<.003)
NO SMOKING SIGN (P<.002)

% Ss FAILING AFTER 18 MINUTES

CONTROL
CARDBOARD
OBSOLETE CALENDAR
CLOUDY MIRROR
CURRENT CALENDAR (P<.003)
INTACT MIRROR (P<.003)
NO SMOKING SIGN (P<.002)

☐ WEAKLY EMBEDDED CONDITIONS
▨ STRONGLY EMBEDDED CONDITIONS

FIGURE I. Probabilities given refer to differences from control condition as determined by Fisher's exact method.

PART II

It was felt that another, more direct, way of testing for the cognitive embeddedness of the string would be informative. The idea was suggested[7] that subjects should be placed in the same experimental room as in Part I, with the "No Smoking" sign hanging in the identical place and manner on the wall, and that the subject should be simply asked to "name all the objects in the room." The subject was accordingly asked to continue enumerating until he could think of nothing more. It was expected that the string would either not be mentioned at all, or would occur late in the subject's enumeration. Of the 20 subjects used, 17 did not mention the string, although all named the "No Smoking" sign. The number of things named ranged from 14 to 61 with a mean of 31.8. Three subjects mentioned the string, two in the first half and one in the last half of their enumerations. A control group of 5 subjects was run, with the string hanging alone as in the original control condition. Every subject mentioned the string. Here the range of naming covered 19 to 73 objects with a mean of 36.6. The string was named by these subjects within the first quarter of their enumeration. In terms of the mean number of objects named, the string was given on the average as the ninth object mentioned. The reader may wonder how so many things could be named in a room previously described as "barren." Actually the room contained only 15 or 20 objects in the "molar" sense (desk, chairs, rings, peg, sticks, wastebasket, etc.). Subjects were able to name up to 60 or 70 things only by breaking down the larger objects into smaller components, i.e., door-doorknob; desk-desk drawer, desk-drawer handle; light fixture-bulb; wall-light switch-plug; etc. The subjects' overwhelming failure to name the string when it suspended the "No Smoking" sign is all the more striking in view of their increasing analytic dismemberment of molar

---

[7] By our colleague, E. L. Wike.

things into molecular parts in response to the demand to enumerate. Thus, each in its own way, this experiment and those of Part I, support the hypothesized cognitive embeddedness.

However, in Part I, relatively more subjects isolated the string even in the E+ condition. This may be accounted for by suggesting that these subjects were more motivated to single out the string because they actually needed it in Part I.

The naming experiment demonstrates further that seeing the sign and naming it as such docs not help to separate the string, although subjects were "molecularizing" other objects. This is in keeping with our hypothesis that the sign must be viewed differently to break asunder the sign-and-string unit.

Conceivably, it might be argued that what we call the cognitive embeddedness of the string is really Duncker's "static" or passive "preutilization": from the start the subject "meets" the crucial object in its customary use without having himself fixed it that way by action. Accordingly, the string's suspending function (F 1) hinders another use (F 2). But the instruction to "name everything in the room" does not call for such reorganization of string into a new, specific F 2. "Naming" is not "using," is not an F 2, and should not be hindered by F 1. Naming calls only for identifying or reading off F 1, and should be easy.

Furthermore, in Duncker's theory, F 1 is conceived to be a self-fixing function of the object proper, and the fixed object is but rarely considered in relation to others; nor is the nature of such other objects dealt with even when the fixed object enters into a relationship with them. Whether, for example, the string suspends an obsolete or a current calendar would not essentially matter, since in both cases the string has the same F 1 (support). Yet it was demonstrated that the string's availability differed greatly in the two cases. This tends to contradict the generality of the preutilization hypothesis. The concept of meaning unit, which includes the functional interaction of the contained objects, can explain this different availability in terms of stronger and weaker cognitive embeddedness.

PART III

Experimental Design and Method

In proposing that cognitive embeddedness derives from meaning units, it was claimed that the part which becomes embedded remains perceptually available. Concerning the method employed in Part I, the question may be raised whether perceptual availability was adequately insured, i.e., whether each subject could readily see the string. In the postexperimental interviews, no subject complained of *not* having seen the string, but we do not consider this to be sufficiently direct and controlled evidence of its perceptual accessibility. Therefore, the following variation in method was conceived:

The subject himself should hang the object on the wall by means of the string. Otherwise the entire procedure was to be identical with that of Part I. This one change would guarantee that the subject had had *recent* manipulatory, tactual, and visual contact with the string while he hung the object in the very position in which he would face it soon thereafter, when trying to solve the two-stick problem. It would then be hard to argue that the string had not been perceptually available. The experimental design of Part III closely parallels that of Part I in that both utilize E + and E − conditions.

So that the subject would neither become suspicious nor connect the hanging of the object with the subsequent two-stick task, plausible settings and "explanations" were provided.

Strongly Embedded ("Introduced") Conditions

The intact mirror and the "No Smoking" sign were introduced from outside the experimental situation as ostensibly unplanned events. First, the subject was given the general part of the instructions (A), "that this was to be an experiment in problem solving," etc. The subject was then asked to solve some puzzles designed to fill in time without biasing him with respect to the two-stick problem. After five minutes, the mirror or "No Smoking" sign was introduced.

For the mirror, the procedure was as follows: the department secretary[8] opened the cubicle door as if unaware that the room was occupied, stopped short on the threshold, and said, "Excuse me, I didn't know there was anyone in here. I have to put these mirrors in all the lab cubicles. They're going to use them for an experiment next week." With an apologetic "I'm sorry," she reached over and laid the mirror on the table, where the experimenter and the subject were seated. The experimenter replied, "That's okay," as she left the room. Since the experimenter was seated behind a table in the corner and could not move his position easily, the experimenter said to the subject, who was on the side of the table having easy access to the room, "I suppose this should be hung up—would you do it for me, please?" The subject then hung the mirror on the only nail in the room (the crucial place for the subsequent two-stick problem). The experimenter thanked the subject and asked him to resume work on the fill-in problems. After fifteen more minutes of this, the rest of the instructions (Parts B, C, and D) for the two-stick problem was presented, and the subject began.

The procedure for introducing the "No Smoking" sign was as follows: again after five minutes, the secretary came in, carrying several "No Smoking" signs and said, "Oh, excuse me, I didn't know there was anybody in here. We just got word today that there's to be no more smoking in the cubicles and I'm taking these signs around." She laid a sign down,

---

[8] Our special thanks to Mrs. Mary Townsend, Secretary of the Psychology Clinic, whose skillful role playing helped to make possible this phase of the experiments.

and, as with the mirror, the experimenter asked the subject to hang it up. From this point on, the procedure was as described above for the mirror.

In both cases the string was tied beforehand by the experimenter, so that when hung it had the identical amount and angle of form visible as in Part I.

Mirror and "No Smoking" sign in these "introduced" conditions were expected to embed the string because (a) the "accidental" introduction of the mirror and sign would be interpreted by the subject to be genuine, and not part of the experimental design, since the subject would "believe" that the experimenter did not know it was to be brought in. To use psychological concepts, the subject would structure the introduction of the object as belonging to a different "sphere of meaning" than that of the experimental situation: "No Smoking" sign or mirror belongs to an administrative province outside the design of this experiment. (b) The explanations of the secretary and the experimenter's request that the subject hang the object both point to future "No Smoking" and imply permanent belongingness of the introduced article on the wall. (c) Once the object was hung on the wall by the subject, it would acquire its usual stay-putness value for him, as if it had always been there.

Our experimental analysis does not attempt to determine which of the cognitive factors hypothesized above is more or less operative and how they are interrelated. We only maintain that they are "intervening variables" which shape the meaning of the situation for the subject such as to imbue the object with a permanent character on the wall.

In addition, as a separate condition the intact mirror was introduced in which the usual white string was replaced by an orange-red one. The purpose was to test whether a more perceptually outstanding string—Duncker's "pregnant signal"— would outweigh cognitive embeddedness.

Predictions

The following predictions were made: despite the subjects' recent experience with the string, the problem difficulty (failure frequency and solution time) with the introduced objects would be significantly greater than in the control group, and would approach that of the hanging E + objects in Part I.

Weakly Embedded ("Dexterity") Conditions

Here, perceptual availability was maintained while the embedding influence of the object meaning was either minimal to begin with, or deliberately reduced by the experimenter. The articles used were the cardboard, the obsolete calendar, and the intact mirror. Each was lying on the desk, in the respective experiment, before the subject entered the room.

The procedure was as follows: the subject entered the room, was seated, and again started with the general part of the instructions (A), after which he was told that the experimenter was interested in correlating people's manual dexterity with the manner in which they went about solving problems. Therefore the subject was next given the O'Connor Tweezer Dexterity Test (subjects familiar with this test were excluded). As a "second part" of the Dexterity Test, the subject was asked to pick up the object by the string, using the tweezers, carry it across the room, and hang it on the nail in the wall (the same crucial position as always). For realism, the subject was timed with a stop watch. As soon as he had done this, the experimenter said, "Okay, sit down please. Now I want you to start with the first problem." The subject was given the same fill-in tasks for the same fifteen-minute period as in the introduced conditions, and, following this, the rest of the instructions for the two-stick problem.

The time needed for hanging the respective object with the tweezers was virtually the same as that required for hanging it "by hand" in the introduced conditions. It was assumed that the perceptual contact with the string would be comparable in both cases and result in equivalent perceptual availability. In the one case, the subject hangs the string over the nail with tweezers and in the other he "makes tweezers" with thumb and forefinger for the same purpose.

It was expected that hanging the object on the wall as completion of the Dexterity Test would interfere with the embedding influence of the string because: (a) the experimenter himself designates string-and-object as *equipment* of the Dexterity Test, which makes the object lose its specific purposive meaning (e.g., whether the object for the Dexterity Test is a mirror or something else does not matter); therefore, the subject can *include* such things more easily in the experimental situation, and may more readily structure them as relevant to the two-stick problem as opposed to the "introduced" and "hanging" conditions; (b) as the subject hangs the object in the context of proving his dexterity, a test which he assumes will be repeated later with other subjects, the object would not acquire temporal belongingness on the wall. This holds not only for the cardboard and the obsolete calendar where the stay-putness character is low to begin with, but also for the intact mirror, whose potent stay-putness character has been demonstrated. (c) The hanging of the object is the termination of the Dexterity Test, and as such does not "fixate" the object anywhere permanently, but "discards" it with the functional meaning of having fulfilled a transiently assigned purpose. Again it is not claimed that our experimental analysis can differentiate among the cognitive factors hypothesized above.

Predictions

We predict that in the dexterity conditions: (a) failure frequency and solution time will not differ significantly from the control; and (b) that these measures will not differ significantly from the values obtained with the same objects in the E — conditions of Part I. (c) In the special case of the intact mirror which potently embedded the string in Part I, we now predict

a decrease of that influence, reducing it to the level of the E −
conditions. Also we predict that success with this mirror will
be greater than in the introduced conditions.

Subjects

A total of 94 subjects including the controls were used in Part
III. The numbers for each group will be presented with the
results. Selection of subjects and assignment to conditions followed the procedure of Part I.

Results

The data were again analyzed according to the failure frequencies, solution time and persistence of embeddedness
through time, using the same statistical methods as in Part I.
Tables III and IV, and Figure 2, present the findings.

TABLE III

Frequency of Failure: All Conditions

Conditions	N	Number Failing	Per Cent Failing	Significance of Difference from Control Condition
Control (string alone)	16	0	0	——
Weakly embedded				
Cardboard dexterity	10	0	0	not sig.
Obsolete calendar dexterity	16	1	6.25	not sig.
Intact mirror dexterity	10	0	0	not sig.
Strongly embedded				
Introd. mirror	16	8	50	$p < .003$
Introd. mirror, red string	10	3	30	$p = .046$
Introd. "No Smoking" sign	16	5	31.25	$p = .022$

TABLE IV

Comparison of Solution Times Under Experimental and Control Conditions

Conditions	N	Mean Solution Time	Significance of Difference from Control Condition
Control	16	2'8''	——
Weakly embedded			
Cardboard dexterity	10	4'00	not sig.
Obsolete calendar dexterity	15	4'12''	p < .05
Intact mirror dexterity	10	3'16''	not sig.
Strongly embedded			
Introd. mirror	8	6'36''	p < .01
Introd. mirror, red string	7	7'26''	p < .05
Introd. "No Smoking" sign	11	6'08''	p < .001

It is evident from Table III that all strongly embedded (introduced) conditions differ significantly from the control in per cent of failures, notwithstanding the fact that the string was made perceptually available by the introduction method. Even the use of the orange-red string with the mirror did not reduce failure frequency significantly.

A comparison was also made between the per cent of failure for the intact mirror and the "No Smoking" sign in the introduced conditions and in the hanging conditions of Part I. No significant differences were found.

The solution time comparison (Table IV) yielded statistically significant differences for all strongly embedded conditions versus the control. Of the weakly embedded (dexterity) conditions, only the calendar differed significantly from the control, contrary to our hypothesis. In summary, of twelve predictions in Part III, eleven were confirmed.

The findings on persistence of embeddedness through time given in Figure 2 closely parallel those of Part I. However, the

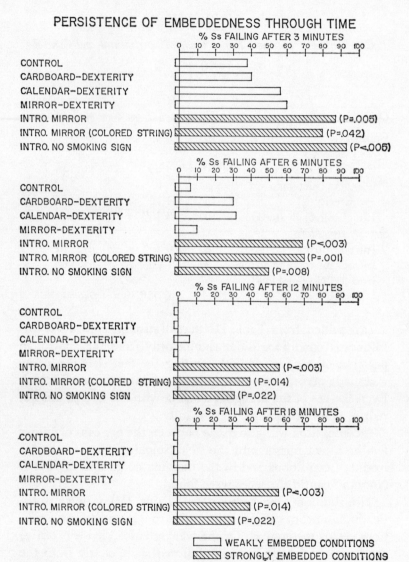

FIGURE 2. Probabilities given refer to differences from control condition as determined by Fisher's exact method.

contrast between the strongly embedded and weakly embedded conditions appears earlier, being statistically significant after three minutes.

DISCUSSION OF PARTS I - III

The problem-solving difficulty our subjects had with the introduced conditions might be attributed to *active* preutilization in Duncker's sense. Specifically, "heterogeneous functional fixedness" occurs when the subject preutilizes an object in its usual function (F 1), and this fixates the meaning of it so that later, within the same problem context, it resists service in an unusual and dissimilar function (F 2). Thus in our "introduced" conditions the subject suspends the object on the wall with the string. This could be interpreted as F 1 which fixates the string so as to make it less available for the two-stick problem (F 2: string to bind sticks). However, this explanation does not seem to apply here.

1. In Duncker's preutilization, "the properties particularly claimed by the function of F 1 stand out, become dominant, 'central' " so that recentering or other potential use (F 2) is hindered (1945, p. 100). By contrast, "the properties" of our crucial item, the string, do not become dominant or central, but are cognitively embedded in the meaning unit of which the string is a part.

2. Duncker's F 1 is defined as the usual or customary function of the critical item; F 2 is an unusual or new function. This distinction does not hold for our experiment, where suspending (F 1) and binding (F 2) are not really heterogeneous and are equally familiar uses of string. Thus "recentering" would occur between two customary and similar functions.

3. Moreover, the data demonstrate that active preutilization is not the crucial variable in determining problem difficulty in our experiments. In both the "introduced" and "dexterity" conditions, the subject hangs the critical object by the string, thus presumably "preutilizing" it. Accordingly, the problem difficulty in the introduced and in the dexterity con-

ditions should be equivalent. Our findings contradict this. The contrasting result between the two situations is, however, accounted for by our theory.

In summary, the evidence presented seems to favor the conclusion that (a) preutilization of the string as a confounding variable can be ruled out in our experiment; and that (b) cognitive embeddedness and preutilization are distinguishable determinants of fixedness of thought material.

It is our premise that if we alter the properties of the suspended object in certain ways, its stay-putness value will change, e.g., the mirror will become "less a mirror" when cloudy. Such changes will be perceptual cues for the subject, reducing the stay-putness function and thereby the cognitive embeddedness of the string. It could be argued that this factor is not the crucial variable in the cases of the cardboard, obsolete calendar, and cloudy mirror. Rather their unusual perceptual appearance might provide a clue to make the subject suspicious: "Why is this odd-looking thing hanging there?" This could lead the subject to suspect a connection between the respective object and the design of the experimenter, i.e., "he put it there on purpose." The genuineness of the article's *raison d'être* on the wall would thereby vanish, bringing the string into the foreground. It may be noted that the experiments were conducted in the basement of a fifty-year-old building where the interior of the psychology offices, laboratory cubicles and equipment had a well-worn appearance. Examination of our data contraindicates the above-suggested interpretation. All subjects were instructed to "think aloud" during the entire experiment and were further reminded to do so at one-minute intervals, if necessary. Any suspicion on the part of the subjects should have been expressed under this intensive demand. In the running verbatim protocols of the 28 successful subjects in the three experimental conditions (cardboard; obsolete calendar; cloudy mirror), only one statement of suspicion was found. This subject commented on the "oldness of the calendar" as bearing on the experiment. Surprisingly, of the subjects succeeding with the hanging cardboard, 5 spontaneously said later that they had at *first* thought it was (variously) a sign, or a calendar, or a sign with its face to the wall. No subjects connected the cardboard with the design of the experiment. This suggests that instead of inducing suspicion, even the blank cardboard tended at *first* to assume some meaningful function on the wall for the subject.

Since all successful subjects were asked in the postproblem interview to describe how the string came to their attention, their responses offer another source of evidence concerning possible suspicion. In principle, if the subject became suspicious of the object to a degree where he would interpret it to be part of the experimenter's *design*, this would have to be *consciously* manifest at some time in the subject's thinking. Only 1 additional subject voiced this suspicion retrospectively, making a total of 2 out of 28 subjects who expressed suspicion. Many of the others never remarked at all on the appearance of the object. Those who did, typically made naïve comments such as "I wondered why there would be an outdated calendar in this room"; or "I noticed the mirror, I don't know why I noticed it other than it looked funny because it looked cloudy." The frequency with which subjects examined or contacted the object on the wall but did not utilize the string at that time also argues behaviorally against suspicion (subjects looked behind the cloudy mirror, touched the screw eyes which held the string, spoke of wrapping the obsolete calendar around the sticks for fastening them, without yet using the string, etc.). The same question could be raised for the dexterity conditions where the subject's suspicion might be aroused when he has to hang the cardboard, the obsolete calendar, and the intact mirror. Of the 35 successful subjects in this case, none expressed suspicion, either in the recorded verbalizations during the experiment, or in the postproblem interview. Furthermore, of the 63 subjects in *all* E − conditions (dexterity and "hanging"), 80 per cent asked the experimenter's permission to take off the string when they expressed the thought of using it for the solution. Had the subjects been suspicious of the experimenter having "planted the thing" there, they would hardly have bothered to ask. Concerning the "introduced" conditions, no successful subject either in the experimental protocols or in the postproblem interview gave any indication of suspicion about the secretary's bringing the object into the room and of himself subsequently hanging it at the request of the experimenter. On the contrary, *both* failing and successful subjects commented that they had thought the object was genuinely destined for the wall. It is noteworthy that even in the E+ conditions subjects would show naïve behavioral orientation toward the "No Smoking" sign or mirror by putting out their cigarettes or by looking into the mirror to "groom" themselves without responding to the string at that moment.

part IV

It is our basic thesis that in all experiments all subjects "saw" the sign with the string, at least in terms of the string being "latently" present perceptually; but that in terms of thought material not all subjects regarded it as relevant to the problem. This perceptual presence may be here defined as form vision or a certain degree of visual discrimination of the string versus other suspending devices, etc. Obviously, for the successful subject, that perceptual presence need not be demonstrated. For the validity of the postulated cognitive embeddedness it is also necessary to establish as clearly as possible this perceptual presence for the failing subjects as well. Since we could not obtain direct evidence for this proposition, efforts were made to support it by indirect methods.

First, all subjects faced the object and string squarely in their line of vision—the string with a visible knot always appearing as two sides of a well-defined triangle (5½ inches to each side). This can be considered a definite figure on the level of visual field organization. Indeed, 95 per cent of the 66 subjects discovered the string, i.e., solved the problem, in all E − conditions. In the E + conditions, the embedding objects were equivalent to the nonembedding ones as far as physical stimulus dimensions and visual field organization were concerned. Here, 50.6 per cent of the 89 subjects succeeded and must have seen the string. Therefore, the inference seems to be justified that in both E + and E − conditions all subjects had equal "opportunity" to see the string on the level of visual field organization.

Second, the setting, where the object was introduced and hung by the subject, was designed expressly to provide undeniable *recent* perceptual-motor commerce with the string, regardless of whether he failed or succeeded.

Third, the procedure in the postproblem interview for *all* failing subjects contains information on this issue (as well as pointing to the strong cognitive embeddedness of the string). The following questions, giving stepwise hints, were asked in order to determine the point where the embeddedness would give way, allowing the subject to see the string's relevance:

1. What about that? (Experimenter points in the general direction of the object on the wall.)

   If no insight, then:

2. What about that "No Smoking" sign (mirror, cardboard)?

   If no insight, then:

3. What about that string? (Experimenter points.)

Of all 47 failing subjects, 5 offered the solution after Question 1; 4 after Question 2; and 38 after Question 3. On the one hand, the preponderance of insight only achieved after the question "What about that string?" attests to its potent cognitive embeddedness. On the other hand, the manner in which the subjects responded bespeaks the string's latent perceptual presence: the vast majority of the subjects, verbally and behaviorally, expressed chagrin, self-reproach, or surprise that they had not *thought* of the string earlier. In addition, 72 per cent of the subjects stated upon direct questioning that they had been aware of the string's presence, but that it had not occurred to them to use it.

Two additional experiments were conducted to tap as directly as possible the perception of the string as defined above. We tried to design a situation that would approximate the psychological condition of an unsuccessful subject. Up to a certain point the procedure for the new group was completely identical with the "No Smoking" sign condition of Part I. It differed only in that the experimenter stopped the subject at the point where he had verbalized the conceptual solution, i.e., "If I had something to fasten the sticks together, I could reach the rings and peg," or "If I had a string or something, I could do it."

Experiment A

The subjects were asked to turn away from the experimental problem, close their eyes, and "name all the prominent objects in the room." If subjects named the sign but not the string, they were asked: "How was the sign attached to the wall?" If they did not spontaneously name the sign, they were asked if they remembered seeing a "No Smoking" sign, and if they did, they were also asked about its attachment.

It was expected that analogous to the naming experiment of Part II, all subjects would mention the sign spontaneously but not the string. They would, however, mention the string when questioned about the attachment. Twelve subjects were used.

Surprisingly, only 3 subjects named the sign spontaneously. Eight more remembered the sign when asked. Of these 11, 9 subjects responded by stating, "It was hung on the wall with string." (The other two said "thumbtacks" and "scotch tape" respectively.) We consider this suggestive evidence for the perceptual presence of the string for the failing subjects, all of whom had also reached the stage of verbalizing the conceptual solution. We were not sure how much of the failure of most subjects to name the sign *spontaneously* could be attributed to the functional stay-putness character of the sign itself, and how much to the wording of the instructions to name "prominent" objects. Inspection of the protocols suggested both possibilities, since they revealed that relatively few objects were named (a mean of 10.7), and these were almost exclusively the furniture and the task material (rings, sticks, pegs). Furthermore, it could be argued that the subjects responded positively to the experimenter's direct question about the sign, because it was a leading question. In order to minimize these possibly confounding variables, a variation of the questioning procedure was devised.

Experiment B

After again reaching the conceptual solution, subjects were taken out of the room. This time they were given a check list of thirty objects arranged in random order among which sixteen were actually in the room (the sign included) and fourteen were not, with the following instructions: "Below are listed a number of objects. Some were in the room; some were not. Please check those that were in the room."

Table____	Door____	Manila Folder____
Window____	Door Knob____	Cigarette Package____
Writing Pad____	No Smoking Sign____	Eye Chart____
Blackboard____	Board Eraser____	Coffee Cup____
Sticks____	Light Fixture____	Chair Cushion____
Chalk____	Window Shade____	Picture____
Hoops____	Light Switch____	Desk Lamp____
Chairs____	Thermometer____	Mirror____
Stop watch____	Calendar____	Paper Cup____
White Line____	Ink Well____	Thermostat____

Since this check list required only recognition, it was expected that this task would reduce the possible interference of the sign's functional stay-putness character with the spontaneous recall of it under other conditions. Since the check list defined the range of items for the subject, the possible former bias in the instructions to name "prominent" objects was obviated. Since the "No Smoking" sign was presented along with four other objects conventionally found on walls, as well as twenty-five other items (some fictitious and some not), it was assumed that any leading character of the inquiry about the sign was minimized.

All subjects who checked the "No Smoking" sign were then questioned: "You checked the "No Smoking" sign. How was it attached to the wall?" Ten subjects were used, and 9 checked the sign, and also responded, "It was suspended by a string." The picture, the mirror, the eye chart, and the calendar were deliberately included so as to allow for mistakes, in case the subject had only a vague recollection of what was on the wall. No subject checked these, indicating that the selection of the sign was not guesswork but genuine recognition. Analyzing the distribution of responses, it was found that the subjects' recall of what was in the room proved highly accurate. In the *total* number of responses of all 10 subjects, a "dummy object" was checked only five times. If every subject had checked all fourteen dummy items, this would have amounted to a total of 140 errors. Thus only 3.6 per cent of the total possible errors were committed by our subjects. Of the sixteen objects actually in the room the subjects averaged 12.9 correct checks (range 11-15), indicating that their recall was quite complete.

Combining Experiments A and B, 18 of 22 subjects stated that the sign was attached to the wall by the string. Such signs are probably just as often attached by other means. The subjects could have responded with "scotch tape; thumbtacks; staples; nails; adhesive backing," etc. They could also have answered, "I don't know," but none did. It therefore seems unlikely that 80.6 per cent of the subjects would designate the string by chance. The inference concerning the perceptual presence of the string, even for the failing subjects, finds support in both experiments.

PART V

Our findings in Part I to IV leave us with a psychological paradox. How is it possible that something may be present in the visual field but not in the cognitive field? We are not prepared to solve this paradox, but will offer some rather speculative hypotheses and one additional experiment which bears on them. If our theory of meaning units is correct, then it would follow that an embedded object is cognitively not registered as long as the meaning unit remains intact and un-analyzed by the subject. In terms of a phenomenological re-construction, the process of breaking down the meaning unit and freeing the string seems to involve the following phases, some of them lasting a very brief time: (a) in seeking to solve the two-stick problem the subject scans the room for some-thing to "bind." Usually he verbalizes the need for a fastener such as a clamp, scotch tape, or string. (b) In order to suc-ceed, the subject must "de-center" the functional stay-putness character of the unit on the wall. He "suspends" the given meaning of the unit. Thus, for example, instead of seeing the mirror on the wall, he views it as merely a hanging object ("nonmirror"), even if *only for a fleeting moment*. (c) This object can now appear as having other possibilities, and can be in-spected in relation to the subject's needs for a fastener. (d) This allows the subject to break down the unit "hanging object" into its components, and the string becomes cognitively ac-cessible. Once this is accomplished, a new unit of mirror-and-string is constituted, in which the string is cognitively present. (e) What was originally accepted as a stay-put unit functional-ly belonging on the wall is now recentered into a unit "mirror-with-a-*string*" from which the string may be used or "bor-rowed." The presumed phases (a) to (e) are elusive to experi-mental test. Some support may be offered for (e) in that an impressively high proportion of subjects, before taking the string off, asked the experimenter if it was all right to use it. In addition, after having used it, many subjects spontaneously replaced the string as if the cognitive unit had to be restored.

Phenomenologically these phases may be further characterized as a transition from an *unreflective* experience of the
given meaning unit (e.g., the mirror) to a *reflective* approach
to it; during this transition the subject increases the psychological distance between himself and the meaning unit as it
was initially present in his direct experience. Considering the
unsuccessful subjects from this point of view, they may never
"de-center" the meaning unit in question and maintain an unreflective attitude toward it. In the postproblem interview of
the 47 failing subjects, when the experimenter pointed to the
object and said, "What about that?" 5 de-centered it and
achieved insight. When the experimenter pointed again, asking, "What about that mirror?" (or "No Smoking" sign, etc.),
only 4 more subjects de-centered it. The rest (38 subjects)
continued to view the mirror as as mirror and the sign as a sign.
They said, "What about it?" or just named it again. But even
if such a subject reached the stage of de-centering and of en-
visaging other possibilities, he still may make an incorrect
choice and become "fixated" on it. Among these subjects,
some persisted in considering the "No Smoking" sign or calendar for use as a wrapper to bind the sticks or as a shovel-
like ending to be attached to one of the sticks for "scooping"
the rings onto the peg. Still others thought of using the screw
eyes on the back of the mirror. In general we could describe a
variety of other patterns of rigidity and "fixations" in our unsuccessful subjects. They parallel the types of fixation analyzed
by Duncker and Krechevsky (1939). But the failing majority,
even after considering verbally the object on the wall for a
moment as "something one could use," rejected it. This lends
some support to the interpretation that the unreflective approach to the given meaning unit as a whole was never fully
abandoned in these cases.

The Observation Experiment

Many writers have associated reflectiveness with psychological distance or ego detachment (Goldstein, 1939; Werner,

1940; Lewin, 1935). Too much involvement in a situation, for example, can lead to a lessening of both a reflective approach and psychological distance.

It was therefore thought that by manipulating the variable of psychological distance we would concomitantly influence reflectiveness. An experiment was conceived in which the subject would naïvely observe, from outside the situation, the problem-solving attempts of someone else without being himself directly engaged in the action. At the same time he would acquire all the relevant facts necessary for the solution. It was expected that in the position of a naïve observer, the subject would be less ego-involved than the person actually performing in the situation. It was predicted that subjects would solve the problem with ease after they had watched a "plant" go through all the usual actions of a *bona fide* experimental subject to the point where the conceptual solution had been expressed. This would be the case even when the observation took place under $E+$ conditions, which in Part I had produced a significant amount of failures.

Procedure

Two groups of subjects were told, "You are going to observe a demonstration in problem solving. Afterwards you will be asked some questions. Please do not speak to each other from now on." Then they were taken into the experimental room with all the usual equipment present. With one group of 15 subjects an eye chart (of the same dimensions as the previously used objects) was hanging on the wall with the string in the same manner as always. With another group of 7 subjects, the usual "No Smoking" sign hung. Both groups were told, "This is the room in which the experiment will take place. You will watch it from behind that mirror" (one-way vision screen which constituted one wall of the room). After each group was seated in the observation room accompanied by an experimenter, the subjects were again reminded not to speak to each other. A second experimenter and the planted subject entered the experimental room in which the "No Smoking" sign (or eye chart) hung on the wall directly opposite the one-way vision mirror. The standard instructions were given to the planted subject, and the problem proceeded until the subject expressed the need to fasten the two sticks together and had verbalized his need for a fastener or a string (conceptual solution). Following this, with a few minutes of further futile effort, the planted subject was stopped by the second experimenter and told, "I'll stop you here. Please wait in the outer room and I'll tell you the solution later." At this point each observer was given a questionnaire as follows:

> Now we would like you to try your hand at the problem. What would you suggest to the subject in the experiment? Maybe you will choose to begin by continuing where he left off, that is, where you observed him trying to put the sticks together in order to reach the rings. We would like you to describe the solution which you suggest to the subject for this problem in complete detail. Specifically, of the things in the room, what would you propose to him to use here in order to get the rings onto the peg.
>
> In giving your specific advice to this subject, you should remember the conditions under which he is required to operate. For this reason, we repeat to you the instructions he received.

The verbatim standard instructions followed the above, and the subjects were assured that the problem could be solved by using what was in the room. Each subject was instructed to write his solution down at once on the questionnaire sheet, and on a subsequent page he was asked questions about the experimental objects. All subjects were also informed verbally that they were to remain anonymous and should not put their names on the questionnaire. Since no subject wrote "I don't know," the responses were scored "correct" or "incorrect."

Results

Of the 15 subjects with the eye chart, 11 immediately wrote down the correct solution (73 per cent). Of the 7 subjects with the "No Smoking" sign, 6 succeeded at once (86 per cent). No subject reported that he discovered the solution because string had been mentioned during the planted subject's thinking aloud, or made any comments about this.

The conditions in this experiment were considered to be E + conditions; the percentage of failures is much lower than in the other E + conditions of Part I, and in fact almost represents a reversal of the Part I results.

Using Fisher's exact method, no significant difference between the frequency of success and failure between the eye chart and "No Smoking" sign conditions was found. It was therefore considered justifiable to pool the results of the two groups. Because of the procedural differences between this experiment and the E + conditions of Part I, it was felt that only a gross comparison was in order. Therefore, all E + conditions (hanging intact mirror, "No Smoking" sign, and current calendar) were pooled and compared with the pooled observation experiments, using the X^2 technique. With one degree of freedom the obtained X^2 of 6.74 was significant at the .01 level of confidence. This indicates that there was significantly more success in the observation experiments than in the individual E + conditions.

COMMENTS

The framework in which cognitive embeddedness may be explored is a flexible one, extending beyond our specific experimentation. The near-to-life situations which can be devised to study such embeddedness are limited only by the experimenter's ingenuity. For illustration, we list the following possible designs: one could study the degree of embeddedness of the string by having it support (1) a poster which announces a coming social event as opposed to one that has already taken place; (2) a "Wet Paint" sign in a freshly painted room versus the same sign on a shabby wall; (3) a hanging "No Smoking" sign or mirror versus the same object leaned against the corner with its string loose. Another possibility could involve a string wrapped around a package lying in the room. Different degrees of the string's embeddedness could also be explored by having *several* objects hung on the wall, each with a different functional stay-putness; the test would be, which object is selected *first* by the subject, and so on. The area of different cultural taboos may also be a fruitful source for demonstrating cognitive embeddedness derived from social attitudes.

Another interesting design has been reported which we feel is a case of cognitive embeddedness: the subject has to remove a ping-pong ball from a pipe, a task that can only be accomplished by floating it out with water. In one version dirty water in a bucket was available and was readily used. In the other clean water in a pitcher with glasses was not used.

Although the case for cognitive embeddedness seems to have been established in our study, a complete theory would have to answer several questions not yet dealt with. All concern variables which influence the meaning unit.

1. The chief question centers around the problem of what determines, within a given meaning unit, which object is the embedding and which the embedded one. Without being in the position to offer a solution at this point, a direction for further inquiry may be suggested. The first step would be to consider the possibility of whether there are general functional characteristics of certain classes of things which predispose them to enter into a relationship with other things where they can become embedded. This would imply that certain objects have *relatively* little meaning in themselves save that of a general utility or instrumentality. Examples of such objects would be water, cotton, paper, tape, cork, string, cardboard, sticks, clay, glue, rubber bands, and the like. These appear chameleonlike in their functional meaning in that they tend to take on the "coloring" of the context to which they belong. They have a kind of incompleteness; they invite being used *for* or being applied *to* something. They call for association with other objects or solicit plastic manipulation. The functional properties of these objects, though versatile, are by no

means unlimited. Tape has only so many uses, and is of no value as a rigid support or as a weight. Such objects may be categorized as having a functionally fluid meaning versus other objects which have more defined, "self-sufficient" and stable functional meaning. This distinction does not propose a dichotomy but rather a polarity spanned by a continuum of varying degrees of functional self-sufficiency. It is possible that this dimension represents one determinant of which objects tend to become more easily embedded in a meaning unit, and which not.

In a pilot study a rating sheet was administered to 55 college students in an attempt to obtain differentiating responses between the functional properties of such "fluid-meaning" objects and their polar opposites. The subject was asked to rate each object on five functional aspects (many vs. few uses; used alone vs. used with something; fixed vs. nonfixed size, form, location). We expected that the ratings between the "fluid" and "stable" objects would diverge on these aspects. Using a X^2 analysis we found the "fluid meaning" objects to be rated as predicted either on four or all of the five aspects. The ratings of the "stable" objects were not as clear-cut on most expected aspects, but also tended toward the predicted direction.

Analysis of the results of this pilot study revealed certain faults in the design of the rating scale (overlapping of certain categories, etc.) which need correction. Such difficulties might be overcome by the use of established rating techniques like the Semantic Differential (Osgood et al., 1957).

The "fluid-stable" dimension as a determinant of potential cognitive embeddedness must also be investigated in relation to the broader context in which a meaning unit is formed. An example where a usually "fluid" object dominates the meaning unit, instead of becoming embedded in it, is the legend of Damocles seated under the sword hung by a hair.

2. There are certain normative expectations about the characteristics of objects in meaning units, based on past

experience. Alterations of these standards affect the cohesive-
ness of the unit. In our experiments, the functional stay-putness
was altered by manipulation of such norms involving appearance. Other norms, needing further exploration, are, for example, style, size, and form of the unit. These may influence
the interrelation of the contained objects and thereby modify
the balance of the embeddedness. We may think of a small
rococo mirror or a very large cardboard sign with "No Smoking" in very tiny lettering hung in a laboratory cubicle. This
would weaken the embeddedness of the string. In principle,
the problem of congruence and incongruence *within* the structure of a meaning unit and its relation to the broader *context*
to which the contents of the meaning unit must be apposite,
is still an open field.

3. In our experiment we have been theoretically and empirically concerned with variables which lie in the dimension
of object qualities, functions and relationships influencing
cognitive embeddedness. There is another set of relevant variables which lies in the province of intraorganismic functions,
e.g., individual differences. As the Gottschaldt figures have
been employed by Witkin (1950), by Gardner et al. (1960)
tapping personality factors, and by Teuber and Weinstein
(1956) for determining the intellectual sequellae of brain
pathology, the phenomenon of cognitive embeddedness could
be similarly utilized in exploring personality organization,
normal and abnormal. This would also call for a study of
meaning units and cognitive embeddedness in reference to
developmental sequences. Werner's contributions to our
knowledge of genetic laws of thinking and of microgenesis
(1956) and also Piaget's work on child development have
laid the foundation for such research.

Finally the concepts of meaning unit and cognitive embeddedness may be applicable to fixedness of thought material where the thought content refers to relationships among
"ideas" or symbols, instead of among abjects. Some of
Wertheimer's (1945) analyses of instances of productive

thinking could be cited as illustrative, especially Einstein's reformulations of the traditional concepts of time and space.

SUMMARY

The concept of cognitive embeddedness was introduced and theoretically developed as another type of fixedness of thought material. The concept was applied to problem-solving difficulties encountered in natural life situations where the crucial object needed for solution becomes camouflaged (embedded) in the meaning unit it forms with another object. Thus something can be present in the visual field but not in the cognitive field, as, for example, a string suspending a mirror on the wall. The focus of the investigation was twofold: to demonstrate cognitive embeddedness experimentally, and to explore different degrees of influence of this factor. For this purpose seventeen different experiments were performed using a total of 240 subjects. The results of these experiments both demonstrated the factor of cognitive embeddedness and supported specific predictions generated from its theoretical formulation.

BIBLIOGRAPHY

Carnap, R. (1937), Testability and Meaning, IV. *Philosophy of Science*, 4:1-40.
Duncker, K. (1945), On Problem Solving. Translated by Lynne S. Lees. *Psychological Monographs*, *58*, No. 5.
——— & Krechevsky, I. (1939), On Solution Achievement. *Psychological Review*, *46*:176-185.
Finney, D. J. (1948), The Fisher-Yates Test of Significance in 2 x 2 Contingency Tables. *Biometrika*, *35*.
Gardner, R. S.; Holzman, P. S.; Klein, G. S.; Linton, H.; Spence, D. P. (1959), Cognitive Control: A Study of Consistencies in Cognitive Behavior. *Psychological Issues*, *1* (4). New York: International Universities Press.
Goldstein, K. (1939), *The Organism*. New York: American Book Company.
Gottschaldt, K. (1926, 1929), Über den Einfluss der Erfahrung

302 *Martin Scheerer and Maurice D. Huling*

auf die Wahrnehmung von Figuren, I and II. *Psychologische Forschung*, *8*:261-371; *12*:1-87.

Köhler, W. (1917), *Intelligenzprüfungen an Anthropoiden*, I. Abh. Königl. Preuss. Akad. Wiss. Phys. Math. Kl. No. 1.

────── (1931), *The Mentality of Apes*. New York: Harcourt, Brace.

Latscha, R. (1953), Test of Significance in a 2 x 2 Contingency Table: Extension of Finney's Table. *Biometrika*, *40*.

Lewin, K. (1935), *A Dynamic Theory of Personality*. New York: McGraw-Hill.

Osgood, C. E.; Suci, G. J.; & Tannenbaum, P. H. (1957), *The Measurement of Meaning*. Urbana: University of Illinois Press.

Scheerer, M. (1959), Spheres of Meaning: An Analysis of Stages from Perception to Abstract Thinking. *Journal of Individual Psychology*, *15*:50-61.

Teuber, H. L. & Weinstein, S. (1956), Ability to Discover Hidden Figures after Cerebral Lesions. *A.M.A. Archives of Neurology and Psychiatry*, *26*:369-379.

Werner, H. (1940), *Comparative Psychology of Mental Development*. New York: International Universities Press, 2nd rev. ed., 1957.

────── (1956), Microgenesis and Aphasia. *Journal of Abnormal and Social Psychology*, *52*:347-353.

Wertheimer, M. (1945), *Productive Thinking*. New York: Harper.

White, C. (1952), The Use of Ranks in a Test of Significance for Comparing Two Treatments. *Biometrics*, *8*:33-41.

Witkin, H. A. (1950), Individual Differences in Ease of Perception of Embedded Figures. *Journal of Personality*, *19*:1-15

Instinctive Behavior, Maturation— Experience and Development

T. C. SCHNEIRLA, Sc.D.

Museum of Natural History

All animals display patterns of adaptive action characteristic of their species, normally appearing within a typical range of developmental conditions. Moth caterpillars at maturity spin cocoons, female carnivores commonly wean and leave their young when these near the end of infancy, and human babies commonly begin to smile at faces around three months after birth. Advocates of "instinct" theory think of such actions as due to inborn, innate impulses blindly impelling actions appropriate to reaching the respective ends. Others (e.g., Schneirla, 1948, 1956), skeptical of the instinct dogma, prefer the less presumptive term "instinctive behavior" for a set of problems concerning the evolutionary and ontogenetic origins of species-typical behavior. These are the real problems raised by the instinct tradition, and the fact is that no common theoretical formula is yet available to meet them on all functional levels.

It is a strong probability that heredity is basically involved in the development of all behavior. The issue is not whether heredity or environment dominates in particular cases, nor is it a matter of their relative strengths. It is very likely that the real contributions of American anti-instinctivists have been obscured by the impression that their goal was to lock out genetics from the discussion. Although they may have gone "too far," as Hunter (1947) concluded, in the case of Watson (1914), for example, I believe an objective historical appraisal raises his pioneer studies on terns and on neonate human infants to a significance well above that of his post-experimental lectures questioning the role of heredity in human development. The principal contribution of this group rather was its emphasis on objective, experimental investigations of behavior development to replace the phenomenistic, descriptive type characteristic of the classical instinctivists.

To an alarming extent scientists are still bound up in the main confusion of the traditional instinct problem, through a tendency to substitute for the "outworn" (Beach, 1947) nature-nurture dichotomy equivalent dogmas such as the distinction of the innate and the acquired in behavior. The problem is thus often stated as one of innate behavior, and a common answer among ethologists is that the genes pass on a code which through encapsulated intraneural processes directly determines development of instinctive patterns. Another variation, not uncommon among child psychologists, is that genic determiners install an organic growth through which innate behavior arises, to be modified through learning as infancy advances. The objective of this essay is to mark out, from the standpoint of comparative psychology, some concepts that promise to facilitate the avoidance of instinctivistic obscurantism and that may improve our perspective in the investigation of development (Schneirla, 1956).

How are these problems to be solved? Of course, the criterion of *early appearance* has been weakened by evidence for prenatal conditioning in certain birds and mammals. On the other hand, the changes so produced lack clarity, and thus far their postnatal effects have not been traced. Of course, *universality* is doubtful as a criterion, in view of the fact that common habits tend to prevail in species living under similar natural conditions; it is doubtful, however, that beavers learn to build dams, and patterns such as hoarding in rats and nesting in birds seem very difficult to explain except as innate. To many, the conventional criteria of the innate seem thus defensible; also, perhaps most impressive, characteristic patterns often appear in animals *isolated* from their kind and from their species environment from birth. And although it is admitted, with Hebb (1953), that the nature of *learning* is not yet sufficiently well understood to be distinguished readily from the hypothetical innate in behavior, the problem of demonstrating how learning influences early stages of ontogeny still seems very hazy, and the possibility of assigning a role for learning in many species-typical patterns such as the predatory patterns of solitary wasps seems negative. Even the hardest-headed epigeneticists may be impressed by the genic-behavior correspondences described by the psychogeneticists (Hall, 1951), although such evidence may not do much more than emphasize the problems of ontogeny without solving them. Even if all of these difficulties are considered, there are nevertheless grounds for holding that no infallible rules exist for differentiating the innate from the acquired, as both are hypothetical, and that questions of instinctive behavior must be investigated along other lines.

The fact cannot be emphasized too often that the central problem of instinctive behavior is one of development (Maier and Schneirla, 1935, Chaps. VI, XI), working comparatively not just with higher mammals and a few other convenient types but through the widest possible range. Furthermore, experience shows that the gains will come not only through comparisons of ontogeny in closely related animals, as is usual in psychogenetics, for example, but also in very different phyletic types. Jellyfish take food with tentacles and manubrium, carnivores with forepaws and jaws—how different are these processes in their development? It is doubtful, for example, that a perception of "food" arises in both cases. How are we to account for the development of functional differences often more striking in closely related species than are those between more distantly related types? Clark, Aronson, and Gordon (1954) have shown that the "isolating mechanisms" opposing the crossing of two closely related species of fish involve not only structural and physiological, but also behavioral processes. As yet there have been very few experiments on this problem, so that, for example, we cannot say whether the behavioral components of isolating mechanisms in lower vertebrate and in mammalian species are similar or are very different.

Investigators are still hampered by various types of reductionistic tendencies, a common one being the generalization of "learning" and "perception" through the animal series, with all behavior modifications classed as the former and all sensitivity classed as the latter. For these matters, comparisons should be developmental and go far beyond the scope of adult properties. If scientists are to compare lower and higher animals insightfully, the entire causal nexus intervening between the fertilized egg and later stages in ontogeny must be studied analytically, with the functional properties of each stage always examined in relation to those of the preceding and the following stages. The concept of *intervening variables*, denoting all types of processes mediating between initial and later stages in development, has great potential utility for the study of instinctive behavior.

Appropriate methods are needed for studying development and the involved causal nexus both analytically and synthetically in each important species, to discern what common processes and what specialized differences prevail in the ontogeny of each. It is now recognized that what the individual really inherits in each species is a characteristic set of genes, the *genotype*, with an accompanying cytoplasm, as distinguished from possible *phenotypes*, the developing organism and its properties at successive stages in ontogeny. It is of course the phenotype that can be studied more or less directly, whereas investigations of the genotype are necessarily indirect. This unavoidable fact unfortunately encourages nativistic conceptions of species templates in the genes, directly uncoded or translated through growth into the functional patterns of later stages.

But in reality the idea of a direct uncoding of ontogenetic patterns from the genes remains hypothetical. Its application even to early stages seems unclear, as may be gathered from statements such as the following by Weiss, an embryologist:

> It is evident that every new reaction must be viewed in terms of the cellular system in its actual condition at that particular stage, molded by the whole antecedent history of transformations and modifications, rather than solely in terms of the unaltered genes at the core . . . no cell develops independently, but . . . all of them have gone through a long chain of similar environmental interactions with neighboring cells and the products of distant ones [1954, p. 194].

The genes are involved in interactions with their medium from the start, and the fact is that science has barely touched the problem of how genic factors influence organic development (Stern, 1954). The most comprehensive and reasonable attitude for investigators of functional development therefore seems to lie along the lines of Dobzhansky's (1950) statement to the effect that all development is both genotypic and environmental, rather than preformistic. Our premise consequently is that the hypothetical genic effects are mediated at each ontogenetic stage by systems of intervening variables characteristic of that stage in that species under prevalent developmental conditions, and that from initial stages these variables include both factors indirectly dependent on the genotype and others primarily dependent on the situation and environs of development.

Very probably most if not all functional and behavioral properties as well as structural properties of organisms have figured in minor or major ways, separately or in patterns, as factors in natural selection, related *pro* or *con* to survival. In the list of factors having relatively greater weightings in species evolution must be included the intervening variables of all developmental stages, for, as Orton (1955) has pointed out, the evolutionary role of developmental properties at earlier stages may often have exceeded that of adaptive properties at mature stages. A complex array of very different types of organisms has resulted, with contrasting adaptive properties from those of the viruses to those of the primates. It is very advantageous as a conceptual procedure to characterize and differentiate these major adaptive types as *levels* (Needham, 1929; Werner, 1940; Schneirla, 1947), in that they may be classed as higher or lower with respect to the status of abilities and types of organization underlying their adaptive adjustments.

The concept of levels has great potential significance for comparative psychology, as a comprehensive basis for the analysis and synthesis of evidence concerning similarities and differences among the varied adaptive patterns of major phyletic types. What, for example, have similar or different ontogenetic processes to do with the manner in which insects, fishes, and mammals modify their adaptive adjustments under somewhat equivalent conditions. But considerations of the "molecular" as in specific movements and the "molar" as in mating patterns (e.g., Roe and Simpson, 1958) are a different type of theoretical exercise, and do not answer such questions. They are directed at the analysis of functional properties at different stages in individual ontogeny, and should not be confused with "levels" theory, which is directed at phyletic comparisons. For excellent reasons on both biological (Allee et al., 1950) and psychological (Werner, 1940) grounds, re-capitulation doctrine has only a limited significance for the study of ontogeny at any phyletic level in relation to its evolutionary background.

In psychological literature complexity is often used as a criterion to distinguish the adaptive patterns of higher and lower animals. But although animals may be differentiated to some advantage in terms of the complexity of cell aggregates, levels theory concerns psychological properties, and its hypothetical units of ability and organization can differ greatly among the levels. The definition of "simple" or "complex" in the psychological sense at different levels, therefore, must depend upon the nature of adaptive processes and the status of organization attained in the respective animals. This cannot be a matter of what totals of hypothetical molecular components (or complexities) are attained, but of how the sub-systems of each pattern are interrelated, what degrees of plasticity are possible among them, the nature of perceptual re-arousal and of self-excitation processes and the like. As an example, I have found that *Formica* ants and pigmented rats learn the "same" maze problem very differently, the former making a really *complex* problem of it and advancing gradually by distinct stages, the latter behaving as though the problem were much *simpler* and mastering it in less than half the trials (Schneirla, 1959a). What is much more important, the rats exhibit a superior organization in the learning, whereby processes (distantly) similar to those appearing in the ant's second and third stages appear even in the first runs. How are we to determine what the "units" are, so that the learning of these two animals may be compared as to "complexity"? The dilemma can be solved only by viewing the two adjustments as qualitatively different, if we are to derive a theory appropriate to the wholistic nature and the psychological properties of the different animal types.

Notwithstanding a contemporary tendency among behavior investigators to disavow teleology, the practice persists of naming reactions in terms of their adaptive results (e.g., "courtship," "threat reactions"). Subjective impressions rather than objective criteria tend to dominate when common descriptive terms are used—the adjustments of insects and apes, for example, seem to become more alike psychologically—and the possibility wanes of distinguishing functional levels. By hypothesis, however, all existing animals are successful in adapting to their respectively different environments, and the efficiency of adaptive actions to which common names (such as "feeding") are applied therefore cannot be a valid criterion of psychological levels. For example, insects in general in all probability are able to carry out the reproductive adjustments ("courtship," "mating") at least as efficiently as man and often more smoothly, but without proving thereby any appreciable equivalence in the underlying psychological processes.

The task of the developmental psychologist, therefore, is to find formulae appropriate to the ontogenetic patterns of the respective phyletic levels. One important disadvantage of instinct theory, in scientific as in popular writing, is that the same terms are used for adjustments on very different levels, with the result that important differences are obscured. To use a broad contrast, feeding in a jellyfish and in a cat might both be called instinctive, since both acts are products of ontogeny in the normal species habitat, both are species-typical and adaptive. Yet the developmental processes underlying the acts are relatively brief in the former and lengthy in the latter, and the two are organized very differently from a psychological standpoint.

In the lower vertebrates, patterns such as food-taking are stereotyped in that they are obtainable through adequate arousal of species-characteristic tissues in routine ways. The component processes of feeding in the jellyfish depend upon the functional properties of tentacles, manubrium and bell as affected by adequate stimulation, and with suitable techniques comparable reactions may be obtained even from the operatively separated parts. The integration of these part processes into a serial action pattern depends on the conductile functions of the nerve net; their order of participation in action thus depends chiefly on their spatial locations as determined through growth. By virtue of arousal-threshold properties, on adequate stimulation (glutathione at a low concentration), the manubrium (mouth tube) bends adaptively to the given side; on adequate (i.e., high intensity) stimulation both manubrium and bell contract strongly. Although behavior in this animal is variable, stereotypy predominates in the essential components, and modifications in the pattern seem to be limited to relatively short-lived changes in the nature of sensory adaptation or muscular tonus.

Feeding in the domestic cat also is a species-typical pattern developing in the standard habitat. But the chief properties and integration of this mammalian act differ vastly from those in coelenterates. The ontogeny of feeding in kittens passes through long and involved stages, that in the jellyfish is relatively short and essentially a product of tissue growth. In his well-known experiments with feline rodent-killing, Kuo (1930) found evidence that development normally brings several part processes into a functional pattern. Organic components were indicated such as those adapting the cat to being excited by small moving objects, others to pouncing on, to seizing, and to devouring small animals. Other ways of feeding developed instead of this pattern under appropriate extrinsic conditions, and by suitably regulating the kitten's experiences with rodents Kuo produced subjects that preyed upon, feared and avoided, or lived placidly with rodents.

It is apparent that in lower invertebrates and in mammals, patterns such as feeding or mating develop through the mediation of very different intervening variables in radically different ontogenetic progressions. In coelenterates, growth processes impose relatively narrow limits upon action at all stages; in mammals, the involved factors greatly exceed the limits of growth and exploit them very differently according to the developmental conditions. The mammalian pattern is *plastic* in the sense that, under appropriate conditions, onto-genetic systems rather divergent from the species norm may arise; but in coelenterates, change is a matter of variability on a relatively fixed basis, and is not to be confused with the characteristic of plasticity.

Research on instinctive behavior generally has not advanced much beyond an introductory or descriptive stage of study, in which the investigator deals with his problem in terms of vague, categorical terms (e.g., "displacement reaction"). To illustrate the difficulty, we might say that the adaptive patterns of both coelenterates and insects are stereotyped, without recognizing the significant fact that the term "stereo-typy" may have significantly different meanings in the two cases.

Because insects are often cited for their instinctive, stereo-typed behavior, investigations going beyond the descriptive into the analytical stage are needed for insight into the de-velopmental background of typical patterns. It is convenient to point to the fact that the arrangement of tracts and centers, together with properties of rapid conduction over short arcs, promotes a domination of activities by organic mechanisms and by sensory conditions. Among insects species, systems are found in a bewildering variety which illustrate this generaliza-tion broadly, but typically these have involved organizations resisting analytical investigation. As an example, Spieth (1952) found the mating patterns of closely related *Drosophila* species so well differentiated as to be taxonomically reliable. In such cases, it is conventional to emphasize the role of innate deter-mination as effective through endogenous factors; however, the ontogenetic background of such factors remains obscure. Investigating such behavioral phenomena in relation both to their organic setting and to their developmental situation promises to be fruitful, as the following studies have shown.

One of the outstanding investigations of behavior in a soli-tary insect was the study of spinning activities in the *Cecropia*

silkworm by Van der Kloot and Williams (1953). Under natural conditions, the mature caterpillar of this lepidopteran
stops feeding and wanders for a time, then posts itself in a
twig-crotch and spins a cocoon with a thin apex through
which the adult escapes at the end of pupation. The experi-
menters found the termination of feeding in this caterpillar
due to glandular changes marking the period, as was also
shown for the wandering, which was absent in caterpillars
deprived of their silk glands. Furthermore, the removal of
these glands eliminated two movements, the stretch-bend and
the swing-swing, basic to normal spinning which was thereby
shown to depend at least partly on sensory input from the
spinning apparatus itself.

Although the genesis and temporal order of activities essential to the typical *Cecropia* spinning pattern thereby are shown
to depend to an important extent upon processes in the individual's changing internal condition, their occurrence and
function in the pattern involves relationships of these processes with tactual and gravitational cues dependent on relationships with the external situation. Thus it was found that
the initiation of spinning requires contact of mouth parts
with a surface, also that the termination of either of the two
critical spinning movements depends upon contact of spinner-
ets with a surface when the caterpillar is at full flexion or full
extension. Accordingly, the pattern of the species-typical
cocoon may be considered a compound resulting from the
merging of processes based on metamorphosis with sensory-
input processes depending on the spatial and other properties
of the extrinsic situation. Consequently, in a uniform environment such as the interior of a balloon, the caterpillar spun a
flat layer of silk as a lining, tethered to a peg; the larva spun
a cone-shaped tent—both structures arising by virtue of the
very different physical properties of the extrinsic situation.
The typical behavior pattern thus arises through a complex
progressive relationship between changing organic conditions
and the sensory input from these states, fused with that from

sets of external circumstances which may change in their effects as the act progresses.

For the social insects, much evidence indicates that morphological and functional properties of the individual contribute critically to relationships arising in the group situation. Thus, in ants such as *Formica*, it is possible that early mouth-part reactions may be modified from initial passive feeding, through group interactions, into active feeding of others and then into foraging outside the nest (Schneirla, 1941). In these events a simple conditioning process, perhaps beginning with larval feeding in the nest situation, may implement and enlarge the function of organic factors involved in mouth responses and in regurgitation. In the social situation, other individuals function as key agents facilitating such integrations, thus in a sense equivalent to (but far more specialized in their developmental role than) certain properties of the general environment (e.g., food-plant odors) in solitary insects.

In the social insects, different specialized processes have evolved concurrently in the various types of individuals within a community, indispensable for the rise and maintenance of functional patterns in the colony as a unit. The army ants, for example, exhibit regular functional cycles with phases characteristic of the species, which owe both their timing and their integrity to the degree and nature of stimulative effects exerted on the adult population by the great developing broods (Schneirla, 1957). The massive broods appear in regular succession, and each, as it develops, is the source of excitatory tactual and chemical stimulation which dominates adult behavior but varies radically in intensity according to the developmental stage. A brood when in the larval stage arouses the workers maximally, so that large daily raids and nightly emigrations then are carried out regularly by the colony; but when this brood enters the quiescent pupal stage, and social stimulation falls abruptly to a low level, daily raids are small and emigrations cease.

At first sight, from the fact that the single colony queen lays the eggs producing successive broods in regular periods somewhat more than one month apart, one might think that a rhythmic process endogenous to the queen must serve as "clock" for the cycle. But the pacemaker is not in the queen, as investigation reveals the presence of recurrent changes in the extrinsic colony situation capable of influencing the queen's reproductive condition in critical ways. The relationship is complex, as these extrinsic changes concern the amount of tactual and chemical stimulation and of food received by the queen from the workers, and periodic changes in these factors depend in their turn upon developmental brood changes. When a brood is passing through the larval stage and its stimulative effect on the workers is high, responses of the workers to the queen fall off and her reproductive processes advance only slowly; when, however, this larval brood is mature, ceases to feed, and begins spinning cocoons, workers continue to be excited by brood activities but divert their responses appreciably to the queen, whose reproductive processes at once accelerate toward maturation and laying of the eggs. The large-scale reproductive processes of the army-ant queen are thus controlled extrinsically, running their course according to the level of stimulative and nutritive conditions in the colony.

The necessary cause evidently lies in complex stimulative relationships depending on the brood and changing with its development, but depending indirectly on the queen as the broods initiate with the queen. Each rearousal of the queen is timed rather precisely through changes in this set of factors. Clearly, the army-ant cyclical pattern does not pre-exist in the genes of any one type of individual—workers, brood, or queen—nor is it additive from these sources. Rather, organic factors basic to the species pattern have evolved in close relationship with extrinsic conditions which in the evolved pattern supply key factors essential for integrating processes from all sources into a functional system (Schneirla, 1957).

Whatever general principles may hold for behavior development, it is likely that they express themselves very differently according to the phyletic level. Traditional sharp distinctions such as that between the native and the acquired in ontogeny now seem untenable for any level. Instead, conceptual tools are needed to mark off the principal sources of ontogenetic factors, without the implication that either is ever independent of or altogether distinct from the other in normal development in any animal (Schneirla, 1956).

The conceptual terms to be used on this basis are "maturation" and "experience." The differentiation of these terms is considered here a conceptual convenience rather than one assuming a dichotomy of factors clearly separable in reality. It is improbable that any clear distinction can be made between what heredity contributes and environment contributes to the ontogeny of any animal, and no such distinctions are implied here. As a guide to investigation, the view that development is a natively determined unfolding of characters and integrations is no more valid than that development is directed only by extrinsic forces or by learning. Instead, concepts are needed which do not carry traditional biases into research on the real problem, namely: how development occurs in individuals at each level under conditions both typical and atypical of the species "niche."

The contention here is that, in all animals, individual genic equipment influences ontogeny throughout its course, but indirectly, and in relation with the developmental situation according to a formula characteristic of functional level and of species. The distinction between the sets of processes denoted by these terms is therefore a relative one, in view of the impossibility of separating the intrinsic strictly from the extrinsic (McGraw, 1946). *Maturation*, therefore, designates factors contributed to ontogeny essentially through processes of growth and differentiation at all stages, *experience* designates factors contributed through the effects of stimulation at all stages.

"Maturation" as used in this sense includes the effects of

growth and differentiation without implying that these effects are exerted in a pattern directly derived from genic templates, as does Gesell (1950) in speaking of "the innate processes of growth called maturation." The dogma of a direct hereditary determination of development is thus excluded, and instead we emphasize the principles of genic factors indirectly influencing growth in different ways and of growth and differentiation as differently related to extrinsic conditions according to phyletic level, developmental situation, and ontogenetic stage. The doctrine of a genic "code" that is directly "uncoded" in development is opposed by evidence concerning genotypes, not only with respect to organic growth and differentiation but also with respect to behavioral ontogeny. As an example, in experiments with pure strains of fruitflies, Harnly (1941) found that the same genes may influence differently the development of wings and other structures affecting locomotion, according to what temperature prevails during ontogeny. With different temperatures stimulating growth differently, phenotypes capable of normal flight, erratic flight, or no flight were produced from the same genotypic strain. Under the different conditions, factors such as wing size, wing articulation, and neuromuscular control were indicated as variables affecting behavior differently in the phenotypes. Accordingly, the term *maturation* denotes here an expanding system of effects dependent on growth but operating at all stages intimately in connection with effects from the developmental situation; not a closed system of forces operative exclusively through organic growth.

Nativists frequently consider the nervous system as encapsulating a "code," derived from the genes, which through passive growth processes directly controls the development of specific behavior patterns. Coghill's (1929) results with larval salamanders are conventionally regarded as strongly supporting this theory. Yet these studies involved no analysis of behavior, but rather demonstrated histologically and descriptively a correspondence between successive new types of neural connections and changes in motility. Carmichael's (1928) experiment with larval salamanders is accepted by many as further proof. In this investigation, embryos immobilized with chloretone through early developmental stages, when tested as adults, were reported as swimming within thirty minutes after recovery, and in a manner indistinguishable from that of undrugged controls. These findings have been interpreted as excluding peripheral factors and effects of action in favor of an intraneural determination of development in amphibians. But Fromme (1941), replicating the experiment with tadpoles and with emphasis on analysis of the behavior, reported that drugged experimental subjects on recovery swam not only more slowly than the normals but with indications of deficient coordination. The effects of action, therefore, along with other possible feedback effects of function which have not yet been clearly identified, may play a role in the behavioral development of these amphibians.

Frequently cited also as evidence for an intraneural determination of patterns in lower vertebrates are the operative experiments of von Holst (1935), with teleosts and other fishes, from which rhythmic movements were reported in sections of trunk ostensibly deprived of their sensory connections. But Lissman (1946) in similar research found that carrying deafferentation beyond a certain point abolished the locomotor rhythms completely; hence these activities evidently require some degree of afferent supply to function.

The fact deserves emphasis that these experiments were carried out with advanced or *adult* stages of lower vertebrates, hence can furnish no clear picture of how the respective patterns develop. Furthermore, their applicability to behavioral development in higher vertebrates remains unstudied, notwithstanding the frequency of textbook use of the results. How can such evidence be validly applied to higher levels while the extent of its relevance to the ontogeny of lower vertebrates remains unclear?

Rather than a strict intraneural rise of patterns, a view more in keeping with the evidence is that the nervous system develops in functional relationships to its setting, and that systems of intervening functional variables link it to the genes on the one hand and developing behavioral processes on the other. This view is strongly favored by a variety of evidence (Schneirla, 1956), as, for example, from experiments on the micturition pattern of the dog. Although the concept of a direct hormonal priming of an intraneural mechanism appeared to find support in earlier studies, subsequent research has shown that without its afferent components the adult pattern cannot function. Such mechanisms, also related deviously to hormonal processes, may well be essential to the development of neural properties underlying species-typical action patterns.

In view of the little-explored aspect of functional relationships in ontogeny, Coghill's conclusion that in behavioral development, generalization is primary, individual secondary, may need heavy qualification. Serious questions pointing against the generalization-to-individuation view are raised by the finding of Carmichael and Smith (1939) with early guinea pig embryos. They showed that stimulation of one limb produces discrete movement of that member or mass action according to whether stimulus intensity is weak or strong, respectively. In birds and mammals, particularly, early activities tend to be variable and indistinctly patterned. The pioneer investigations of Kuo (1932) with chick embryos, which disclosed varying successions of local and inclusive action as routine in that animal at early stages, also indicated significant relationships between movements and local actions as of leg and thorax. A swinging head movement was observed in those stages which might then in one sense have been considered specific, but which would have to be regarded as generalized in relation to different head responses appearing at later stages as in feeding, preening, and attacking. Moreover, the latter types are all in a developmental sense successors of the former.

Development must be examined from a functional and behavioral approach, going beyond the limits of embryology and genetics, for an adequate theory of the interrelationship of maturation and experience variables as differently related at successive stages. The mature chick embryo could not chip the egg, nor after hatching initiate and improve its discriminative pecking, unless increasing muscular strength and sensitivity facilitated the head lunge together with adequate postural support. Certainly, in different types of organisms, typical developmental systems may involve many close and subtle interrelationships of these variables characteristic of phyletic level and species, not readily understandable in terms of sharp differentiation of intrinsic and extrinsic factors. Such processes should become better understood when developmental research graduates from the descriptive to the systematic analytical stage.

To illustrate how involved these relationships can be even on an elementary level in vertebrates, we may consider the results of Tracy (1926) on toadfish ontogeny. At an early stage the larva of this fish, lying quiescent on the bottom for regular intervals, intermittently exhibits quick jerking movements, which the investigator termed "spontaneous" because they have no apparent extrinsic cause. But these movements, from Tracy's evidence, occur during each quiescent period through accretion in the blood of metabolic products as growth processes reduce available oxygen. Then, at a critical point in the build-up, an excitation somehow arises. Perhaps the existing biochemical condition (anoxia) directly causes motor neurones to fire, perhaps it acts indirectly as by altering thresholds—at any rate, sensory impulses from somewhere arouse a motor discharge to muscles. The rhythmicity of the process seems to rest on the fact that each movement phase serves to alter the embryo's condition, restoring the oxygen supply so that a further resting phase ensues—then a new accumulation of metabolites sets off another action phase, and so on. It is difficult to understand these processes from the facts of growth alone (Tracy, 1959).

The developmental role of the medium is emphasized

strikingly by Waddington's (1959) experiments in which in-bred strains of fruitflies, after being subjected for many successive generations to an extrinsic agent, ether vapor, exhibit a distinct new structural character evidently due to the existence of genotypic changes. The point is that not only extreme extrinsic stresses (perhaps accounting for exceptional phenotypes) but also normal effects of the "standard" developmental situation are to be reckoned with at all stages in ontogeny. Clearly, the idea of an "original nature" in each species, innately determined through direct genic effects and modified only at "later stages" as through learning, must be held invalid. Who has determined, for any organism, the stage at which the "original nature" is established and ready for modification? A growing file of evidence shows that developing organisms enter into constant and progressively changing interactions with their environs, and that the developmental medium therefore participates crucially in ontogeny at all stages. It is these effects we are representing by the term "experience," which is not at all reducible to *learning*, although nativists often indulge in this reductionistic misinterpretation. "Learning" is to be considered one prominent outcome of experience at later stages in organisms capable of it.

Through a different kind of reductionist practice, characteristic rhythmic processes are conventionally considered "endogenous" because "no apparent external cause" is involved. But, as in the example already considered, the "cause" may be a set of external effects readily overlooked because they enter into subtle reactions with intraorganic processes. Sometimes the key external agent is not highly evasive once adequate investigative methods are used. For example, Harker (1953) found that the normal day-night activity rhythm of adult mayflies does not appear unless the individual has been subjected to at least one 24-hour light-dark cycle in the egg or larval stage. This rhythm accordingly does *not* appear in mayflies raised as eggs and larvae in continuous light or in continuous darkness. Somehow, specific physical changes act-

ing for only a limited time early in ontogeny set up trace
effects so implicated in growth that adult behavior is influenced. Despite the popularity of the "innate clock" concept, a prominent investigator in this field (Brown, 1959) has
been led by a variety of evidence to conclude that the species-
typical rhythmic functions of many animals may owe their
timing to periodic external energy effects so low as to escape
detection save by the most delicate techniques.

A useful generalization therefore is that, in any animal, extrinsic agencies common or exceptional to the developmental
medium may contribute to ontogeny in ways characteristic of
level and species, entering into developmental functions by
merging with maturative processes appropriate to the stage.
Knowledge of such phenomena often is arrived at only indirectly and by degrees. Now, however, the evidence seems
strong enough to justify the deductive term "trace effects" for
organic changes introduced through experience in early stages,
even though they may not demonstrably influence action until
much later in the individual's life. One example has been
given from Harker's work; another one of importance comes
from the research of Hasler and Wisby (1951) with Pacific
salmon. These fish, initially spawned and raised to the down-
stream-migration phase in specific headwater streams, leave
the ocean and ascend the river system prior to spawning. And
in a reliable frequency, field tests and related laboratory experiments show that individual salmon tend to turn at
branches toward the tributary carrying the chemical essence
of headwaters in which the individual developed from the egg.
What the organic trace effect may be is not yet known; that
one exists to affect adult behavior seems clear.

Factors of *experience* influence development constantly and
vitally. This concept covers a wide range of effects from biochemical changes set up variously (as illustrated) to more
specialized types of afferent input including patterns having
trace effects usually classed as "learning." Although, in studies
of conditioning in embryonic chicks, Gos (1935) found no

evidence of specific training to a touch-shock pairing before about sixteen days of age, simpler forms of change were indicated before that. In subjects given the test pairings after about the tenth day, there was observed a change in general responsiveness to the extrinsic stimuli used. Some trace effect, although a diffuse one, was thereby indicated. Accordingly, it is possible that, normally, experiences common in the species environment, such as a periodic turning of the eggs or knocking about in the incubative routine, might set up trace effects significant for later behavior, as perhaps in the form of a relative susceptibility to emotional excitement under certain general conditions. The response in such cases may be a different one in the animal's repertoire at the later stage. For example, it is possible that exposure of a larval solitary wasp during feeding to the odor of its typical species prey may induce a susceptibility of the sexually mature adult to this odor when that prey is encountered, eliciting the responses of stinging and ovipositing (then in the individual's repertoire).

The time at which conditioning and learning enter as influences in development, in animals having these abilities, is therefore likely to prove a relative matter, subject to how strict the definition is. Although evanescent conditioning results have been demonstrated in a few cases in birds and mammals prior to hatching or birth, the question remains as to when specific and more lasting patterns become possible. In tests with young puppies at different ages, Fuller et al. (1950) found no evidence before the twentieth day of a definite conditioning of the flexion response by electrical shock to exteroceptive stimuli such as a buzzer sound.[1] Since then, however, other investigators have demonstrated general conditioned responses to gustatory and tactual stimuli in neonate mammals only a few hours or a few days old. The latter

---

[1] The growth process prerequisite to such attainments may be a sufficient myelinization of fibers in the corticospinal motor tracts known to occur at about that age in the dog.

finding is consistent with results of studies in our laboratory (Rosenblatt et al., unpubl.) showing that significant changes appear in kittens soon after birth in their orientation to the mother, with individually differentiated responses appearing within the first few hours. These adaptations concern both a gradually more efficient approach to the female's abdominal surface and processes in local orientation leading to attachment at a given zone in the nipple series (e.g., fore or aft). These adjustments clearly form an important basis for wider social adaptation in the litter situation. Learning processes are no doubt implicated, although (as preliminary analysis indicates) rudimentary and general in nature.

Recently there has been a great increase in studies directed at demonstrating the effects of early experience in mammals, with results indicating that for young rats and dogs experiences in the later part of the litter period, from trauma to varying environmental heterogeneity, may identifiably affect later behavior. Although such research is still generally preliminary in nature, the results suggest that early experience may have a variety of effects, from a differential reaction to stimuli (Gibson and Walk, 1956) to general effects as of emotional excitability level and susceptibility to stress. To understand how varied such effects may be, particularly in their significance for the typical species behavior pattern, we must again widen our theoretical perspective to include very early stages and lower vertebrates.

We must first discard the traditional notion, still prevalent among ethologists, that specific behavior patterns arising in an organism raised in isolation from the "natural" environment and from species mates must *ipso facto* be "innate" or "inherited" in the sense of being exclusively gene-directed. Although the method of isolation is clearly useful, a compulsive nativistic interpretation of results is doubtful, as it involves a serious *non sequitur*. Perhaps the worst of the unexamined assumptions is that the experimenter knows *a priori* that the environment of isolation is not equivalent in any important respect to the typical species environment and the influence of species mates. This is a difficult matter to test, but let us consider the possibility that the isolated individual may influence its own development, through its own properties, in ways somewhat equivalent to the effects of species mates. Some time ago I suggested (1956) this might be possible through odor effects in social insects, and through visual effects (e.g., self-reflection) in fish. The latter possibility has been investigated in our laboratory (Shaw, unpubl.). Platyfish fry were removed from the female by Caesarian operation and raised in individual aquaria, isolated from stimuli from species mates and other animals until they were sexually mature. Individuals raised alone, surrounded by plates of ground glass, scored much lower in mating tests at maturity than subjects raised in community tanks during the first month with species mates and then placed in isolation. Early social experience thus proves essential to the normal development of the mating pattern in this fish. Experiments testing the hypothesis that self-stimulation may account for the lower scores of these isolated subjects are now under way. Scattered evidence suggests that in lower mammals, the female's experience in touching and licking her genital zones and posterior body contributes a perceptual orientation to those areas as familiar, and also facilitates a perceptual adjustment, by licking and not biting, to objects such as neonate young bearing equivalent olfactory properties.

Results from our investigations (Tobach et al., unpubl.) of maternal behavior in the domestic cat militate against assumptions of an inborn pattern, and speak in favor of progressive self-stimulative processes. Earlier development contributes certain specific organic processes; evidently also an orientation to her own body and perceptual differentiation of the genital area in particular. Analysis of results points to the crucial importance of organic processes such as uterine contractions and of their by-products: birth fluids, afterbirth, the neonate and the membranes—each in its turn with potent stimulative effects. The processes of licking in particular, occurring in response to the attractive birth fluids, account for a progressive transfer of the female's attention from her own body to fluids on the substratum, and through responses to these (as an incidental outcome) to the still wet neonate kitten. Abdominal contractions arouse attention and direct it posteriorly; fluids and further products promote and channelize the adjustment in ways basic for the establishment of a reciprocal stimulative relationship between female and kitten. Thus the pattern of parturitive behavior seems not to be organized from within, but rather to be assembled through the effect of stimuli furnished incidentally via the organic changes of parturition, literally a series of feedback effects of an essentially self-stimulative nature, merging into a perceived environment.

Self-stimulative processes appropriate to the stage evidently contribute to development in many and varied ways typical of the level. A notable example offered for an early vertebrate stage is Kuo's (1932) evidence that from early organic functions in the chick embryo, such as beating of the heart and rhythmical pulsations of the amniotic membrane, stimulative effects may arise contributing to the ontogeny of the species-characteristic head-lunge response. His evidence indicates that in these early stages, self-stimulative processes (e.g., an incidental pushing up of the head by the thorax with dilatation of the heart) give rise to extrinsic stimuli such as tactual effects which (through their combination with proprioceptive stimuli and other causes) later can produce the head action alone. It is not that the heart "teaches the chick to peck," as a facetious nativist once remarked, but that incidentally its beating contributes to the development of a significant pattern. Actually, the process effected here resembles *sensory integration* (Maier and Schneirla, 1942) more than it does the typical conditioning pattern.

The isolation method is often as significant for what *does not* appear in the absence of the typical developmental situation or of species mates as for what does appear. Many lepidopteran larvae, when transferred away from their food plant, cannot survive; emphasizing the fact that, by laying her eggs in that situation, the female normally insures the presence of a set of experiences to which the caterpillar can adapt. At an early age, marsupial embryos shift from the mother's uterus to the pouch, a different situation still intimately associated with the mother and also involving a standard set of experiences to which the normally developed embryo can adapt. In ungulates the mother is a prominent feature of the environment to which the neonate soon adjusts by means of olfactory and visual stimulation she furnishes (Blauvelt, 1955). Oriented also by her directionalized licking, the neonate soon establishes a nursing relationship. Developmental environments in general tend to be species-standardized, so that experiences are more or less prestructured at all stages. This state of affairs indicates that developmental processes must have been significant factors in evolution (Orton, 1955), also that behavior must have had a prominent role in processes of natural selection prerequisite to species-typical adjustments and the environmental conditions of development.

In mammals generally, important aspects of the environment for embryo and neonate are prestructured by the mother. From our research, her role in patterning the situation of parturition has already been described for the domestic cat. In this animal the young are altricial, or blind-born, and the nest, localized and odor-saturated at the time of parturition, furnishes an orientative base for the young in their early perceptual development (Rosenblatt et al., unpubl.). Soon after delivery, the female insures the presence of the neonates in this place by retrieving the scattered ones; she also introduces a directionalization to their variable movements by lying down and arching her body around them. The kittens, aroused to action and further directionalized by the female's licking of their bodies, are attracted to the female's abdomen by tactual and thermal stimulation from her. Thus, through a

variety of experiences centering around the parent, the neonates arrive at the abdomen, nuzzle and attach to a nipple.
Our studies show that from the first hour the neonate kittens
not only improve in their ability to reach the female and re-
attach but also to arrive at a given part in the nipple series.

Early experiences with a prestructured environment thereby furnish the basis for a social bond between parent and
kittens, as well as a home base for the young. As our research
suggests, attainment both of parent and of the nest reduces
tension and introduces gratifications facilitating learning.
During the first neonate week the adaptations of the kittens
to female and nest improve steadily, paralleling sensory and
locomotor development but also being clearly dependent
upon processes of progressive learning and perceptual development. Sound production, "crying," indicates disturbance in disoriented kittens, and reductions in the intensity
and pitch of this reaction in orientation tests through the
first week offer clues to an orientative adjustment of increasing
scope.

These early perceptual advances occur through integrations
of tactual and olfactory cues progressively expanding the kitten's space from the home site. Navigation about the home
cage improves slowly on this basis, based on proximal cues
from walls and floor. Although the eyes open at about one
week, the proximal pattern of organization continues in force
for a few days thereafter; then in a few days the kitten begins
to make its way more freely on a visual basis, now reaching
the home corner on the diagonal in tests instead of near the
walls as before. The role of direct experience in this process is
revealed particularly by the fact that kittens given the daily
tests are definitely superior to untested kittens in attainment
of the stage of visual perceptual control.

As analyses of results show, the gains of this stage are not
altogether new but represent a reorganization in visual terms
of earlier and more restricted patterns of proximal control on
which visual perception is based. These results impressively

illustrate the principle of qualitative advancement in perceptual development through an overlapping of stages in which gains from the maturational and experiential integrations of earlier stages provide a basis for new patterns under new conditions. On a lower vertebrate level, it is possible that tactual and proprioceptive integrations controlling head movements in the embryo provide a basis for the prompt ("spontaneous") responsiveness of early terrestrial stages in amphibians and reptiles with head-lunging to visual movement (Maier and Schneirla, 1935, Chap. IX).

Operation of the same principle at a higher vertebrate level is represented by the findings of Nissen et al. (1951), who reduced and modified the normal opportunities of young chimpanzees for tactual and manipulative experience, first by binding the arms from birth, then after the fifth week by encasing all four extremities in tubes. When the subjects were freed of these impediments at thirty-one months, they were markedly deficient, compared to normal subjects, not only in discriminating touched points on the body but also in their perceptual adjustments to seen objects. In the same sense, not only growth but also action through experience impels normal processes of perceptual development in the human infant (Werner, 1940).

I have suggested (1959b) that "The socialization of early physiologically given biphasic excitatory states and the specialization of motivation and emotion advance hand in hand in the education of the infant mammal in perceptual processes and action." This principle, found applicable to more limited developmental attainments at lower phyletic levels, is illustrated in the ontogeny of the smile and of reaching, two adjustive processes crucial to man's perceptual and motivational development. Although actions such as head-turning and arm extension toward the stimulated side, and a fleeting oral grimace, have been observed in neonate infants and even in the embryo, it is unlikely that these actions then represent "seeking" tendencies as Schachtel (1959) has suggested for the former, or innate social responses as Koehler (1954) has suggested for the latter. Rather, it is significant that both of these actions first arise as crude and variable responses to a variety of stimuli, but evidently always as incidental "weak" responses to low-energy stimulation. Neither can be called "purposive" in early stages; rather, analysis shows that reaching, through "progressive integrations of vision with pre-existing tactuoproximal adjustments, becomes first a specific approach response, then a perceptually directed seeking response," and that the grimace becomes a "smile" or social approach response only through comparable processes in perceptual development (Schneirla, 1959b).

The purposive adjustments of the older human infant are therefore not themselves given as "instincts," but rather are the products of an involved perceptual development through which maturative-experiential processes of earlier stages are radically modified into externally meaningful patterns. This principle, concerning the appearance of adaptive behavioral adjustments through ontogeny, has been illustrated before in this essay in terms of ontogeny at lower phyletic levels—but always intimately in relation to the developmental context appropriate to the level.

Each type of animal grows into its own world with different properties and acquires its adaptive patterns, whatever their nature or scope, through the functioning of successive sets of intervening variables operating in the global situations of respective developmental stages. The emergence of psychological properties peculiar to the developmental circumstances will become increasingly understandable in the future, as investigators correct the limitations of concepts such as "growth" and "learning" by devising improved explanatory Gestalts in better tune with reality.

BIBLIOGRAPHY

Allee, W. C.; Emerson, A. E.; Park, O.; Park, T.; and Schmidt, K. P. (1950), *Principles of Animal Ecology*. Philadelphia: Saunders.

Beach, F. A. (1947), Evolutionary Changes in the Physiological Control of Mating Behavior in Mammals. *Psychological Review*, *54*:297-315.

Blauvelt, Helen (1955), Dynamics of the Mother-Newborn Relationship in Goats. *Group Processes, 1st Conference.* New York: Josiah Macy, Jr. Foundation, pp. 221-258.

Brown, F. A. (1959), The Rhythmic Nature of Animals and Plants. *American Scientist*, *47*:147-168.

Carmichael, L. (1928), A Further Experimental Study of the Development of Behavior. *Psychological Review*, *34*:253-260.

—— L. and Smith, M. F. (1939), Quantified Pressure Stimulation and the Specificity and Generality of Response in Fetal Life. *Journal of Genetic Psychology*, *54*:425-434.

Clark, Eugenie; Aronson, L. R.; and Gordon, M. (1954), Mating Behavior Patterns in Two Sympatric Species of Xiphophorin Fishes: Their Inheritance and Significance in Sexual Isolation. *Bulletin of the American Museum of Natural History*, *103*:139-335.

Coghill, G. E. (1929), *Anatomy and the Problem of Behavior*. New York: Macmillan.

Dobzhansky, T. (1950), Heredity, Environment and Evolution. *Science*, *111*:161-166.

Fromme, A. (1941), An Experimental Study of the Factors of Maturation and Practice in the Behavioral Development of the Embryo of the Frog, *Rana pipiens. Genetic Psychology Monograph*, *24*:219-256.

Fuller, J.; Easler, C. A.; and Banks, E. M. (1950), Formation of Conditioned Avoidance Responses in Young Puppies. *American Journal of Physiology*, *160*:462-466.

Gesell, A. (1950), Human Infancy and the Ontogenesis of Behavior. *American Scientist*, *37*:529-553.

Gibson, Eleanor and Walk, R. D. (1956), The Effect of Prolonged Exposures to Visually Presented Patterns on Learning to Discriminate Them. *Journal of Comparative and Physiological Psychology*, *49*:239-242.

Gos, M. (1935), Les reflexes conditionnels chez l'embryon d'oiseau.

Bulletin de la Société Scientifique de Liège, 4-5:194-199; 6-7:246-250.

Hall, C. S. (1951), The Genetics of Behavior. *Handbook of Experimental Psychology*, Chap. 9:304-329. New York: Wiley.

Harker, Janet E. (1953), The Diurnal Rhythm of Activity of Mayfly Nymphs. *Journal of Experimental Biology*, 30:525-533.

Harnly, M. H. (1941), Flight Capacity in Relation to Phenotypic and Genotypic Variations in the Wings of *Drosophila melanogaster*. *Journal of Experimental Zoology*, 88:263-274.

Hasler, A. D. and Wisby, W. J. (1951), Discrimination of Stream Odors by Fishes and Its Relation to Parent Stream Behavior. *American Naturalist*, 85:223-238.

Hebb, D. O. (1953), Heredity and Environment in Mammalian Behaviour. *British Journal of Animal Behaviour*, 1:43-47.

Hunter, W. S. (1947), Summary Comments on the Heredity-Environment Symposium. *Psychological Review*, 54:348-352.

Koehler, O. (1954), Das Lächeln als angeborene Ausdrucksbewegung. *Zeitschrift für menschliche Vererbungs- und Konstitutionslehre*, 32:390-398.

Kuo, Z. Y. (1930), The Genesis of the Cat's Response to the Rat. *Journal of Comparative Psychology*, 11:1-30.

——— (1932), Ontogeny of Embryonic Behavior in Aves. IV. The Influence of Embryonic Movements upon the Behavior after Hatching. *Journal of Comparative Psychology*, 14:109-122.

Lissman, H. W. (1946), The Neurological Basis of the Locomotory Rhythm in the Spinal Dogfish (*Scyllium canicula, Acanthias vulgaris*). II. The Effect of De-afferentation. *Journal of Experimental Biology*, 23:162-176.

Maier, N. R. F. and Schneirla, T. C. (1935), *Principles of Animal Psychology*. New York: McGraw-Hill.

——— ——— (1942), Mechanisms in Conditioning. *Psychological Review*, 49:117-134.

McGraw, Myrtle (1946), Maturation of Behavior. *Manual of Child Psychology*, Chap. 7:332-369. New York: Wiley.

Moore, K. (1944), The Effect of Controlled Temperature Changes on the Behavior of the White Rat. *Journal of Experimental Psychology*, 34:70-79.

Needham, J. (1929), *The Skeptical Biologist*. London: Chatto.

Nissen, H.; Chow, K. L.; and Semmes, Josephine (1951), Effects of Restricted Opportunity for Tactual, Kinesthetic and Manipulative Experience on the Behavior of a Chimpanzee. *American Journal of Psychology*, *64*:485-507.

Orton, Grace (1955), The Role of Ontogeny in Systematics and Evolution. *Evolution*, *9*:75-83.

Roe, Anne and Simpson, G. G. (1958), *Behavior and Evolution*. New Haven: Yale University Press.

Rosenblatt, J. S.; Wodinsky, J.; Turkewitz, G.; and Schneirla, T. C. (unpubl.), Analytical Studies on Maternal Behavior in Relation to Litter Adjustment and Socialization in the Domestic Cat. II. Development of Orientation. III. Maternal-Young Relations.

Schachtel, E. G. (1959), *Metamorphosis—On the Development of Affect, Perception, Attention and Memory*. New York: Basic Books.

Schneirla, T. C. (1941), Social Organization in Insects, as Related to Individual Function. *Psychological Review*, *48*:465-486.

——— (1947), Levels in the Psychological Capacities of Animals. *Philosophy for the Future*. New York: Macmillan, pp. 243-286.

——— (1948), Psychology, Comparative. *Encyclopaedia Britannica*, *18*:690-760. Chicago: Encyclopaedia Britannica, Inc.

——— (1956), Interrelationships of the "Innate" and the "Acquired" in Instinctive Behavior. *L'Instinct dans le Comportement des Animaux et de l'Homme*. Paris: Masson & Cie., pp. 387-452.

——— (1957), Theoretical Consideration of Cyclic Processes in Doryline Ants. *Proceedings of the American Philosophical Society*, *101*:106-133.

——— (1959a), L'Apprentissage et la question du conflit chez la fourmi. Comparaison avec le Rat. *Journal de Psychologie*, in press.

——— (1959b), An Evolutionary and Developmental Theory of Biphasic Processes Underlying Approach and Withdrawal. *Nebraska Symposium on Motivation, 1958*. University of Nebraska Press, pp. 1-42.

Shaw, Evelyn (unpubl.), Studies on Sexual Behavior in Platyfish Reared Under Altered or Reduced Environmental Conditions.

Spieth, H. T. (1952), Mating Behavior Within the Genus *Drosophila* (Diptera). *Bulletin of the American Museum of Natural History*, *99*:401-474.

Stern, C. (1954), Two or Three Bristles? *American Scientist*, *42*:212-247.

Tobach, Ethel; Campbell, Marie Lou; Cohn, Ruth; and Schneirla, T. C. (unpubl.), Analytical Studies on Maternal Behavior in

Relation to Litter Adjustment and Socialization in the Domestic Cat. I. Parturition.

Tracy, H. C. (1926), The Development of Motility and Behavior Reactions in the Toadfish (*Opsanus tau*). *Journal of Comparative Neurology, 40*:253-369.

—— (1959), Stages in the Development of the Anatomy of Motility of the Toadfish (*Opsanus tau*). *Journal of Comparative Neurology, 111*:27-81.

Van der Kloot, W. G. and Williams, C. M. (1953a), Cocoon Construction by the Cecropia silkworm. I. The Role of the External Environment. *Behaviour, 5*:141-156.

—— —— (1953b), Cocoon Construction by the Cecropia silkworm. II. The Role of the Internal Environment. *Behaviour, 5*:157-174.

von Holst, E. (1935), Über den Prozess der zentralnervösen Koordination. *Pflügers Archiv, 236*:149-158.

Waddington, C. H. (1959), Evolutionary Systems—Animal and Human. *Nature, 183*:1634-1638.

Watson, J. B. (1914), *Behavior: An Introduction to Comparative Psychology*. New York: Holt.

Weiss, P. (1954), Some Introductory Remarks on the Cellular Basis of Differentiation. *Journal of Embryology and Comparative Morphology, 1*:181-211.

Werner, H. (1940), *Comparative Psychology of Mental Development*, 3rd ed. New York: International Universities Press, 1957.

The Problem of Individuality
In Development

HERMAN A. WITKIN, Ph.D.

State University of New York

In concluding his most recent general contribution to developmental theory, Heinz Werner (1957) wrote: "The original aim of developmental theory, directed toward the study of universal genetic changes, is still one of its main concerns; but side by side with this concern, the conviction has been growing in recent years that development conceptualization, in order to retain its truly organismic character, has to expand its orbit of interest to include as a central problem the study of individuality." Over the past half dozen years Hanna Faterson, Ruth Dyk, Donald Goodenough, Stephen Karp,

The research described in this paper has been supported mainly by a grant (M-628) from the United States Public Health Service, National Institutes of Health.

and I have been conducting studies of development in which we have attempted to keep the individual to the fore.

The fact that our investigations of perception-personality relationships turned some years ago toward issues of development bears the mark of Werner's influence. Werner has persistently emphasized the necessity of considering psychological processes in their developmental aspects; and this viewpoint has impressed itself upon the general theoretical atmosphere in which those of us concerned with cognitive functions have been conducting our research. The conceptual system that he devised pointed out the directions—sometimes general, sometimes quite specific—which an interest in cognitive development might pursue. In addition, during the time we spent together at the same institution, I had many discussions with Werner about our work. These contributed to the realization that the "person-centered" approach to cognition we were then pursuing would be greatly enriched by an approach which was developmentally oriented as well.

Our studies have shared the interest of developmental theory in the sequence of changes occurring during cognitive growth and in the laws governing these changes. Even more have they been concerned with identifying the nature and source of individual differences in direction and pace of growth. This is another manifestation of an interest in the problem of individuality which has been centrally present in our work from its inception more than a decade and a half ago.

I should like to describe here selected portions of our work[1] which will illustrate our attempt to keep the individual in focus while investigating problems of development. First, we observed performances of the same children in a series of perceptual and intellectual tasks and thereby determined the nature and extent of individual self-consistency in patterns of cognitive functioning. Through studies with children of differ-

---

[1] This work will be reported more fully in a forthcoming book.

ent ages we were able to establish more "primitive" and more "advanced" ways, developmentally speaking, of performing some of these tasks. Second, we sought to relate the observed patterns of cognitive functioning to differences in level of differentiation of personality structure. This phase of the studies focused attention on the affective and motivational aspects of growth, supplementing the preoccupation of developmental theory with problems of cognitive growth. It was also concerned with how "things hang together" in the individual child during his development. Finally, through an investigation of children's early family experiences, particularly in relation to their mothers, we tried to obtain some insight regarding the forces that may influence the direction of cognitive growth. The last-mentioned inquiries, in particular, brought to the forefront problems of individual differences in pace of growth.

Our studies have used some of the general concepts of developmental theory and yet, in their broad concern with individual functioning, have gone beyond these concepts. We have delineated some of the broad patterns of interrelationship that exist among the perceptual, intellectual and personality aspects of children's development. Much remains to be done in identifying the source of these patterns.

SELF-CONSISTENCY IN COGNITIVE FUNCTIONING

Our work in this area grew out of earlier studies (Witkin, 1949, 1950, 1952; Witkin and Asch, 1948; Witkin, Lewis, Hertzman, Machover, Meissner, and Wapner, 1954) of the "field-dependence-independence" dimension of perceptual functioning. One of the situations we devised for evaluating individual differences along this dimension was the "body-adjustment test." The apparatus for the test consists of a small room which the experimenter can tilt to any degree, left or right, containing a chair for the subject that also can be tilted to the left or right. The structure and "interior decoration" of the room provide many clearly defined lines that accentuate its vertical and horizontal axes. With room and chair tilted by set amounts, the experimenter moves the chair at the subject's direction until the subject reports himself to be upright. The room—the limited world in which we have placed him—remains meanwhile at its initial tilted position. If, when the subject finally believes that he is "straight," the chair is tipped far over toward the axes of the tilted room, we may reasonably infer that he is determining body position mainly by reference to the visual field. On the other hand, if the chair is close to the true upright, he is able to determine body position independently of the influence of the surrounding field, or to maintain the separateness of his body from the visual field.

A second test enabled us to study individuals' perception of the "straightness" of objects other than their own bodies. The subject sits in complete darkness, facing a luminous rod centered in a luminous frame; the rod and frame can be moved independently of each other. He sees them first in tilted positions. Then, while the frame remains tilted, he directs the experimenter to move the rod until it appears upright. In some trials the subject sits erect, and in others his chair, too, is tilted to one side. If the subject reports that the rod is straight when objectively it is tipped far toward the tilt of the frame, he is strongly influenced by the directional axes of the field that surrounds the rod. If he adjusts the rod close to the true upright, however, he is demonstrating ability to deal with an object without reference to its context, relying mainly on his own body position to do so.

A third situation, the "embedded-figures test," makes use of modified Gottschaldt figures. The subject is asked to locate a simple geometric figure "hidden" within a large complex figure designed to obscure it. People who tend to perceive the complex figure in accordance with its dominant pattern find it difficult to locate the simple figure within it. People who can readily break up the complex figure identify the simple figure quickly.

All these situations require the individual to separate some item (his own body, a rod, or a simple geometric design) from its background or context. To achieve this he must resist the embedding influence of a surrounding field, "break up" a given organization and deal with it analytically. We applied the label "field independent" to people who in each situation showed a ready capacity to differentiate objects from their backgrounds. Conversely, we designated as "field dependent" those whose performance reflected relatively passive submission to the domination of the background, and inability to keep an item separate from its context. In any random group of subjects drawn from the general population perceptual performances do not fall into two distinct types but range in a continuum between extreme field dependence and extreme field independence. When in the discussion that follows we use designations as "field-dependent children," for example, we shall be referring to subjects whose performances place them on the field-dependent side of the mean in a continuous distribution of scores.

As part of a broad attempt to understand the origin of these individual differences, we undertook studies of changes in perception during growth. We gave our battery of perceptual tests to groups of boys and girls of various ages between eight and twenty years. Supplementing these cross-sectional studies of perceptual development we also conducted longitudinal studies in which, at intervals over a period of years, we tested one group from the time they were ten until they reached seventeen, and another group from age eight to age thirteen. These studies all led to the same conclusion: children tend to be field dependent early in their perceptual development and to become more field independent as they grow up. This tendency is seen clearly in Figures 1, 2, and 3 which show curves for each of the three perceptual tests composed from the data obtained by the cross-sectional method. Ability to determine the position of the body apart from the tilted room, to perceive the position of the rod independently of the tilted

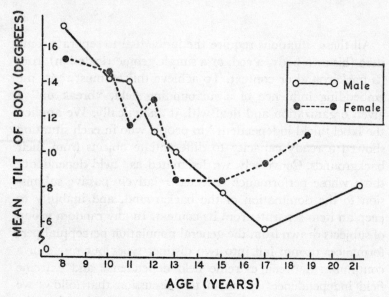

FIGURE 1

Developmental curves for body-adjustment test.

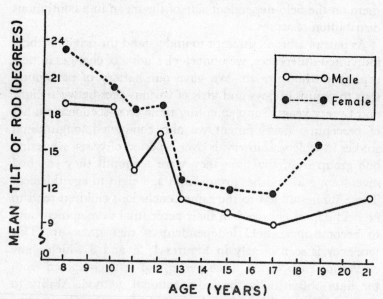

FIGURE 2

Developmental curves for rod-and-frame test.

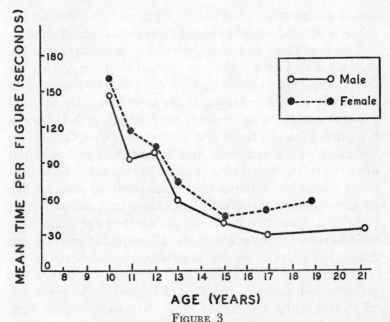

FIGURE 3

Developmental curves for embedded-figures test.

frame, to pick out a simple geometric figure obscured by a complex context, all improve, on the whole, as children become older. The change is particularly marked in the eight- to thirteen-year period. After that there is a tendency to level off, and even a slight tendency to "regress."

A field-dependent mode of perceiving is, by these results, identified with earlier stages of growth and in this sense is more primitive. The finding that with growth objects are better differentiated from their surroundings effectively illustrates, in perception, at least part of Werner's cardinal regulative principle of development—namely, that it proceeds from a state of relative globality and lack of differentiation to one of increasing differentiation, articulation, and hierarchic integration.

If, concerned more particularly with the problem of individuality, we go beyond such a general statement of growth trends to an examination of individual performances, the result is a rich harvest of important additional information.

This is evident, first of all, when the performances of the *same* children in the various perceptual tests are considered. Such a comparison shows that the child who in the rod-and-frame test is, by comparison to his peers, relatively field dependent is likely to be relatively field dependent in the body-adjustment test and embedded-figures test as well. Conversely, the child who is relatively field independent in one test is apt to be relatively field independent in the others. Stated another way, some children tend consistently to perceive like children younger than themselves, others tend consistently to perceive in a way that is "advanced" for their age group. This self-consistency is reflected in the following intercorrelations among test scores for a group of young college men, the largest single group we have studied thus far: body-adjustment test vs. rod-and-frame test .61 (P < .01); body-adjustment test vs. embedded-figures test .54 (P < .01); rod-and-frame test vs. embedded-figures test .64 (P < .01).

The longitudinal study of one group of children from the time they were ten years old until they reached seventeen provided an opportunity to check self-consistency over a long period of time. Tracing the performances of individual children from the initial test occasion to the final retesting seven years later, we find that in each of the perceptual situations children tended to maintain their relative positions within their group as they grew older, even though group averages changed with age. This consistency is reflected in the following test-retest correlations computed on the basis of composite perceptual index scores for the three tests combined. For boys, 10 years vs. 14 years, .64; 14 years vs. 17 years, .87; and 10 years vs. 17 years, .50. For girls, the corresponding values are .90, .91 and .79 (P < .01 for all values for boys and girls).

Both cross-sectional and longitudinal findings on self-consistency suggest, first, that a child is likely to perceive in his own characteristic fashion under diverse conditions; and, second, that the child who is relatively field dependent or field independent at one age will show the same tendency at later ages as well. We seem, then, to be dealing with ways of perceiving that are pervasive in the individual child. Moreover, on the basis of "perceptual style" we can identify the pace of the child's perceptual development—that is, the degree to which he "lags" behind his age group or is relatively "advanced" as he grows up.

Recent investigations by ourselves and others have extended the picture of self-consistency to include *intellectual* functioning as well as perceiving. There is now considerable evidence that field-independent people are significantly better at intellectual tasks in which essential elements must be isolated from the context in which they are presented and recombined in new relationships.

Harris (1957) has shown, for example, that people who are relatively field dependent in their perception find it very difficult to solve Duncker's well-known insight problems. They show great "functional fixity," being unable to restructure a situation so that "parts" are extracted from one functional context and made to serve in another.

Goodman (1957) has reported that subjects who are more field dependent in our perceptual tests take significantly longer than field-independent subjects to solve the extinction problem in the *Einstellung* situation. It is possible to think of the set-breaking process required to solve the extinction problem in terms analogous to those we have used in describing the perceptual situations. The initial set-inducing problems in the *Einstellung* series can be solved by one method only. If the three jars are designated A, B, and C, the fixed solution takes the form A-C-$2B$; that is, the required amount of water may be obtained by filling A and emptying it once into C and twice into B. Since the extinction problem cannot be solved by this method, the induced set must be broken. The elements, A, B, C may no longer be used in the A-C-$2B$ pattern, but must be fitted into a new organization. Subjects who in the perceptual tasks cannot readily separate item from context also experience difficulty in thus "breaking up" an existing pattern in order to place its constituents in a new relationship.

As a final illustration that people tend to use a common approach to perceptual and intellectual situations we may cite a study done in our laboratory by Goodenough and Karp (1960) with children aged ten and twelve as subjects. The matrix of intercorrelations among their scores for the three perceptual tests, the subtests of the Wechsler Intelligence Scale for Children, and a series of specially devised cognitive tasks was submitted to a factor analysis. Three major factors emerged. On one of these, which is of particular interest here, the perceptual tests and three subtests of the W. I. S. C. (block design, picture completion, and object assembly) had a high loading. The requirements of the tasks presented by these three W. I. S. C. subtests may be broadly conceived as similar to those posed by the perceptual tests. Of the other two factors, one was identified as a verbal and the other as an attention-concentration factor; and none of the three perceptual tests appeared on either. There was a significant correlation ($-$ .66, P $<$ .01) between perceptual index scores and composite scores for the three W. I. S. C. subtests named above, but not between perceptual index scores and the composite scores for the W. I. S. C. subtests that appeared on the verbal factor or the attention-concentration factor.

These results permit us to interpret more meaningfully than before the often-reported finding that field-independent children are likely to achieve significantly higher total I. Q.'s in standard tests of intelligence. It is now clear that the over-all superior I.Q.'s of such children result specifically from their relatively better performance on those parts of intelligence tests that like the perceptual tests require "analytical ability." They do not significantly surpass field-dependent children in other parts of the tests, concerned with vocabulary, information, and comprehension, or demanding attention and concentration. Field-independent children cannot be considered as superior in *general* "tested" intelligence.

These and many other studies have shown that the style of functioning which the individual shows in his perception is manifested in his intellectual behavior as well. The way in which one perceives is an expression of a more general dimension of cognitive functioning. The terms we now use to designate contrasting ways of functioning in this dimension are "active-analytical" and "passive-global" field approach. Our studies of the perceptual component of the dimension have inclined us to consider the passive-global field approach as the more primitive, developmentally.

A first outcome, then, of emphasizing "individuality" in a study of development was the identification of broad individual styles of cognitive functioning, "pegged" as to developmental status.

MODE OF FIELD APPROACH AS RELATED TO
LEVEL OF DIFFERENTIATION

The finding that a passive-global field approach is associated with earlier stages of growth suggested the general hypothesis that children who persist in such a field approach, by comparison with most children their own age, may have made less progress in general psychological development. That it is appropriate to infer broader aspects of psychological functioning from cognitive behavior is strongly suggested by a large body of recent evidence regarding the relation between cognition and personality.

On the basis of experimental data and theoretical considerations that need not be reviewed here, we hypothesized that an active-analytical field approach is likely to be found in children who have developed a differentiated psychological structure and a passive-global approach in children who are relatively undifferentiated. Like variations within the field-approach dimension, differences in extent of differentiation may also be broadly defined in terms of developmental status.

To test the hypothesis that mode of field approach is related to level of differentiation, it was necessary to identify
some of the ways in which extent of differentiation may be
manifested. We postulated that a child's achievement of a
fairly high level of differentiation would be manifested principally in the following ways: a relatively developed conception of his body; a better sense of his own identity and of his
separateness from others; a relatively clear awareness of the
world around him and of his own needs and characteristics;
more developed controls and defenses; a greater capacity for
directed activity. On the premise that children with an
active-analytical field approach are likely to be more differentiated, we anticipated that such children would be apt to
show these characteristics to a greater degree than children
with a passive-global field approach.

The results of our own intensive studies and those carried
out by a number of other investigators have amply confirmed
these expectations. We cannot report them in any detail here.
We can only review briefly one or two studies bearing on each
of the above-named indicators of differentiation, in order to
illustrate the approaches used and the results obtained. The
examples may also help clarify the nature of each of the postulated indicators of differentiation.

Nature of Body Concept

We had conjectured that children with an active-analytical
field approach, as one sign of greater psychological differentiation, would show a relatively developed body concept. In
one analysis, we considered that the nature of a child's body
concept would be observably expressed in his drawings of human figures. Our colleague, Hanna Marlens, developed a
five-point rating scale designed to reflect the degree of primi-
tiveness or sophistication represented in such drawings. The
scale was based directly on particular features of the drawings, and both the male and female figures were considered
in making a rating. The most primitive and infantile draw-

ings, given a rating of 1, were characterized by a very low level of form and integration and the absence of any evidence of role or of sexual identity. The most sophisticated drawings rated 5, showed a high form level; successful integration of parts of the figure; and appropriate, even imaginative detailing. The intervening points on the scale were defined with reference to these two extremes.

Ratings made of figure drawings according to this "sophistication of body-concept" scale were significantly related to perceptual index scores. Children with an active-analytical field approach tended to demonstrate in their drawings a more sophisticated conception of the human body.

Sense of Separate Identity

In this area we hypothesized that children with an active-analytical approach would have a better sense of identity and of their separateness from others. Two investigations, one by Linton (1955), the other by Rudin and Stagner (1958), are illustrative of a very large number of studies bearing on this hypothesis. Both dealt with what may be regarded as observable behavioral manifestations of a developed sense of separate identity. One such manifestation, involved particularly in Linton's experiment, is the capacity to maintain one's own "direction" in the face of contradictory attitudes of others, through reliance on internal frames of reference. A second manifestation, represented in the study by Rudin and Stagner, is a relatively stable self-view, which survives fluctuations in the prevailing social context.

Linton's subjects were given several of our perceptual tests as well as tests designed to evaluate their reactions to group pressure. Included among these was the autokinetic situation in which a planted confederate attempted to influence the subject's judgments, following the method developed by Sherif. In addition to determining changes in judgment, under the influence of the confederate, Linton also made several kinds of ratings of the subject's way of functioning in the situation. The matrix of correlations among the variables obtained from this study was subjected to a factor analysis. Two factors were identified, on each of which both social and cognitive variables appeared. One of them is of particular relevance here. Loaded on this factor were measures of field dependence from the body-adjustment and embedded-figures tests and three measures from the autokinetic situation. Field dependence was associated with a tendency to change judgments in the direction of the confederate's judgments, the absence of active attempts to achieve a stable basis for making judgments, and the absence of conscious effort to resist the influence of the confederate. People with a passive-global field approach, in the absence of standards of their own, are thus likely to adapt their views to conform with those held by others.

Rudin and Stagner devised for their study a Self-Contextual Influence Test. The subject was asked to think of himself in four situations and to describe himself in each in terms of specially prepared rating scales. The scoring reflected the extent of similarity among a subject's self-descriptions for the four situations. The similarity scores correlated significantly with measures of perceptual field dependence. Relatively field-dependent subjects showed greater fluctuation in their views of themselves in different contexts. Field-independent subjects tended to be less influenced by changes in the imaginary contexts. These findings are consistent with the thesis that people with an active-analytical field approach tend to have a stable self-view, which we regard as reflecting a developed sense of identity.

Level of Awareness

For one test of the hypothesis that children with an active-analytical approach would show more developed awareness an interview was conducted with a number of ten-year-old boys, with the aim of determining the quality of their experience of themselves and of the world around them, including other people. An analysis was then made of the level of each child's "cognitive clarity." We consider that children show cognitive clarity if they experience the world and themselves in a relatively clear and organized way and lack cognitive clarity if their experiences are blurred and poorly integrated. A child in the first category is aware of relationships among events, as well as among people. His view is not limited to the immediate present, but includes past, present, and future in a continuous association. He is aware that people, including himself, have reasons for doing things; he defines people by attributes that go deeper than their actions or physical characteristics. The amount of knowledge a child has is not so important in assessing cognitive clarity as is the degree of integration of his knowledge. Even though circumstances and interests may have limited his fund of information, he may yet display great cognitive clarity. In our interpretation this concept refers to level of awareness in the very broadest sense.

A five-point rating scale of cognitive clarity, applicable to the data provided by the interview, was devised. Criteria for the ratings included awareness of means-end relationships, orientation with regard to time and space, awareness, of motives of oneself and others, evidence of interest in augmenting one's fund of information and of activity directed to that end, clarity of expression and relevance of responses, and ability to abstract and generalize about people and events.

The ratings were significantly related to the children's perceptual index scores. As we had anticipated, children who demonstrated an active-analytical field approach showed the kind of clear, integrated awareness of themselves and their surroundings that signifies a high degree of cognitive clarity.

Nature of Controls and Defenses

A major feature of progress toward differentiation is the formation of structured controls and defenses for the channeling of impulses. We predicted that children with an active-analytical field approach would present a picture of comparatively greater development in this respect. A representative analysis carried out to test this prediction involved a broad clinical evaluation of the three projective test records (Rorschach, TAT, and Figure-drawing) of each of a group of ten-year-old boys. These records were turned over to our colleague, Meta Steiner, for classification according to degree of structure of controls and defenses, within a scale defined by two extreme categories. Boys at one end of the scale would be characterized by an obsessive-compulsive structure; their controls would be adaptive and fairly easily carried out, or they might be tight and rigid. Boys at the opposite extreme would be characterized by a fluid structure, perhaps to the point of diffusion and hysteria, or by a lack of structure. They might present a picture of poorly controlled impulses, of chaos and disorganization, or, on the other hand, of "emptiness," lack of resources and a low level of impulse or energy requiring control.

Within this scale the children were classified in five categories; and the classifications corresponded significantly with their perceptual index scores. Again the initial hypothesis was confirmed.

Capacity for Directed Activity

The achievement of ability to direct activity is of course intimately linked to the development of controls for the channeling of impulse. Directed activity may be invested as much in intellectual as in physical pursuits; and it may involve either participation in and leadership of social groups or functioning in isolation from others.

One way in which we tried to discover whether or not children with an active-analytical field approach show greater capacity for directed activity was to analyze children's behavior while taking the TAT. The TAT session was recorded and transcribed, so that a full account of the child's side-comments was available. The examiner's recorded observations of the child's behavior, attitudes, and apparent feelings while taking the test added to the transcribed record. Thus we usually had a good deal of information about a child's manner of dealing with the task.

The TAT records of some children conveyed strong impressions of a "storyteller in action." The child could be perceived "behind the scenes," going about the task of developing and organizing a sequence of ideas. These impressions were derived particularly from the child's comments about his general plans, stated in advance, for a given story, about the pros and cons of various possibilities he was considering, and the use he was making of particular parts of a card; from his expressed judgment of the story he had told; and from his interpolated references to his own experience. Because such comments often involved the use of the first-person pronoun, we have come to speak of them as providing "evidence of an I." The records of some other children lacked this kind of evidence of active, purposeful enterprise.

We considered "evidence of an I" to be indicative of a capacity for directed activity, and classified the TAT records of children according to whether they did or did not show such evidence. The content of the stories themselves was not considered in this evaluation. As we had anticipated, the children whose records received a positive rating for "evidence of an I" showed an active-analytical field approach to a significantly greater degree than children whose records lacked "evidence of an I."

All these studies, representative of a much larger number of investigations, lend confirmation to the general thesis that mode of field approach is related to level of differentiation. Each of them, of course, considered only one indicator of differentiation at a time. We have also conducted intensive case studies of many individual children, in which all aspects of differentiation could be viewed in their complex interrelations. Basically, they confirmed the picture suggested by the studies of separate indicators. Few of the children, however, consistently displayed all the personality tendencies generally associated with their particular mode of field approach; and along with the salient trends shown in common by children in the same cognitive group we also observed important differences among them in other areas of personality functioning.

The case studies, moreover, highlighted a significant fact already evident in our earlier investigations: that the apparently greater differentiation of children whose field approach is active-analytical does not necessarily imply better adaptation to life situations or an absence of pathology. Maladjusted children are found both among those who tend toward an active-analytical approach and those who tend toward a passive-global approach. Personality disturbances in the latter group tend to be of the kind that stem from relatively primitive, amorphous, chaotic personality structure; whereas in the former group they are more likely to take such forms as overcontrol, overintellectualization, and emotional isolation. Cognitive style and level of cognitive development do not of themselves indicate whether or not a child will have a "healthy" personality; they may, however, suggest the form that pathological developments may take.

In summary, it may be said that the work reported in this section, and other similar work, suggests a linkage between the level of a child's cognitive development and the extent of his psychological differentiation. We are now inclined to consider that an active-analytical field approach is itself an indicator in the cognitive sphere of progress toward differentiation, and that a passive-global approach is indicative of limited differentiation.

When we introduce issues of personality formation and personality dynamics into the consideration of perceptual and intellectual growth we take, in effect, a broader view of the child as we study his development. The interrelatedness of perceptual, intellectual, and personality aspects of growth implies individual differences in pace of growth, which involve the "total system."

THE ROLE OF EARLY LIFE EXPERIENCES IN DEVELOPMENT

The question of possible sources of these individual differences in pace of development next engaged our interest. Pursuit of this problem again focuses attention on "individuality." It requires consideration of the forces acting on the individual—and comparison of the forces exerted on different individuals—that may serve to accelerate or "arrest" development. A comprehensive program of research is needed to deal with such large, complex issues, and we have made only a very small beginning on such a program.

Before describing what we have done, it is well to state that we undertook these studies with an "interaction" approach. A child's development proceeds by way of the unique interaction between his initially present, constitutionally determined characteristics and the particular environmental forces surrounding him as he grows up. A fully effective investigation of the nature of this interaction requires a longitudinal study which begins with observations of the family even before the child is born.

For practical reasons we have not been able to carry out that ideal kind of study. As the only realistic alternative we took a cross-sectional view of the interaction process. We considered first a particular aspect of the interaction process—the relation between a child and his mother. Within the wide range of relationships children have with their environments (both in the family and in society) the mother occupies a strategic position in influencing development. The most effective way of studying the mother-child interaction, it seemed to us, was to approach it from the standpoints of both mother and child. An impression of the mother's view of her relation to her child was obtained through an intensive interview with her. An impression of the child's view of his relation to his mother was derived from an analysis of his account of parental role as projected in the TAT and as given in an interview

Although these studies were undertaken with an interaction point of view, our observations are necessarily reported from the vantage point of one member or the other of the interacting pair. Thus, the results of the interview with the mother are cast in terms of her behavior, attitudes, and feelings toward her child.

With these reservations as background, we may consider some of the specific studies performed. They were guided by the broad hypothesis that children with a passive-global field approach have had the kind of relations with their mothers that would tend to hamper their opportunities for progress toward psychological differentiation.

Our first study was made with the group of ten-year-old boys whose perception, intellectual functioning, and personality had already been investigated. Each boy's mother was interviewed at home by a staff member who did not know the child or the child's test results. The interview was "free-wheeling" in character rather than restricted to a set schedule of questions. It sought to explore the mother-child relationship as a cross-section of the immediate present as well as in longitudinal perspective. Three areas of mother-child interaction were given particular attention: the mother's general orientation toward child rearing, her goals for the child, and her complaints about him; her response to the child's behavior in critical situations such as cleanliness training, eating, exploratory activities, illness; and her evaluation of the child's adaptation to school, to his companions, and to various extracurricular activities.

On the basis of the data obtained in the interview, and still without knowledge of the child's test results, each mother's role in relation to her son was evaluated in terms of whether its total impact seemed predominantly to have fostered or hampered his development of differentiation. Such judgments were of course quite complex and encompassing. To "anchor" them a set of nine "clues" was formulated. Expressed in terms of characteristics attributed to mothers judged as hampering differentiation, the clues are listed below.

1. The mother markedly limits the child's activities, either through her fears and anxieties for him, or her strong ties to him. For example, one mother withdrew her boy from the Boy Scouts because the play was too rough and not sufficiently supervised. Another still escorted her son to school when he was nine years old.

2. The mother regards her child as delicate, needing special attention or protection. Thus, some mothers thought of their children as too weak to engage in certain sports, or not able to perform some chores at home.

3. The mother expresses strong approval of social conformity and propriety. Some mothers, for example, stressed "proper" dress for their sons and set high standards of personal appearance.

4. The mother's control, directed against self-assertion, is not calculated to help the child achieve increasing and appropriate responsibility. Some mothers interpreted any assertiveness in their children as disobedience and freshness and regarded these as chronic problems which they were trying to correct. Others were overindulgent, yielding to the child's every display of temper. Some used methods of control that surely had the effect of generating great guilt in their children about the expression of strong feelings. One mother used to admonish her child by asking: "What would happen if I should die when you are yelling at me?"

5. The mother's physical care of the child seems inappropriate to his age. Some of our mothers still bathed and dressed their ten-year-old sons.

6. The mother limits the child's curiosity. An example is one mother who expressed strong annoyance whenever her child asked questions.

7. The mother does not encourage her son to assume a masculine role. Thus, one mother preferred to have her son play

with girls because such play was quieter and so disturbed her
less.

8. The mother does not feel confident about her methods of
rearing the child, and relies on authorities rather than on her
own judgment and feelings. Some mothers of this kind tried to
turn the interview into an opportunity for obtaining advice
about how to handle their children and for seeking approval
of the practices they were following.

9. The mother does not experience pleasure and self-fulfillment in the care of her child and in her home responsibili-
ties. One mother, for example, complained: "I feel drained. I
cannot pour that much of myself into my child."

Comparable clues, contrasting with these, were used to infer
"differentiation-fostering" rather than "differentiation-ham-
pering" relations between our boy subjects and their mothers.

It is important to note that the attitudes of mothers characterized as interacting with their sons in a way that fostered
differentiation did not always help their children make comfortable, effective adjustments. Some of these mothers, viewing their children as especially capable and urging them on
to greater achievement, set standards too high for those particular boys. One of our mothers promised her son a dollar
for every point above 95 per cent in his school grades at the
end of a semester. Such pressure, understandably, had serious
adverse effects on the child.

The mothers' classifications proved to be significantly related to the perceptual performances of their children. Boys
with a passive-analytical field approach more commonly had
mothers who were characterized as fostering differentiation;
boys with an active-global approach more often had mothers
characterized as hampering differentiation.

Confirmation of this relationship was obtained when the
study was repeated with a second group of ten-year-old boys
and with a group of fourteen-year-old boys. Moreover, the
ratings of the mothers made on the basis of the interviews also
agreed significantly with the children's performances in tasks

that evaluated field approach in the intellectual area; and they were significantly related as well to most of the measures of differentiation considered earlier.

Our analyses of the children's views of parental role, as projected in their TAT stories, gave further evidence that the nature of a child's experiences in the family bears a relation to the nature of his cognitive functioning. Every story with a theme of parent-child interaction was placed in one of eight categories. In four of these categories, the parent in the story was portrayed as being negatively oriented toward the child— as expressed in coercive actions, hostile feelings, punishment, hitting, injury, or even killing. In the other four categories, the parent in the story was portrayed as positively oriented toward the child—as giving guidance and direction, providing support when the child was in difficulty, showing warm, approving feelings toward the child or concern for him.

Each child was given a composite score for his "mother" stories, his "father" stories and for both combined. In the first group of ten-year-old boys, ratings of both "mother" and "father" stories were significantly related to perceptual test scores. For a second group of ten-year-old boys the ratings of father stories, although not those of mother stories, agreed significantly with perceptual performance. In the group of fourteen-year-olds, ratings of both mother and father stories related significantly to perception.

Considered in terms of the content of the stories, these results indicate that under the permissive fantasy conditions of the TAT, children with a passive-global field approach tend to project impressions of parents as physically aggressive, brutalizing, and dominating toward their children. Parental authority is seen as exercised in an arbitrary, tyrannical, and inflexible fashion. The child in the story is usually required to comply with the parent's wishes, with no reason given or implied. By contrast, the stories of children with an active-analytical field approach tend to portray parents as reasonable and flexible, and the pressures they apply as mild. Even when a parent acts against the child's immediate wishes, the parent's actions are likely to have positive consequences for the child's later life. Parents are able to offer informed guidance to their children, and they support and comfort them in adversity.

The results for the children's TATs are consistent with the results for the interviews with their mothers. In all three groups, the correlations between the total composite TAT ratings and ratings of the mothers are in significant agreement. Boys who in their TAT stories portrayed parents as negatively oriented toward their children were more likely to have mothers who, on independent evaluation, were judged as hampering differentiation; boys who portrayed parents as positively oriented tended to have mothers characterized as fostering differentiation. The agreement in outcome of these two quite different analyses of parental role justifies greater confidence in each.

Still further evidence supporting the view that a child's cognitive functioning is related to the nature of his family experiences comes from a study, not yet published, conducted by Seder (1957) at Harvard University. Each of a group of sixty boys and sixty girls, all ten years of age, was given the embedded-figures test, as a means of evaluating extent of perceptual field dependence. Each child's mother had already been interviewed in connection with the Newton Reading Project. The interviews were based on a questionnaire specifically devised for that project, in which the questions were designed to obtain specific information about various areas of child rearing and family relations. The areas included feeding procedures, toilet-training practices, techniques of discipline, sleeping arrangements, intrafamily relationships and so on. The interview data were coded and evaluated according to hypotheses suggested by our studies of mother-child interactions in relation to mode of perceiving and by various theories concerning parent-child relationships.

The over-all results are very similar to ours. A few of the

significant relationships reported by Seder may be mentioned. Children who were relatively field dependent had parents who discouraged them from expressing aggression and severely punished assertive behavior. The punishments administered by the mothers of such children were likely to be dictated by personal needs, and whims, and were often aggressive and violent. Fathers of field-dependent boys spent comparatively little time with their children. The pastimes they shared with them were passive ones, such as watching TV together. Seder found that the parents of field-independent children presented a contrasting picture in these and other areas.

It is apparent, from all the accumulated evidence, that passive-global and active-analytical field approaches in children are associated with quite different sorts of parent-child relationships. In general, the parents of youngsters who demonstrate a predominantly passive-global approach—and particularly their mothers—seem to have had the kinds of relations with their children that served, basically, to interfere with the process of separation. Parents of children whose field approach tends to be active-analytical, on the contrary, have had the kinds of relations that encouraged development toward autonomous, assertive functioning. If we follow the postulate suggested earlier that mode of field approach is an expression of level of differentiation, these results may be taken to reflect the impact of different kinds of parent-child relations upon children's progress toward self-differentiation.

We have taken only a small step toward understanding a very complex problem. The evidence we have been able to accumulate so far permits us to say that given modes of cognitive functioning in children occur in significant association with particular kinds of parent-child relationships. We are not yet in a position to make definitive statements about the important issue of causality. How much of what we have observed is a product of parental influence? To what extent does parental behavior itself represent a reaction to the particular characteristics of a child?

We recognize, indeed, that differences in early life experiences cannot account fully for the broad psychological differences we have observed among children. There can be little doubt that constitutional differences may also be extremely important. We have recently begun studies that may clarify the connection between characteristics observed in infancy and the kinds of pervasive differences we have found in later development. Through the generous cooperation of Dr. Lois Murphy and Dr. Sibylle Escalona, seventy-two children studied in infancy by Escalona and her collaborators in Topeka were recently tested again by Carol Johnson of our laboratory when they were six to eight years old. They were given a series of modified versions of our perceptual tests, as well as a number of personality tests and an intelligence test; and the mother of each child was interviewed. The data are yet to be analyzed. One aim of this analysis will be to evaluate particular characteristics discernible in the infancy records, as they relate to the modes of functioning observed later. These records also offer an opportunity to extend the study of mother-child relationships to earlier stages of the child's development than we have thus far explored.

The evidence summarized in this section suggests some of the routes that may be profitably pursued for an understanding of the forces which contribute to individual differences in direction and pace of growth.

In the developmental studies we have carried out, described here in part, our central interests in differences in growth trends fostered a greater concern with problems of individuality than has until quite recently been shown by developmental theory. The results of the first small steps we have taken in pursuit of this interest offer perhaps some glimmerings of the advantages that may accrue to developmental theory from an expansion of "its orbit of interest to include as a central problem the study of individuality."

BIBLIOGRAPHY

Goodenough, D. R. and Karp, S. A. (1960), A Factor Analysis of Cognitive Functioning With Special Reference to the Field-Dependence Dimension. In preparation.

Goodman, B. (1957), Field Dependence and *Einstellung* Performance. Unpublished.

Harris, F. (1957), Experimental Investigation of a Relationship between a Perceptual and Cognitive Function. Unpublished.

Linton, H. B. (1955), Dependence on External Influence: Correlates in Perception, Attitudes and Judgments. *Journal of Abnormal and Social Psychology*, *51*:502-507.

Rudin, S. and Stagner, R. (1958), Figure-ground Phenomena in the Perception of Physical and Social Stimuli. *Journal of Psychology*, *45*:213-225.

Seder, J. A. (1957), The Origin of Difference in Extent of Independence in Children: Developmental Factors in Perceptual Field Dependence. Thesis submitted to Harvard University.

Werner, H. (1957), The Concept of Development from a Comparative and Organismic Point of View. In *Concept of Development*, ed. D. B. Harris. Minneapolis, Minn.: University of Minnesota Press.

Witkin, H. A. (1949), Perception of Body Position and of the Position of the Visual Field. *Psychological Monographs*, No. 302, Vol. 63, No. 7.

———— (1950), Individual Differences in Ease of Perception of Embedded Figures. *Journal of Personality*, *19*:1-15.

———— (1952), Further Studies of Perception of the Upright When the Direction of the Force Acting on the Body Is Changed. *Journal of Experimental Psychology*, *43*:9-20.

———— and Asch, S. E. (1948), Studies in Space Orientation: IV. Further Experiments on Perception of the Upright with Displaced Visual Fields. *Journal of Experimental Psychology*, *38*:762-782.

———— and Lewis, H. B.; Hertzman, M.; Machover, K.; Meissner, P. B.; Wapner, S. (1954), *Personality Through Perception*. New York: Harper.

Publications of Heinz Werner

Books and Monographs

1916

Zur Psychologie des ästhetischen Genusses. Ph.D. dissertation. University of Vienna.

1917

Die melodische Erfindung im frühen Kindesalter. Vienna: Sitzungsbericht der kaiserlichen Akademie der Wissenschaften, *182*, No. 4.

1919

Die Ursprünge der Metapher (Veröffentlichungen des Leipziger Forschungsinstituts). Leipzig: Barth.

1922

Grundfragen der Intensitätspsychologie (Zeitschrift für Psychologie, Ergänzungsband 10). Leipzig: Barth.

1924

Die Ursprünge der Lyrik. München: Reinhardt.

1926

Einführung in die Entwicklungspsychologie. Leipzig: Barth (2nd ed., 1933; 3rd ed., 1953; 4th ed., 1959).

1932

Grundfragen der Sprachphysiognomik. Leipzig: Barth.

1935

Compendio de Psicologia Evolutiva. Barcelona: Salvat Editores.

1937

Dynamics in Binocular Depth Perception (Psychological Monographs, *49*, No. 2, Whole No. 218). Columbus: Psychological Review Co.

1940

Comparative Psychology of Mental Development. New York: Harper; 2nd ed., Chicago: Follett, 1948; 3rd ed., New York: International Universities Press, 1957.

1945

Perceptual Behavior of Brain-injured, Mentally Deficient Children. Genetic Psychology Monographs, *31*, 51-110.

1952

(with Kaplan, E.) *The Acquisition of Word Meanings: A Developmental Study* (Monographs of the Society for Research in Child Development, *15*, No. 1, Serial No. 51). Evanston: Child Development Publications.

1955

(ed.) *On Expressive Language* (Clark University Monographs in Psychology and Related Disciplines, *1*). Worcester: Clark University Press.

1957

(with Wapner, S.) *Perceptual Development* (Clark University Monographs in Psychology and Related Disciplines, *2*). Worcester: Clark University Press.

Articles

1912

Begriffstafel auf genetischer Grundlage. *Archiv für systematische Philosophie und Soziologie, 18*:45-62.

Ein Beitrag zur Lehre logischer Substitutionen. *Archiv für systematische Philosophie und Soziologie, 18*:431-444.

1913

Über künstlerisch-individuelle Prozesse. *Archiv für systematische Philosophie und Soziologie, 19*:429-441.

Untersuchungen über den "blinden Fleck." *Pflüger's Archiv für die gesamte Physiologie des Menschen und der Tiere, 153*:475-490.

Ein Phänomen optischer Verschmelzung. *Zeitschrift für Psychologie, 66*:263-270.

1914

Eine psychophysiologische Theorie der Übung. *Vierteljahrsschrift für wissenschaftliche Philosophie und Soziologie, 38*:417-441.

1915

Begriffspsychologische Untersuchungen. *Archiv für systematische Philosophie und Soziologie, 21*:162-172.

1918

Über optische Rhythmik. *Archiv für die gesamte Psychologie, 38*:115-163.

1919

Die Auslese befähigter Volksschüler in Hamburg: Das Ordnen von Begriffsreihen. *Zeitschrift für angewandte Psychologie und Charakterkunde, 18*:49-56.

Rhythmik, eine mehrwertige Gestaltenverkettung. *Zeitschrift für Psychologie, 82*:198-218.

1923

Prüfung der Fähigkeit der Geschwindigkeitsschätzung und Bremsführung an Triebwagenführern. *Praktische Psychologie, 4*:113-117.

1924

(with Lagercrantz, E.) Bericht betreffend die experimentell-psychologischen Studien über die Wortstruktur. *Mémoires de la Société Finno-Ougrienne, Helsingfors, 52*:316-339.

Studien über Strukturgesetze I: Über Strukturgesetze und deren Auswirkung in den sogenannten geometrisch-optischen Täuschungen. *Zeitschrift für Psychologie, 94*:248-264.

Studien über Strukturgesetze II: Über das Problem der motorischen Gestaltung. *Zeitschrift für Psychologie, 94*:265-272.

(with Lagercrantz, E.) Studien über Strukturgesetze III: Experimentell-psychologische Studien über die Struktur des Wortes. *Zeitschrift für Psychologie, 96*:316-363.

1925

Studien über die Strukturgesetze IV: Über Mikromelodik und Mikroharmonik. *Zeitschrift für Psychologie, 98*:74-89.

1926

Studien über Strukturgesetze V: Über die Ausprägung von Tongestalten. *Zeitschrift für Psychologie, 101*:159-181.

1927

(with Creuzer, H.) Studien über die Strukturgesetze VI: Über einen Fall von Schichtspaltung beim Bewegungssehen. *Zeitschrift für Psychologie, 102*:333-337.

Über die Intensität der Empfindungen. *8th International Congress of Psychology. Proceedings and Papers.* Groningen: Noordhoff, pp. 85-93.

Über physiognomische Wahrnehmungsweisen und ihre experimentelle Prüfung. *8th International Congress of Psychology. Proceedings and Papers.* Groningen: Noordhoff, pp. 443-446.

(with Lagercrantz, E.) Über Gestaltbildung in den Dialekten der lappischen Sprache. *Zeitschrift für Psychologie, 104*:201-223.

(with Zietz, K.) Studien über Strukturgesetze VIII. Über die dynamische Struktur der Bewegung. *Zeitschrift für Psychologie, 105*:226-249.

1928

Über allgemeine und vergleichende Sprachphysiognomik. *Deutsche Gesellschaft für Psychologie. Bericht über den 10. Kongress für experimentelle Psychologie, 10*:184-186.

Über die Sprachphysiognomik als eine neue Methode der vergleichenden Sprachbetrachtung. *Zeitschrift für Psychologie, 109*:337-363.

Über magische Verhaltungsweisen im frühen Kindesalter. Beitrag zu Stern's *Psychologie der frühen Kindheit.*

Über magische Verhaltungsweisen beim Kinde und Jugendlichen. *Zeitschrift für pädagogische Psychologie und Jugendkunde, 29*:465-476.

1929

Über das Empfinden und seine experimentelle Prüfung. *Deutsche Gesellschaft für Psychologie, 11*:190-191.

1930

Untersuchungen über Empfinden I: Das Problem des Empfindens und die Methode seiner experimentellen Prüfung. *Zeitschrift für Psychologie, 114*:152-166.

Untersuchungen über Empfinden II: Die Rolle der Sprachempfindung im Prozess der Gestaltung ausdrucksmässig erlebter Worte. *Zeitschrift für Psychologie, 117*:230-254.

1931

Zeit und Raum in den Urformen der Künste. *Beiheft der Zeitschrift für Aesthetik und allgemeine Kunstwissenschaft, 25*:68-86.

Das Prinzip der Gestaltschichtung und seine Bedeutung im kunstwerklichen Aufbau. Festschrift Stern, *Zeitschrift für angewandte Psychologie und Charakterkunde, 61*:241-256.

(with Zietz, K.) Untersuchungen über Empfinden III: Gegenseitige Beeinflussung von Farb- und Tonerlebnissen. *Zeitschrift für Psychologie, 121*:257-356.

1932

Sprache und Ausdruck. *Deutsche Gesellschaft für Psychologie. Bericht über den 12. Kongress für experimentelle Psychologie, 12*:201-210.

(ed.) Untersuchungen über Empfinden IV: (v. Schiller): Das optische Verschmelzen in seiner Abhängigkeit von heteromodaler Reizung. *Zeitschrift für Psychologie, 125*:249-289.

(ed.) Untersuchungen über Empfinden V: (v. Schiller): Die Rauhigkeit als intermodale Erscheinung. *Zeitschrift für Psychologie, 127*:265-289.

1934

L'Unité des sens. *Journal de Psychologie, 31*:190-205.

1935

Studies on Contour: I. Qualitative Analyses. *American Journal of Psychology, 47*:40-64.

1937

Process and Achievement. *Harvard Educational Review, 7*:353-368.

1938

Approaches to a Functional Analysis of Mentally Handicapped Problem Children. *American Journal of Mental Deficiency, 43*:105-108.

On Musical Microscales and Micromelodies. *Psychological Bulletin, 35*:700.

(with Strauss, A.) Deficiency in the Finger Schema in Relation to Arithmetic Disability. *American Journal of Orthopsychiatry, 8*:719-725.

Binocular Depth Contrast and the Conditions of the Binocular Field. *American Journal of Psychology, 51*:489-497.

William Stern's Personalistics and Psychology of Personality. *Character and Personality, 7*:109-125.

1939

Deficiency in the Finger Schema: Finger Agnosia and Acalculia. Bethlehem: Psychological Cinema Register.

(with Strauss, A.) Types of Visuo-motor Activity in Their Relation to Low and High Performance Ages. *American Journal of Mental Deficiency, 44*:163-168.

Finger Agnosia in Children with a Brief Discussion on Defect and Retardation in Mentally Handicapped Children. *American Journal of Psychiatry, 95*:1215-1225.

(with Strauss, A.) Problems and Methods of Functional Analysis in Mentally Deficient Children. *Journal of Abnormal and Social Psychology, 34*:37-62.

1940

Studies on Contour II: Strobostereoscopic Phenomena. *American Journal of Psychology, 53*:418-422.

Perception of Figure and Background in Brain-injured Children. *Psychological Bulletin, 37*:440.

Perception of Spacial Relationship in Mentally Retarded Children. *Journal of Genetic Psychology, 57*:93-100.

(with Strauss, A.) Causal Factors in Low Performance. *American Journal of Mental Deficiency, 45*:213-218.

(with Strauss, A.) Qualitative Analysis of the Binet Test. *American Journal of Mental Deficiency, 45*:50-55.

Musical Microscales and Micromelodies. *Journal of Psychology, 10*:149-156.

1941

(with Bowers, M.) Auditory-motor Organization in Two Clinical Types of Mentally Deficient Children. *Journal of Genetic Psychology*, *59*:85-99.

Old and New Conceptions of Stereopsis. *Archives of Ophthalmology*, *25*:1076-1078.

(with Strauss, A.) Experimental Analysis of Conceptual Thinking in Brain-injured Children. *Psychological Bulletin*, *38*:538.

(with Thuma, B. D.) A Disturbance in the Perception of the Motion in Brain-injured Children. *Psychological Bulletin*, *38*:712.

(with Strauss, A.) Pathology of Figure-background Relation in the Child. *Journal of Abnormal and Social Psychology*, *36*:236-248.

Psychological Approaches Investigating Deficiencies of Learning. *American Journal of Mental Deficiency*, *46*:233-235.

(with Strauss, A.) The Mental Organization of the Brain-injured Mentally Defective Child. *American Journal of Psychiatry*, *97*: 1195-1203.

1942

(with Strauss, A.) Experimental Analysis of the Clinical Symptom "Perseveration" in Mentally Retarded Children. *American Journal of Mental Deficiency*, *47*:185-188.

Functional Interdependence of the Senses. *Filosofia Letras Mexicanas*, *3*:35-48.

(with Carrison, D.) Measurement and Development of the Finger Schema in Mentally Retarded Children: Relation of Arithmetic Achievement to Performances on the Finger Schema Test. *Journal of Educational Psychology*, *33*:252-264.

(with Thuma, B. D.) Deficiency in the Perception of Apparent Motion in Children with Brain-injury. *American Journal of Psychology* *55*:58-67.

(with Thuma, B. D.) Critical Flicker-frequency in Children with Brain-injury. *American Journal of Psychology*, *55*:394-399.

Binocular Vision—Normal and Abnormal. *Archives of Ophthalmology*, *28*:834-844.

(with Strauss, A.) Disorders of Conceptual Thinking in the Brain-injured Child. *Journal of Nerve and Mental Disease*, *96*:153-172.

1943

Principles and Methods of Teaching Arithmetic to Retarded Children, *American Journal of Mental Deficiency*, 47:1-9.

Comparative Psychopathology of the Brain-injured Child and the Traumatic Brain-injured Adult. *American Journal of Psychiatry*, 99:835-838.

(with Strauss, A.) Impairment in Thought Processes of Brain-injured Children. *American Journal of Mental Deficiency*, 47:291-295.

1944

(with Carrison, D.) Animistic Attitudes in the Reasoning of Two Clinical Types of Mentally Subnormal Children. *American Journal of Mental Deficiency*, 48:258-260.

(with Bijou, S. W.) Analysis of the Vocabulary of Subnormal Children. *American Journal of Mental Deficiency*, 48:364-366.

Development of Visuo-motor Performance on the Marble-board Test. *Journal of Genetic Psychology*, 64:269-279.

(with Carrison, D.)Animistic Thinking in Brain-injured Mentally Retarded Children. *Journal of Abnormal and Social Psychology*, 39:43-62.

Experimental Genetic Psychology. In: *Encyclopedia of Psychology*. New York: Philosophical Library, pp. 219-236.

1945

Rorschach Method Applied to Two Clinical Groups of Mental Defectives. *American Journal of Mental Deficiency*, 49:304-306.

(with Bijou, S. W.) Language Analysis in Brain-injured and Non-brain-injured Mentally Deficient Children. *Journal of Genetic Psychology*, 66:239-254.

Motion and Motion Perception: A Study on Vicarious Functioning. *Journal of Psychology*, 19:317-327.

1946

Subnormal and Abnormal Rigidity. *Journal of Abnormal and Social Psychology*, 41:15-24.

1947

The Effect of Boundary Strength on Interference and Retention. *American Journal of Psychology*, 60:598-607.

1949

A Genetic Study of Development of Word Meaning through Verbal Contexts. *American Psychologist*, 4:250-251.

Thought Disturbance with Reference to Figure-background Impairment in Brain-injured Children. *Confina Neurologica*, 9:255-263.

Interrelationships between Perception and Personality: A Symposium. Part I. Introductory Remarks. *Journal of Personality*, 18:2-5.

(with Wapner, S.) Sensory-tonic Field Theory of Perception. *Journal of Personality*, 18:88-107.

Review of "Brain and Intelligence" by W. C. Halstead. *Journal of Abnormal and Social Psychology*, 44:426-428.

1950

(with Kaplan, E.) Development of Word Meaning through Verbal Context: An Experimental Study. *Journal of Psychology*, 29:251-257.

Review of "The Unfolding of Artistic Activity" by H. Schaefer-Simmern. *Psychological Bulletin*, 47:165-166.

(with Wapner, S.) Sensory-tonic Field Theory of Perception. In: *Perception and Personality, A Symposium*, ed. J. S. Bruner and D. Krech. Durham, N. C.: Duke University Press.

(with Klapper, Z.) Developmental Deviations in Brain-injured (Cerebral-palsied) Members of Pairs of Identical Twins. *Quarterly Journal of Child Behavior*, 3:288-313.

(with Kaplan, B.) Introduction to Bibliography and Addenda. In: W. Stern, *Allgemeine Psychologie*. Haag: Nijhoff.

Perception of Spatial Relationship in Mentally Retarded Children. In: Hartley-Birch, *Readings in Psychology*. New York: Crowell.

(with Crain, L.) The Development of Visuo-motor Performance on the Marble Board in Normal Children. *Journal of Genetic Psychology*, 77:217-229.

Introductory Remarks to the Symposium on Perception and Personality. In: *Perception and Personality*, ed. J. S. Bruner and D. Krech. Durham: Duke University Press.

1951

On the Development of Word Meanings. *Cybernetics. Transactions of the Seventh Conference*. New York: J. Macy Foundation.

(with Wapner, S., and Chandler, K. A.) Experiments on Sensory-tonic Field Theory of Perception. I. Effect of Extraneous Stimulation on the Visual Perception of Verticality. *Journal of Experimental Psychology*, *42*:341-345.

(with Wapner, S., and Chandler, K. A.) Experiments on Sensory-tonic Field Theory of Perception. II. Effect of Supported and Unsupported Tilt of the Body on the Visual Perception of Verticality. *Journal of Experimental Psychology*, *42*:346-350.

(with Wapner, S., and Morant, R. B.) Experiments on Sensory-tonic Field Theory of Perception. III. Effect of Body Rotation on the Visual Perception of Verticality. *Journal of Experimental Psychology*, *42*:351-357.

Symposium on Genetic Psychology. I. Introduction: The Conception of Genetic Psychology, *American Journal of Orthopsychiatry*, *21*:472-475.

(with Wapner, S.) Perception and Body Motion. *American Psychologist*, *6*:287.

1952

(with Wapner, S.) Experiments on Sensory-tonic Field Theory of Perception. IV. Effect of Initial Position of a Rod on Apparent Verticality. *Journal of Experimental Psychology*, *43*:68-74.

(with Wapner, S.) Experiments on Sensory-tonic Field Theory of Perception: V. Effect of Body Status on the Kinaesthetic Perception of Verticality. *Journal of Experimental Psychology*, *44*: 126-131.

(with Gunter, R. C., Jr., Chandler, K. A., and Wapner, S.) A Device for Measuring Angular Movements of the Body around Its Axes. *American Journal of Psychology*, *65*:609-613.

(with Solomon, P.) Studies on Contour: III. Studies on Negative After-effects. *American Journal of Psychology*, *65*:67-74.

A History of Psychology in Autobiography, Vol. IV. Edited by H. S. Langfeld, E. G. Boring, H. Werner, R. M. Yerkes. Worcester: Clark University Press.

(with Wapner, S.) An Experimental Study of Configurational Dynamics. *American Psychologist*, *7*:242.

(with Wapner, S.) Toward a General Theory of Perception. *Psychological Review*, *59*:324-338.

Review of "The Principles of Semantics" by Stephen Ullman. *Language*, *28*:249-256.

1953

(with Wapner, S., Bruell, J. H., and Goldstein, A.) Experiments on Sensory-tonic Field Theory of Perception: VI. Effect of Position of Head, Eyes, and of Object on Position of the Apparent Median Plane. *Journal of Experimental Psychology, 46*:293-299.

(with Wapner, S., Bruell, J. H., and Goldstein, A.) Experiments on Sensory-tonic Field Theory of Perception: VII. Effect of Asymmetrical Extent and Starting Positions of Figures on the Visual Apparent Median Plane. *Journal of Experimental Psychology, 46*:300-307.

(with Wapner, S.) Effect of Meaning-Induced Sets on the Position of the Apparent Median Plane. *American Psychologist, 8*:450.

(with Krus, D. M., and Wapner, S.) Studies in Vicariousness: Motor Activity and Perceived Movement. *American Journal of Psychology, 66*:603-608.

1954

Change of Meaning: A Study of Semantic Processes through the Experimental Method. *Journal of Genetic Psychology, 50*:181-208.

(with Kaplan, E.) The Word Context Test. *British Journal of Psychology, 45*:134-136.

(with Wapner, S.) Studies in Physiognomic Perception: I. Effect of Configurational Dynamics and Meaning-induced Sets on the Position of the Apparent Median Plane. *Journal of Psychology, 38*:51-65.

(with Wapner, S.) Gestalt Laws of Organization and Organismic Theory of Perception: Effect of Asymmetry Induced by the Factor of Similarity on the Position of the Apparent Median Plane. *American Psychologist, 9*:488.

1955

(with Kaden, S., and Wapner, S.) Studies in Physiognomic Perception: II. Effect of Directional Dynamics of Pictured Objects and of Words on the Position of the Apparent Horizon. *Journal of Psychology, 39*:61-70.

(with Wapner, S.) Gestalt Laws of Organization and Organismic Theory of Perception: Effect of Asymmetry Induced by the Factor of Similarity on the Position of the Apparent Median Plane and Apparent Horizon. *American Journal of Psychology, 68*:258-265.

(with Kaplan, B.) Introductory Remarks. In: *On Expressive Language*, ed. H. Werner. Worcester: Clark University Press.

(with Wapner, S.) The Innsbruck Studies on Distorted Visual Fields in Relation to an Organismic Theory of Perception. *Psychological Review*, *62*:130-138.

Psychological Analysis of Expressive Language. In: *On Expressive Language*, ed. H. Werner. Worcester: Clark University Press.

(with Wapner, S.) Margin of Safety: Changes in Psychological Distance under Danger. University Park: Psychological Cinema Register.

(with Wapner, S.) Changes in Psychological Distance under Conditions of Danger. *Journal of Personality*, *24*:153-167.

1956

Microgenesis and Aphasia. *Journal of Abnormal and Social Psychology*, *52*:347-353.

(with Weir, A.) The Figure-ground Syndrome in the Brain-injured Child. *International Record of Medicine*, *169*:362-367.

(with Kaplan, B.) The Developmental Approach to Cognition: Its Relevance to the Psychological Interpretation of Anthropological and Ethnolinguistic Data. *American Anthropologist*, *58*:866-880.

(with Wapner, S., and Comalli, P. E., Jr.) Space Localization under Conditions of Danger. *Journal of Psychology*, *41*:335-346.

(with Wapner, S.) The Non-projective Aspects of the Rorschach Experiment: II. Organismic Theory and Perceptual Response. *Journal of Social Psychology*, *44*:193-198.

(with Wapner, S.) Sensory-tonic Field Theory of Perception: Basic Concepts and Experiments. *Revista di psicologia*, *50*:315-337.

1957

(with Kaplan, B.) Symbolic Mediation and Organization of Thought: An Experimental Approach by Means of the Line Schematization Technique. *Journal of Psychology*, *43*:3-25.

The Concept of Development from a Comparative and Organismic Point of View. In: *The Concept of Development: An Issue in the Study of Human Behavior*, ed. D. B. Harris. Minneapolis: University of Minnesota Press.

(with Miller, A., and Wapner, S.) The Effect of Ascending and Descending Tones on Autokinetic Motion. *American Psychologist,* *12*:456.

(with Wapner, S., and Krus, D. M.) Studies in Physiognomic Perception: IV. Effect of Muscular Involvement on the Dynamic Properties of Objects. *Journal of Psychology,* *44*:129-132.

(with Wapner, S., and Krus, D. M.) The Effect of Success and Failure on Space Localization. *Journal of Personality,* *25*:752-756.

(with Liebert, R. S., and Wapner, S.) Studies in the Effect of Lysergic Acid Diethylamide (LSD-25): Visual Perception of Verticality in Schizophrenic and Normal Adults. *A.M.A. Archives of Neurology and Psychiatry,* *77*:193-201.

(with Wapner, S., and Comalli, P. E., Jr.) Effect of Boundary on Perception of Head Size. *Perceptual and Motor Skills,* *7*:69-71.

(with Comalli, P. E., Jr., and Wapner, S.) Studies in Physiognomic Perception: III. Effect of Directional Dynamics and Meaning-induced Sets on Autokinetic Motions. *Journal of Psychology,* *43*: 289-299.

1958

(with Krus, D. M., and Wapner, S.) Studies in Vicariousness: Effect of Muscular Involvement on Visual Threshold. *American Journal of Psychology,* *71*:395-398.

(with Miller, A., and Wapner, S.) Studies in Physiognomic Perception: V. Effect of Ascending and Descending Gliding Tones on Autokinetic Motion. *Journal of Psychology,* *46*:101-105.

(with Wapner, S., and Comalli, P. E., Jr.) Effect of Enhancement of Head Boundary on Head Size and Shape. *Perceptual and Motor Skills,* *8*:319-325.

(with Liebert, R. S., and Wapner, S.) Studies in the Effect of Lysergic Acid Diethylamide (LSD-25): Self and Object Size Perception in Schizophrenic and Normal Adults. *A.M.A. Archives of Neurology and Psychiatry,* *79*:580-584.

1959

(with Comalli, P. E., Jr., and Wapner, S.) Effect of Muscular Involvement on Size Perception. *Perceptual and Motor Skills,* *9*:116.

(with Comalli, P. E., Jr., and Wapner, S.) Perception of Verticality in Middle and Old Age. *Journal of Psychology,* *47*:259-266.

(with Comalli, P. E., Jr., and Wapner, S.) Perception of Part-whole Relations in Middle and Old Age. *American Psychologist,* *14*:349.

Index

DATE DUE

AP 20 00			
MY 19'89			
MR 6'70			
MR 20'70			
AP 3'70			
DE 4 79			
MR 31 '81			
GAYLORD			PRINTED IN U.S.A.